Guide to America's Outdoors

Pacific Northwest

Guide to America's Outdoors
Pacific Northwest

By Bob Devine
Photography by Phil Schofield

NATIONAL GEOGRAPHIC
WASHINGTON, D.C.

Contents

Cover: Beargrass at Eunice Lake, Mount Rainier National Park, Washington *Page 1:* Sea stacks, Oregon coast *Pages 2-3:* Blackwell Peak, Manning Provincial Park, B.C.
Opposite: Tom McCall Preserve, Oregon

Treading Lightly in the Wild

He may be friendly but don't feed him.

NATIONAL GEOGRAPHIC GUIDE TO AMERICA'S OUTDOORS: PACIFIC NORTHWEST takes you to some of the wildest and most beautiful natural areas in a region remarkable for its misty, emerald rain forests, high-desert plateaus, ancient volcanos, and old-growth woodlands.

Visitors who care about this spectacular region know they must tread lightly on the land. Ecosystems can be damaged, even destroyed, by careless misuse. Many have already suffered from the impact of tourism. The marks are clear: litter-strewn acres, polluted waters, trampled vegetation, and disturbed wildlife. You can do your part to preserve these places for yourself, your children, and all other nature travelers. Before embarking on a backcountry visit or a camping adventure, learn some basic conservation do's and don'ts. Leave No Trace, a national educational program, recommends the following:

Plan ahead and prepare for your trip. If you know what to expect in terms of climate, conditions, and special hazards, you can pack for general needs, extreme weather, and emergencies. Do yourself and the land a favor by visiting if possible during off-peak months and limiting your group to no more than four to six people. To keep trash or litter to a minimum, repackage food into reusable containers or bags. And rather than using cairns, flags, or paint cues that mar the environment to mark your way, bring a map and compass.

Travel and camp on solid surfaces. In popular areas, stay within established trails and campsites. Be sure to choose the right path, whether you are hiking, biking, riding, skiing, or four-wheel-driving, and travel single-file in the middle of the trail, even when it's wet or muddy, to avoid trampling vegetation. When exploring off the trail in pristine, lightly traveled areas, have your group spread out to lessen impact. Good campsites are found, not made. Travel and camp on sand, gravel, or rock, or on dry grasses, pine needles, leaf litter, or snow. Remember to stay at least 200 feet from waterways. After you've broken camp, leave the site as you found it.

Pack out what you pack in—and that means *everything* except human waste, which should be deposited in a cathole dug away from water, camp, and trail, and then covered and concealed. When washing dishes, clothes, or yourself, use small amounts of biodegradable soap and scatter the water away from lakes and streams.

Be sure to leave all items—plants, rocks, artifacts—as you find them. Avoid potential disaster by neither introducing nor transporting non-native species. Also, don't build or carve out structures that will alter the environment. A don't-touch policy not only preserves resources for future generations; it also gives the next guy a crack at the discovery experience.

Keep fires to a minimum. It may be unthinkable to camp without a campfire, but depletion of firewood does harm the backcountry. When you can, try a gas-fueled camp stove and a candle lantern. If you choose to build a fire, first consider regulations, conditions, weather, skill, use, and firewood availability. Where possible, employ existing fire rings; elsewhere, use fire pans or mound fires. Keep your fire small, use only sticks from the ground, burn the fire down to ash, and don't leave the site until it's cold.

Respect wildlife. Watch animals from a distance (bring binoculars or a telephoto lens for close-ups), but never approach, feed, or follow them. Feeding weakens an animal's ability to fend for itself in the wild. If you can't keep your pets under control, leave them at home.

Finally, be mindful of other visitors. Yield to fellow travelers on the trail, and if you encounter pack stock, step quietly toward the downslope to let them pass. Above all, keep voices and noise levels low so that the sounds of nature can be heard.

With these points in mind, you have only to chart your course. Enjoy your explorations. Let natural places quiet your mind, refresh your spirit, and remain as you found them. Just remember, leave behind no trace.

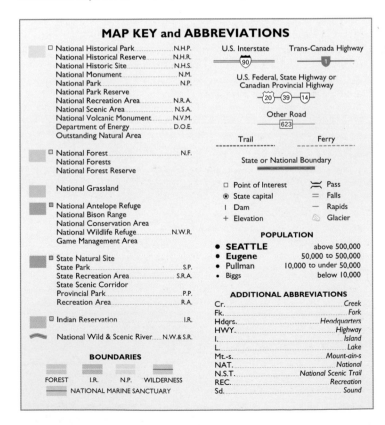

MAP KEY and ABBREVIATIONS

National Historical Park	N.H.P.
National Historical Reserve	N.H.R.
National Historic Site	N.H.S.
National Monument	N.M.
National Park	N.P.
National Park Reserve	
National Recreation Area	N.R.A.
National Scenic Area	N.S.A.
National Volcanic Monument	N.V.M.
Department of Energy	D.O.E.
Outstanding Natural Area	

National Forest	N.F.
National Forests	
National Forest Reserve	

National Grassland

National Antelope Refuge	
National Bison Range	
National Conservation Area	
National Wildlife Refuge	N.W.R.
Game Management Area	

State Natural Site	
State Park	S.P.
State Recreation Area	S.R.A.
State Scenic Corridor	
Provincial Park	P.P.
Recreation Area	R.A.

Indian Reservation   I.R.

National Wild & Scenic River   N.W.&S.R.

BOUNDARIES

FOREST	I.R.	N.P.	WILDERNESS

NATIONAL MARINE SANCTUARY

U.S. Interstate   Trans-Canada Highway

90   1

U.S. Federal, State Highway or Canadian Provincial Highway

20   39   14

Other Road

623

Trail   Ferry

State or National Boundary

▫ Point of Interest	≍ Pass
⊛ State capital	= Falls
I Dam	— Rapids
+ Elevation	Glacier

POPULATION

● **SEATTLE**	above 500,000
● **Eugene**	50,000 to 500,000
● Pullman	10,000 to under 50,000
· Biggs	below 10,000

ADDITIONAL ABBREVIATIONS

Cr.	Creek
Fk.	Fork
Hdqrs.	Headquarters
HWY.	Highway
I.	Island
L.	Lake
Mt.-s.	Mount-ain-s
NAT.	National
N.S.T.	National Scenic Trail
REC.	Recreation
Sd.	Sound

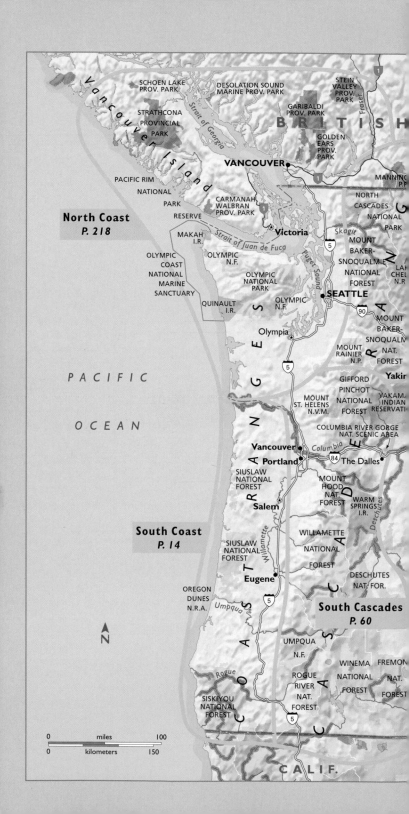

North Coast
P. 218

South Coast
P. 14

South Cascades
P. 60

BRITISH

SCHOEN LAKE
PROV. PARK

DESOLATION SOUND
MARINE PROV. PARK

STEIN
VALLEY
PROV.
PARK

GARIBALDI
PROV. PARK

STRATHCONA
PROVINCIAL
PARK

GOLDEN
EARS
PROV.
PARK

VANCOUVER

MANNING
P.P.

PACIFIC RIM

NORTH
CASCADES
NATIONAL
PARK

NATIONAL

CARMANAH
WALBRAN
PROV. PARK

PARK

RESERVE

Strait of Juan de Fuca

Victoria

Skagit

MOUNT
BAKER-
SNOQUALMIE
NATIONAL
FOREST

LAKE
CHELAN
N.R.

MAKAH
I.R.

OLYMPIC
N.F.

OLYMPIC
COAST
NATIONAL
MARINE
SANCTUARY

OLYMPIC
NATIONAL
PARK

OLYMPIC
N.F.

SEATTLE

MOUNT
BAKER-
SNOQUALMIE
NAT.
FOREST

QUINAULT
I.R.

Olympia

MOUNT
RAINIER
N.P.

GIFFORD
PINCHOT
NATIONAL
FOREST

Yakima

YAKAMA
INDIAN
RESERVATION

PACIFIC

OCEAN

MOUNT
ST. HELENS
N.V.M.

COLUMBIA RIVER GORGE
NAT. SCENIC AREA

Vancouver

Columbia

Portland

The Dalles

SIUSLAW
NATIONAL
FOREST

MOUNT
HOOD
NAT.
FOREST

WARM
SPRINGS
I.R.

Deschutes

Salem

SIUSLAW
NATIONAL
FOREST

Willamette

WILLAMETTE

NATIONAL

FOREST

DESCHUTES
NAT. FOR.

Eugene

OREGON
DUNES
N.R.A.

Umpqua

UMPQUA
N.F.

Rogue

ROGUE
RIVER
NAT.
FOREST

WINEMA

NATIONAL

FOREST

FREMONT

NAT.

FOREST

SISKIYOU
NATIONAL
FOREST

N

| 0 | miles | 100 |
| 0 | kilometers | 150 |

CALIF.

Strait of Georgia

Vancouver Island

Puget Sound

CASCADE RANGES

COAST RANGES

Essence of the West

As I SAT DOWN to write this introduction, I tried to think of the one sight or experience that for me captures the essence of the Pacific Northwest outdoors. But I couldn't come up with anything. Not with any *one* thing, that is. Instead, a multitude of images and memories played out in my mind.

I've been roaming the Northwest for 25 years, especially since moving to Oregon in 1990. Via canoe, bike, kayak, car, raft, jeep, ferry, plane, boat, train, and, most often, my own two feet, I have explored most of the region—though as-yet-unvisited nooks and crannies always beckon. How can I pick one sight or experience out of all the impressive things I've seen?

Perhaps it would be that early morning hike on a remote beach in Olympic National Park, when I watched the fog curling around the tree-crowned sea stacks. Or the time I sat in a small boat off San Juan Island and listened to the sound of killer whales breathing as they swam past less than 20 feet away. Or perhaps that summer day when I stood on the dazzling white alkali flats of the Alvord Desert and watched a thunderstorm assault the snow-bound heights of Steens Mountain. Or touching the gnarled bark of a hulking thousand-year-old tree in Mount Rainier National Park, or hearing the call of a trumpeter swan at Malheur National Wildlife Refuge, or staring into the smoking maw of Mount St. Helens.

There are far too many possibilities from which to choose. And that's the beauty of the Pacific Northwest outdoors. Though industrial civilization has taken its toll, more natural areas remain in good condition in this region than in most other parts of the nation.

As a visitor to the Northwest, you can help to preserve the region's wild places. Most directly, you can observe proper outdoors etiquette (see pp. 6-7). Indirectly, you can also help by learning. Educate yourself about the natural history of the animals and plants, about the intricate workings of the ecosystems, about the vital contributions these systems make to human welfare. Take the region's renowned old-growth conifer forests. These hulking, moss-draped trees make great calendar fodder, but they're more than pretty faces. These forests purify the water that ends up in my tap. They help prevent floods. They build fertile soils. They slow global warming by trapping carbon. They filter pollutants from the air. As old-growth forests are diminished, so are our lives. Learning such things usually leads to appreciation, and appreciation usually motivates people to use their power as consumers and citizens to protect our nation's embattled wild lands. And if we protect them, future generations of visitors will still find so many wonderful wild places from which to choose.

Bob Devine

Cape Perpetua Scenic Area, Oregon

Discovering the Pacific Northwest

Backpacker in the North Cascades

IMAGINE THAT YOU'RE A PIONEER in the 1840s, heading west on the Oregon Trail. You enter the Pacific Northwest in what is now east-central Oregon. As you look around at the sagebrush grasslands of the high desert you think, so, this is Oregon Country. As the wagon train forges northwest, the land rises and you cross the pine-dotted slopes of the Blue Mountains. Oh, you think, this is Oregon Country. Then you descend the mountains and head west across the dry hills of the central plateau, to the Columbia River and the colossal basalt gorge that contains it. You labor through the high, thickly forested Cascade Range in the shadow of the snow-crowned volcano now known as Mount Hood. By this point you no longer think that each new landscape represents the "real" Oregon Country. By the time you reach your destination—the promised land of the fertile Willamette Valley—you're well aware the Pacific Northwest is a region of infinite surprises.

Travelers of the 21st century likewise will discover the many dimensions of the Northwest. Shaped over time by the forces of nature, the region owes its spectacular geography to a monumental event that took place about 200 million years ago, when the earth's North American plate, inching westward, collided with the floor of the Pacific Ocean, moving eastward. The denser oceanic plate slid beneath the continental plate, which scalped the ocean floor and folded the layer of sediments into a coastal range. Today, the Wallowa Mountains and the Blue Mountains of northeastern Oregon are remnants of that ancient range.

The effects of those shifting tectonic plates and the related volcanic activity that followed eventually consigned the Pacific Ocean roughly to its present position and produced such other land forms as the Coast and Cascade Ranges. With this skeleton in place, nature fleshed out the region, creating rivers, deserts, lakes, and canyons. Ice age glaciers and floods carved such features as the Columbia Gorge and the channeled scablands of eastern Washington. After the ice retreated, the Northwest began developing the surface details of the landscape visitors see today.

We define the Northwest as Oregon, Washington, a swath of southern British Columbia, and slivers of western Idaho and northern California. But because the natural world pays no heed to artificial boundaries, we've followed the contours of nature in organizing this guide. Our natural version of the Northwest falls into six biogeographic regions. Though our divisions don't conform precisely to nature's blueprint—it's much too complex—our regions do hold together broadly in terms of vegetation type, geology, climate, latitude, and other such factors.

The South Coast (Chapter 1) takes in Oregon's coastal region, where the Coast Range tumbles down to meet the sea. The South Cascades (Chapter 2) follows the rugged, densely forested interior mountains that make up the spine of the Northwest, from southern Oregon north to Mount St. Helens, in southern Washington. The High Desert (Chapter 3) takes you to the southeast quadrant of the Northwest, the arid, high-elevation expanse of sagebrush-dotted hills and alkali flats sprinkled with lush wetland oases and pockets of high mountains. The Central Plateau (Chapter 4) examines another dry, sparsely vegetated realm, whose rolling hills and rough canyons sprawl across north-central Oregon and south-central Washington. In contrast, the North Cascades (Chapter 5) reveals a verdant region, ranging from west-central Washington into southernmost British Columbia, in which conifer forests pause only for rivers and high peaks. The North Coast (Chapter 6) ends the book among the wild beaches, misty coastal forests, and backwater islands on the shores of northwest Washington and southwest British Columbia.

As you roam outdoors in the Northwest, you'll no doubt enjoy some of the calendar-photography staples—bears, sky-scraping peaks, ancient forests, salmon, and alpine meadows bright with wildflowers. Your inter-action with the natural Northwest may even delve into the realm of emo-tion and instinct, especially if you slow to nature's pace. You might hear the basso-profundo creaking of a glacier in North Cascades National Park as it grinds another millimeter down a mountain, the sound of the land being shaped. Or one night you might sit in silence atop a 200-foot summit of sand in Oregon Dunes National Recreation Area and watch moon shadows slither across the sea of ghostly dunes. And as you observe flora and fauna along trails and in tide pools, take note, too, of the more obscure elements of the natural Northwest, including millipedes, sage-brush steppe, lichens, murky sloughs, and bluebunch wheatgrass.

Much of the Northwest's biogeographical diversity stems from a like-wise diverse climate. The seaside lowlands on the Olympic Peninsula's west side get about 130 inches of precipitation a year—the most in the 48 contiguous states—but parts of the high desert east of the Cascades receive only six inches annually. However, one pleasant fact does pertain to the entire Northwest: Rain seldom falls during the summer and early autumn, when skies are sunny and temperatures run in the 70s and 80s.

Because the Pacific Northwest is richly endowed with wild places, you might get the impression that it largely has escaped development. Unfor-tunately, that is not true. But perhaps if we all visit enough sublime out-door areas, we'll be motivated to help protect and restore the natural world. Let this book be your guide to some of those areas, but don't let it limit you. Go beyond my suggestions, explore on your own, and, like the pioneers before you, fully discover the treasures of the Pacific Northwest. ■

South Coast

Oregon coastline, north of Samuel H. Boardman State Scenic Corridor

THE SANDY BEACHES on which we love to stroll; the rocky shores where waves reach their crescendo; the limpid tide pools brimming with exotic life; the heavily timbered, mist-cloaked mountains that loom over the shoreline— these are the things that define the southern coast of the Pacific Northwest today. But none of these natural features, not so much as a grain of sand, existed 50 million years ago. Instead, what was to become the south coast lay beneath the ocean, a blank slate awaiting a force of nature that would carve the face of the coast. When shifting tectonic plates scalped the surface of the seabed and began to propel it upward through the water 50 million years ago, this new land emerged. And the earth's sculptors—wind, rain, waves, and streams—went to work and shaped the coastline that we enjoy today.

The 362 miles of the south coast run the length of Oregon, from the mouth of the Columbia River, which forms the boundary with Washington to the north, to the northern edge of the redwood forests, near the California border to the south. To the west the coastal zone extends slightly beyond the water's edge to include some offshore islands and nearshore waters, while to the east the zone encompasses the Coast Ranges. Most of the natural attractions discussed in this section, however, are located close to the sea.

The good condition of such natural attractions as Oswald West State Park (see p. 55), with its pristine beaches and unsullied rocky shores, largely stems from Oregon's farsighted coastal protection laws. Mother Nature's years of labor could have been obliterated by condominiums, oceanfront homes, hot dog stands, and miniature golf courses, but such intrusions have been admirably restrained compared with most other American shorelines. And in 1967 the Oregon legislature decreed that all the state's beaches must remain public, with ample public access. The biggest environmental shortcoming can be found back in the Coast Ranges, where timber companies have clear-cut nearly all of the original forest. Luckily for visitors to the south coast, much of the little remaining coastal old growth cozies up to the shore.

The lushness of those ancient forests is partly due to the South Coast's weather. That extreme green is the result of rain and lots of it. Some locations measure 60 inches a year, some as much as 80, and a fair number of areas even break the century mark. However, the south coast climate is much less forbidding than this sounds. Almost all the rain falls during the winter and early spring; during summer it is common to go weeks without a drop of rain, although fog often cloaks the region in the morning. But even when it seems that the skies have opened up, temperatures remain remarkably mild, typically lingering in the 40s and 50s during the winter and reaching into the 60s and 70s during the summer.

Though few experiences in life relax the mind and body more than a day at the beach, the Pacific Ocean is not a benign body of water; coastal visitors should be alert to a few safety concerns: First, beware of sneaker waves. These unpredictable large waves aren't at all common and they're nowhere near the size of a tsunami, but they come upon you quickly. Their force can sweep wading children out to sea or knock unwary tide-poolers off their feet, so it's advisable to keep an eye on the ocean. Beachcombers must know local tides before they venture out so that they don't stroll around a headland at low tide only to find their return cut off when the tide comes in. Finally, stay clear of logs in the surf; they can turn into killers when tossed about by those muscular Pacific Ocean breakers. Otherwise, come along and see what 50 million years has wrought. ■

View of rugged coastline from a scenic overlook

Samuel H. Boardman State Scenic Corridor

■ 1,471 acres ■ Southern Oregon coast, north of Brookings 4 miles ■ Season year-round ■ Hiking, swimming, beachcombing ■ Some informal trails may be steep, slilppery, or unstable ■ Contact Harris Beach State Park, 1655 US 101 N, Brookings, OR 97415; phone 541-469-2021. www.prd.state.or.us

SAMUEL H. BOARDMAN STATE SCENIC CORRIDOR gives landlubbers the chance to go gunkholing. This isn't as distasteful as it sounds—the term "gunkholing" is nautical slang for boating along a coastline in a leisurely fashion, frequently putting into this cove or that bay. Samuel H. Boardman State Scenic Corridor provides motorists with a similar opportunity: About a dozen well-marked viewpoints and trailheads allow US 101 travelers to dip into this skinny, 13-mile-long coastal park as the spirit moves them. The roadside viewpoints don't disappoint either. Looming over the sea, the lushly forested flanks of the coastal mountains occasionally slant right to the edge of 200-foot oceanside bluffs. The mountains are especially rugged and jumbled because Oregon's far southern Coast Ranges formed with measured but monumental force. As the tectonic plates of the continent and the ocean floor collided, the seabed slid beneath the continental plate. The top layer of the ocean floor was sheared off, and its crumpled form became the coastal mountains. The result could make a flatlander dizzy. But Boardman is more than just the mountains and breathtaking views. A verdant ecosystem of Sitka spruce, ferns, shrubby salal, and grassy meadows thrives there, and can be enjoyed on foot. The Oregon Coast Trail strings the viewpoints together, so hikers can troop from one end of the elongated park to the other or walk any individual segment that appeals to them.

What to See and Do

Cape Ferrelo, located near the park's southern border, is an excellent starting point for exploring Boardman. A trail at the south end of the parking lot winds through wind-stunted conifers and within minutes emerges into the treeless meadows that carpet the cape's seaward portion. A quarter-mile stroll through the open grasslands brings you to the tip of this stubby finger of land, from which you can see well down into California.

A couple of miles north of Cape Ferrelo lies **Whalehead Beach,** a vital stop for visitors who yearn to feel sand between their toes. Most of Boardman lacks beach access, except via numerous informal trails leading down from the bluffs. Take care; some of these trails can be steep and slippery, and others may be unstable. But Whalehead sits at sea level; within a minute of parking your car you can be frisking across wet sand in your bare feet. Sharp-eyed beachcombers may spot green jade pebbles among the grains of sand. Jade often is found near deposits of serpentine, a dark green rock present in large quantities in the southern Oregon Coast Ranges. In addition to beachcombing, explore the driftwood pile at the mouth of Whalehead Creek, or watch for belted kingfishers working the stream.

Travelers who see the sign for **Natural Bridges Cove** and pull off will find an unprepossessing parking area. Located about 5 miles from the park's northern boundary, this forestbound viewpoint seems to be without views. But a one-minute trail from the southern end of the parking lot leads to a cliff-rim view of Natural Bridges Cove. On a foggy morning, you may think you've wandered into a classic Japanese painting. Steep mountainsides and towering offshore rocks frame this acre of azure water. The ghostly mist curls through branches of scattered spruce and fir trees that jut from the cliffs and sea stacks—offshore stone pillars—at improbable angles. Below, kelp sways in the cove as broken waves expire in this sheltered hideaway. Two rock bridges, created by the collapse of an ancient sea cave, arch across the water, giving the cove its name. ∎

Oregon Coast Trail

During your visit to Boardman, you'll encounter trails that parallel the coast. These and many other shoreline routes have been stitched together to form the Oregon Coast Trail, which runs 360 miles from California to Washington. The trail swings inland now and then, but mostly keeps hikers close to the beautiful coast. Sometimes it leads down a beach, so hikers need to keep track of the tides, especially when skirting a headland. For more information, get the "Oregon Coast Trail Guide" from the Oregon Parks and Recreation Department, P.O. Box 500, Portland, OR 97207; 503-731-3293.

Following pages: Arch Rock, Samuel H. Boardman State Scenic Corridor

Touring a cave, Oregon Caves National Monument

Oregon Caves National Monument

■ 480 acres ■ Southwest Oregon, southeast of Cave Junction 20 miles ■ Best season summer; to avoid long waits for cave tours, take early or late tours and get in line early to sign up ■ Hiking, bird-watching, wildlife viewing, cave tours ■ Fee for tours ■ Road to monument covered with snow or ice Nov.-April. Cave is cold and somewhat dim ■ Contact the monument, P.O. Box 128, Cave Junction, OR, 97523; phone 541-592-3400

AS CHILDREN, WE'RE TAUGHT to thank people when they put time into making something nice for us. Well, visitors to Oregon Caves National Monument owe Mother Nature an enormous debt of gratitude. She began working on these caves more than 200 million years ago and is still busy refining her gift.

The caves started as limestone deposits in an ancient ocean basin. A collision of the continental and ocean floor tectonic plates erased the basin and injected molten rock into the area, heating the limestone until it recrystallized into marble (marble and limestone are both made of calcite). Water, slightly acidified by carbon dioxide, filtered through the ground and began eating away at the marble, forming subterranean channels. When the water table dropped, some of these channels drained; the caverns that remained were simply waiting for erosion to expose them to the outer world.

A cavern is sometimes little more than a big hole in the ground. What draws people to the Oregon Caves monument are the elaborate rock formations. Again, water was the engine of creation. Laden with dissolved minerals—including calcite, which is also found in cement and eggshells—rainwater seeping into the caves lost its acidity, which prompted its cache of minerals to precipitate out. Over time these deposits built up into the dripstone sculptures that now astonish visitors.

Not all of the monument's attractions lie underground, however. Up in the sunshine, visitors can explore an unusual wilderness landscape. Oregon Caves is in the Siskiyou Mountains, an anomalous, east-west chain that is almost 20 times older than the Cascades. The Siskiyous stayed just beyond the reach of serious glaciation and thus serve as a sanctuary for pre-ice age plant species. The plant community is exceptionally diverse, as well, due to the region's unusual serpentine soils and to the Siskiyous' location at the confluence of several major biological zones. Animal diversity often follows plant diversity, as evidenced by the fact that the Siskiyous boast the greatest variety of birds and amphibians in the state.

To protect the cave's features, the park service occasionally sets fire to the forest above the cave. Decades of fire suppression have led to a buildup of undergrowth and debris. Acid from the rotting wood leaks into the cave and dissolves some of the formations. The unnatural volume of debris also holds water aboveground for an unusually long time, allowing so much water to evaporate that little seeps down inside the cave to slake the thirst of its inhabitants. Prescribed fire should restore natural conditions in the forest—and in the cave.

What to See and Do

The monument's big draw, of course, is the **guided cave tour,** which takes about 1 hour and 15 minutes. The trail goes up and down about 500 stairs, many of them wet and steep; visitors who take the tour should be reasonably fit. Children must be at least 42 inches tall and able to climb a set of test stairs unassisted in order to tour the cavern.

For just over half a mile, the trail slithers through the dimly lighted cave. (A note to those prone to claustrophobia: During the tour you must often duck your head and occasionally stoop over, but you will not have to squeeze through narrow passageways.) The tour route through the cave is lit, but park staff recommend that you bring flashlights for everyone in your party as an extra safety measure and to illuminate particular cave features. Bring your jackets, too, since the temperature in the cavern stays at a constant 42°F year-round. And don't forget your "oohs" and "ahs" because you'll use them frequently in the place that late-19th-century cowboy poet Joaquin Miller called "The Marble Halls of Oregon."

Some formations immediately grab the eye, such as **Paradise Lost,** a big cluster of tan-and-white marble shapes that look like jellyfish—or maybe hot air balloons, or perhaps open parachutes. Like clouds, these formations invite personal interpretation. Other cave features require closer observation, such as moonmilk, which is a mass of minuscule calcite crystals that looks like cottage cheese. It was used as a folk medicine to treat cuts on livestock. You'll likely see cave popcorn, too. It's a residue created when water evaporates as air flowing into the cave passes over it; the translucent, large white bumps look more like eyeballs than like popcorn. If it's

creatures you're looking for, lucky visitors may spot some of a handful that are native to the cave— perhaps Pallid bats or a flea-size albino springtail, which feeds on the bacteria in little pools of water.

After you return to the surface, you can explore the outer world of the monument via half a dozen trails. They all start in the monument proper, but most extend into the surrounding lands of the **Siskiyou National Forest,** which features some fine old growth. For the best vistas, take the 2.5-mile (one way) **Lake Mountain Trail,** which climbs to the highest point in the area (it requires much uphill huffing and puffing). Along the way, you will likely see mule deer and the occasional black bear. The 3.3-mile loop called **Big Tree Trail** winds amid many enormous trees, including white fir and pine, before culminating at the base of the thickest Douglas-fir in Oregon. This behemoth is between 1,200 and 1,500 years old, and its trunk measures an astonishing 12.5 feet in diameter.. The trail also offers options to visit Bigelow Lakes. ∎

Serpentine Treasures

A significant portion of the Siskiyous' exceptional floral diversity stems from the presence of serpentine. This uncommon rock came to the surface all the way from the earth's mantle (the upper edge of the planet's molten interior). Serpentine is very brittle and shattered and has trouble retaining water; it contains chrome, nickel, and other elements that inhibit plant growth; and it produces nutrient-poor soils.

Needless to say, one doesn't find pansies growing in serpentine outcrops. A suite of rare and hardy plants grows in these impoverished patches, often including plants typically found in deserts. A small exposure of serpentine can be found on the monument, and larger outcrops can be observed a few miles north of Cave Junction at Eight Dollar Mountain or a few miles south at the Rough & Ready Botanical Wayside.

Hiking the Rogue River's Mule Creek Canyon

Rogue Wild and Scenic River

■ 84 miles long ■ Southwest Oregon, from Grants Pass to Gold Beach
■ Best season summer ■ Camping, hiking, boating, boat tours, white-water
rafting and kayaking, canoeing, swimming, fishing, bird-watching, wildlife viewing,
wild-flower viewing ■ Permits required to run river ■ Contact Rand Visitor
Center, Bureau of Land Management, 14335 Galice Rd., Merlin, OR 97532;
phone 541-479-3735. www.or.blm.gov:80/rogueriver

SOMETIMES IT'S A RUSH of white water boiling over boulders and caroming
off canyon walls. Other times it's a glassy flow easing past ancient forest
and mountains 4,000 feet high. Always it's a haven for wildlife, its waters
home to river otter, salmon, and waterfowl; its banks frequented by black
bear, deer, mink, and elk; its skies patrolled by bald eagles, kingfishers,
and ospreys. Most people who visit the lower Rogue River believe it epit-
omizes a wild and scenic river.

The government agrees. This 84-mile section of the Rogue, which
stretches from near Grants Pass to just short of Gold Beach, numbers
among the first eight river segments that Congress designated in the
original Wild and Scenic Rivers Act, passed in 1968. Such unspoiled river
reaches were uncommon then and are downright rare today. Of all the
nation's major rivers, only the Yellowstone still flows unfettered by any of
the 100,000 dams that plug America's waterways. Agricultural and urban
runoff pollute the vast majority of rivers. Logging and mining have
degraded many watersheds and the watercourses that vein them. Irrigation diversions reduce the flows of most western rivers, sometimes drying
them up completely. And subdivisions, factories, golf courses, and other
developments have bulldozed natural habitat along many waterways. A
wild and scenic river is something to be treasured—and enjoyed.

The Rogue can be enjoyed in many ways, ranging from the serene—champagne cruises on glass-enclosed tour boats—to the extreme—swimming the river, rapids and all, with fins duct-taped to one's feet. In between these two points are open-air jet boats, rafts, kayaks, canoes, and a hiking trail. Travelers who want to linger can camp or stay at several riverside lodges, grandfathered in before Congress passed the Wild and Scenic Rivers Act.

What to See and Do

Jet Boat Tours

Most Rogue visitors experience the river from a jet boat, a low-slung, high-powered craft that can maneuver up rapids and around tight bends. Typically they carry a maximum of 30 to 40 passengers. Jet boat tours from the upriver end are run by Hellgate in Grants Pass *(966 SW 8th St., Grants Pass, OR 97526. 541-479-7204)*, and a couple of outfits in Gold Beach run a variety of jet boat trips *(contact Gold Beach Chamber of Commerce, 29279 Ellensburg Ave, Gold Beach,* *OR 97444. 541-247-7526)*. To evaluate the trips they offer, it helps to understand that the Wild and Scenic River Act separates designated stretches of river into three categories: wild, scenic, and recreational, with recreational being the most developed and wild the least. Bear in mind that even the recreational segments typically are much less degraded by development than river reaches not protected under the act.

The jet boat tours run from Grants Pass. They travel for about

Jet boats on the Rogue River

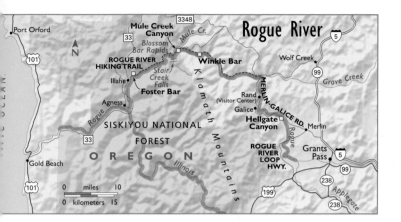

7 miles on an undesignated part of the Rogue and then for some or all of the 30 miles between the **Applegate River** and **Grave Creek,** which are designated recreational. The banks of the unprotected section are lined with houses, but past the Applegate the intrusions of civilization give way to oak-studded hills and willow thickets.

About halfway to Grave Creek you'll motor slowly through the narrow, high-walled stone chasm called **Hellgate Canyon,** where river otters sometimes flirt with the boat. This 30-mile stretch harbors other wildlife, too, especially ospreys. These large, white hawks wearing black masks migrate to the Rogue during the warm months; like many humans, they come for the fish. In a five-hour trip from Grants Pass to Grave Creek and back you'll likely see a couple of dozen ospreys and perhaps a dozen of their huge nests. Lucky visitors get to watch the ospreys fish, diving from 50 feet and slashing into the water with talons outstretched.

From the mouth of the Rogue, at Gold Beach, jet boats on 6-hour trips roar upriver for 30 or 40 miles through recreational and scenic sections of the river. The trips start in the estuary, where you may sight sea lions along with herons, ducks, deer, and other more typical Rogue River fauna. Soon the boat leaves the estuary behind and weaves deep into the Coast Ranges, passing beneath forested mountain slopes. The all-day trips go 52 miles upriver, not stopping until they reach the impassable Blossom Bar rapids. The last 12 miles of these long excursions lie within the wild part of the Rogue, giving passengers a brief taste of the primitive river.

Hiking

To truly savor the untamed waters, you must turn to primitive forms of transportation: non-powerboats or your own two feet. Travelers with four or five days and ample energy can explore all 40 miles of the wild section by walking the **Rogue River Hiking Trail,** an inviting path of moderate grades that winds with the river from Grave Creek to Foster Bar. Hikers can choose among a fair number of established campsites (with pit toilets, picnic tables) or those that are unimproved, or opt for the ease of the wilderness lodges *(541-479-3735; reservations required)*, which happen to be spaced about a day's hike apart. When hiking, be cautious about the heat. Midsummer temperatures in the area typically range in the 80s and 90s; this is warm under any circumstances, but the stone walls of the canyon act as an oven and raise trail-level temperatures to well over 100°F. If you can't avoid visiting in midsummer, consider hiking from west to east so the sun doesn't pound you in the face during the heat of the afternoon.

Whatever the season, don't rush down the trail. Stop and smell the flowers, literally, if you like; there are many different species in this slice of the botanically diverse Klamath Mountains, including rhododendrons, blue irises, lupines, and gold-orange poppies. Note the exceptional variety of trees, too, including Oregon staples such as ponderosa pine, western redcedar, and big leaf maple. Look for the uncommon species, such as Port Orford cedar, Brewer spruce, and Lawson cypress. You also might pack a fishing pole for your travels; anglers come from the world over to try for chinook salmon that weigh up to 40 pounds and steelhead that can weigh 15 pounds.

Boating

Rafting and kayaking are the ultimate means of experiencing the Rogue River. The wild stretch is renowned as one of the nation's classic river journeys. Some 90,000 people a year apply for permits to run the river, but in order to preserve the wilderness experience the Forest Service uses a lottery to limit visitation to about 10,000. Commercial outfits get a share of the permits, however, so you can get aboard by reserving space on an organized tour. And opting for a professional outfitter not only enables inexperienced river runners to go on the Rogue but, more important, it assures them of coming off it safely. Though the Rogue

River Otters

Rivers otters are the clowns of the river. Most visitors who spot otters see little more than a sleek, furry head poking out of the water, its curious eyes framed by a spray of whiskers. But occasionally you'll witness these playful critters chasing each other in the water or tobogganing down muddy slopes and splashing into the river. When not frolicking, these 15- to 40-pound aquatic weasels generally are eating. They must stoke their high metabolisms with vast quantities of fish, eggs, ducks, frogs, shellfish, snails, rodents, and many other sorts of victuals. Their swimming prowess makes otters fearsome predators. Not only can they maneuver gracefully and swiftly in the water, they can stay underwater for as long as four minutes, traveling up to a quarter of a mile before coming up for air—likely holding a snack.

Siskiyou Mountains

doesn't assail river runners with murderous rapids—except when the spring runoff is unusually high—it does have plenty of rapids that shouldn't be attempted by the unskilled on their own.

The vast majority of inexperienced people who opt to go with commercial companies choose rafts over kayaks. Kayaks are fun and exciting, but the typical river kayak only holds one person, so, greenhorn or not, that person will be doing all the steering and paddling alone. Even rookies can still safely and enjoyably kayak the Rogue, if you fit a few criteria: You must be hardy and adventuresome; book a trip with kayakers who are experienced and provide instruction in an emergency; and recognize you will need to portage around the most difficult rapids. On the other hand, almost anyone in good health who doesn't mind getting splashed now and then will do fine in a raft captained by an experienced oarsman.

Most raft trips last three days and embark from the Galice area, about 20 miles northwest of Grants Pass. At first the river is wide and the slope of the low hills gentle, but by the time you reach Grave Creek a few hours later, the river has narrowed and the hills have become mountains. Here you enter the wild section and soon alternate between rapids and flat water. During calm stretches you may spot a bald eagle soaring overhead or great blue herons mincing through the shallows. The forest is a mix of conifers and broadleafs, including canyon live oaks. This evergreen features both smooth-edged leaves and jagged, holly-like foliage. Many creeks feed into the river, sometimes going out in style as little waterfalls.

Camping on the Rogue

For the night, most rafting parties go ashore on gravel bars and camp in sandy areas just above the river, though some trips partake of the lodges. A few people take short hikes, but most settle into folding chairs to chat and watch the river go by. Animals often go by, too. Flights of migrating geese may honk past. Mergansers drift by on the current, their ragged, back-swept crests giving these ducks a perpetually disheveled appearance. American dippers—daredevil birds that dive-bomb into rapids and forage along the river bottom for tasty invertebrates—land on rocks and engage in rhythmic tail-wagging, dancing to a rhumba we humans can't hear. Deer often slip along the river's edge, with fawns trailing behind the does. You'll probably spot black bears around camp once or twice a trip—or several times if you wake up at night when they nose around the rafts and cooking area looking for food. Concerns about lost food, ripped rafts, and close encounters of the furry kind drive many outfitters to keep watch or to string cans along the camp's perimeter as an alarm system. If the bears do awaken you in the middle of the night, take a moment to watch the river sparkle past in the starlight.

During a three-day float you'll encounter many striking sites. Most parties pull over at **Stair Creek Falls** to watch the cool water cascade from ledge to ledge to the river. At **Winkle Bar** you'll pass an old log cabin once owned by Zane Grey, author of sagas about the American West. At ferocious **Blossom Bar** rapids—which you'll probably walk around while your outfitter guides the raft through—sit on the bluff above and watch as guides and kayakers negotiate the minefield of huge boulders and holes.

Mule Creek Canyon is high on everyone's list of favorite places. The sheer, 40-foot rock walls of this mile-long gorge squeeze the Rogue River to as little as 15 feet across, creating strange currents and swirling water, including a semi-whirlpool called the **Coffeepot.** Dangerous for anyone flipped out of a kayak by the big hole at the upper end, Mule Creek Canyon is relatively easy to run in a raft. When you spin, just think of it as a convenient way to get a 360-degree view of this delicious river. ◾

Sea lions near Gold Beach

Cape Arago State Park

■ 134 acres ■ Southern Oregon coast, southwest of Coos Bay 14 miles, at the end of Cape Arago Hwy. ■ Wildlife viewing, especially seals and sea lions ■ Contact Sunset Bay State Park, 89814 Cape Arago Hwy., Coos Bay, OR 97420; phone 541-888-3778, ext. 2. www.prd.state.or.us

AT JUST 134 ACRES, Cape Arago is a pocket park, but it leverages its location to achieve a grandeur far beyond its size. Atop the 150-foot bluff at the tip of the cape, the park's **main overlook** serves as a crow's nest from which you can see thousands of square miles of the Pacific. You can look for the green flash that sometimes flares in the wake of the setting sun, spot migrating gray whales during the winter and spring, and thrill to the thunder of monstrous waves during winter storms.

Another spectacle awaits a few hundred yards northwest of the cape at **Shell Island** and **Simpson Reef.** Pinnipeds—fin-footed mammals—favor these rocky sanctuaries. At various times of the year, you'll see elephant seals, California sea lions, harbor seals, and Steller's sea lions, sometimes by the hundreds, occasionally by the thousands. When the sea lions are in town—their numbers peak in late summer and fall—the park rings with their boisterous barks and moans. Elephant seals aren't as loud as the sea lions, but they make an impression through sheer size: A male elephant seal can measure more than 15 feet in length and weigh 4,500 pounds.

Steep trails lead from the main overlook to three coves that lie within the park. **North Cove** provides a ground-level view of the pinniped parade; the seals and sea lions often swim in the surf and sometimes come ashore (keep your distance). All three coves offer fine tide-pooling. ■

South Slough National Estuarine Research Reserve

■ 4,770 acres ■ South Oregon coast, near Charleston, about 10 miles southwest of Coos Bay ■ Season year-round ■ Hiking, kayaking, canoeing ■ Donations ■ Contact the interpretive center, P.O. Box 5417, Charleston, OR 97420; phone 541-888-5558. www.southsloughestuary.com

"COME ON, KIDS! We're going to the slough to see an estuary!" The slough? An estuary? That doesn't sound quite as compelling as a trip to the seashore or the mountains. In fact, most people don't even know what an estuary is, let alone a slough (pronounced slew).

Which is all the more reason to visit South Slough National Estuarine Research Reserve. Established in 1974, South Slough was the first of more than 20 sites around the nation to be included in the National Estuarine Research Reserve System. Nearly all of the country's estuaries have been seriously degraded by pollution and development, so Congress moved to protect some of the few that were still relatively unspoiled. Estuaries merit such attention because they are among the richest biological areas on earth.

An estuary is a place where fresh water from the land mixes with salt water from the ocean, and that place could be a river mouth, bay, bayou, marsh, inlet, sound, or, yes, a slough, which is a quiet arm of an estuary. Their shallow waters warmed by the sun, their mineral sediments and organic matter constantly stirred by tides and currents, estuaries are extravagantly productive, supporting an array of life from plankton to bears. Exploration of South Slough provides an excellent introduction to estuaries, in part because the reserve is in such fine condition and in part because one of the goals of the reserve system is to teach the public about the importance of estuaries.

What to See and Do

Start at the **interpretive center.** It's small but the displays will give you a context in which to appreciate the 4,770 acres outside. Look through the microscope to examine some of the tiny flora and fauna that float in the water and encrust the mudflats; forming the foundation of the food chain, they carry the ecosystem on their little backs. At another display, read about the economic value of estuaries. More than two-thirds of the nation's commercially important fish and shellfish spend all or part of their lives in these brackish coastal waters.

After you've boned up on estuaries, walk outside and see the real thing. If you have a canoe or kayak and know your way around tides, you can explore the slough by water. But most people opt for one or more of several hiking trails.

Playing in the Mud

As many as 20,000 organisms may live in a single handful of the blend of mud, sand, and organic matter that constitutes the bottom of these intertidal expanses. Find a flat exposed by the outgoing tide, and look for the little holes and mounds that indicate the presence of sub-surface animals. Then dig away with a small tool of some sort. Inexperienced mudflat explorers should avoid soft mud; the unwary have lost shoes and even have gotten so stuck that they had to be rescued. And remember: Due to the danger of getting cut off by incoming tides, it's best to stay close to terra firma.

The **Estuary Study Trail,** the reserve's premier route, starts near the South Slough Interpretive Center and runs 3 miles roundtrip down to the slough and back again. The interpretive center—located on Seven Devils Road, 4 miles south of Charleston—is open June through August, and on weekdays only from September through May.

The trail begins high above the water in a conifer forest. This is the slough's watershed, and its health is critical to the slough's well-being. If, for example, a logging operation polluted it with herbicides and eroded it by building roads, toxic chemicals and sediments would run down into the water. As you descend the forested slope and it begins to level out,

you'll come to a boardwalk that crosses over a swamp thick with deep green plants that in spring and summer sport broad leaves 4 feet long. This is skunk cabbage; take a close sniff and your nose will quickly grasp the origin of the name.

Down in the flats, you'll encounter salt marsh, so called because at high tide saltwater washes over it. This harsh habitat demands special adaptations. Salt grass, for instance, survives by excreting salt through its leaves. And pickleweed hordes freshwater in its succulent foliage to dilute the salt. Survey the marsh and you may spot a raccoon rummaging for food in a little pool or a great blue heron, 4 feet tall with a 6-foot wingspan, regally posed as it waits for unwary fish to pass within spearing distance.

Beyond the salt marsh, the trail delivers you into the heart of the estuary: the mudflats and the open water. During low tide the unvegetated expanse of the mudflats is revealed, but you won't see the community of worms, shrimp, clams, and other denizens that live in there. Nor will you often see the predators, such as perch, crabs, and salmon, that feed in the mudflats when the tide is in. But you will get an inkling of the estuary's richness when you observe shorebirds scurrying about and probing the muck with their bills in search of a tasty ghost shrimp or a nice, plump lugworm. And hungry terns and mergansers patrol the open water, waiting for just the right moment to pluck an unsuspecting herring or flounder from the estuary. ∎

Frolicking at Horsfall Dunes

Oregon Dunes National Recreation Area

■ 40 coastal miles ■ Southern Oregon coast, between Coos Bay and Florence off US 101 ■ Season year-round ■ Camping, hiking, walking, swimming, off-road vehicle riding, bird-watching, wildlife viewing, beachcombing ■ Day use fee, camping fee ■ Contact the visitor center, 855 Highway Ave., Reedsport, OR 97467; phone 541-271-3611. www.fs.fed.us/r6/siuslaw/odnra

IN THE DIM LIGHT of dawn, the sand dunes appear to be an extension of the sea, a series of hulking tsunamis rolling at odd angles toward the bordering forest. As the sky grades from gray to blue, the rising sun unmasks the wavelike dunes, revealing the fine-grained texture of the sand and the sinewy grasses that sprout like whiskers from some of the dune faces. The light illuminates rivers and creeks snaking to the ocean; tree islands—those mysterious oases of forest that punctuate the dunes—small lakes shimmering blue amidst the tan of the sand hills; and the sandy beach that marks the end of land and the beginning of the sea. As the bright light of full morning makes clear, there is much to explore at the Oregon Dunes National Recreation Area.

Oregon Dunes is widely regarded as the foremost coastal dune system on the West Coast. Though the recreation area averages only 1 or 2 miles in width, it stretches for some 40 miles north to south. The individual sand dunes, too, are of impressive size; some reach to 200 feet—about the height of a 20-story building—and range up to a mile in length. One can't say exactly how high or long a particular dune is, however, because the forces that created them are constantly reshaping them.

The Coos Bay Dune Sheet provides the foundation for Oregon Dunes. This gently sloping marine terrace contrasts with the steep seaside bluffs and rocky headlands found along most of the Oregon coast, which prevent sand from blowing inland. That sand, the raw material for the dunes, comes from the ocean floor. Currents, tides, and waves dredge it up and drop it on the area's beaches; from there it is whisked inland and over time builds up to form dunes. The wind blows throughout the year and varies in its direction and intensity, so the topography of this dynamic ecosystem is continually shifting. Dunes can travel as much as 20 feet a year, and their slow, steady march can bury forests, dam creeks to create ponds and lakes, and eliminate existing bodies of water by filling them in. The variation in wind also creates different kinds of dunes. Northwesterly summer winds, for example, produce waves of sand from 5 to 20 feet high called transverse dunes. In winter, however, southwesterly winds smooth over the transverse creations of summer, continuing the cycle of sand.

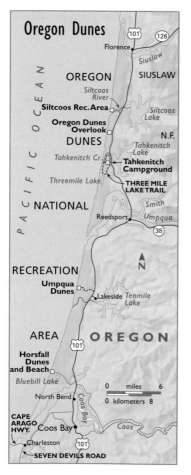

What to See and Do

Let's start at the south end of Oregon Dunes and work our way north. From North Bend/Coos Bay, drive 4 miles north on US 101. Turn off on Horsfall Road and head west to Horsfall Dune and Beach. About a quarter mile short of the beach, pull into the parking lot for the **Bluebill Trail,** a 1-mile loop around **Bluebill Lake,** an old lake bed that becomes a wetland during the rainy season. You'll pass through western hemlock-and-shore-pine forest and walk along boardwalks above the marsh. Birds love this area; look for downy woodpeckers hammering on trees, northern harriers cruising for rodents, and the radiantly white sheen of great egrets stalking through the shallows.

You may also spot your first ORVs here. Not an acronym for a bird species, ORV is short for off-road vehicles, such as dune buggies or four-wheelers. The presence of these loud, fast vehicles on the beaches and dunes has generated much controversy over the years

Alien Invader

By the middle of the 21st century, the open waves of sand that define Oregon Dunes NRA may have vanished beneath a shroud of vegetation. The culprit is an alien plant called European beachgrass.

Worried that the ever shifting dunes would roll over waterways, roads, railroad tracks, and other development, people in the late 1920s began planting beachgrass on some of the dunes near Florence in an effort to stabilize them. It worked. Native plant-eaters don't like beachgrass, and this invasive species thrives when repeatedly buried by sand. From these and other plantings, beachgrass spread rapidly along the Pacific coast.

Beachgrass isn't overrunning the vast expanses of open sand, however; its effect has been more that of a long siege than an overwhelming attack. The conditions that favor beachgrass exist right along the back edge of the beaches. As it grew tall and thick, its leaves intercepted most of the sand that usually blew inland. Within a few decades the beachgrass had intercepted enough sand to form the 20- to 30-foot foredunes that now run the length of the recreation area. Hardly any new sand reaches the inland dunes anymore.

As the existing inland dunes continue migrating east, eventually dissipating in the forest, there are no freshly supplied waves of sand coming behind them to take their place. European beachgrass is starving the dune system to death. Native vegetation is now encroaching on areas where shifting sands used to prevent plants from growing. If a removal program doesn't eradicate significant amounts of beachgrass, the dunes area will continue to shrink until it disappears.

Hikers on the Umpqua Dunes, in Oregon Dunes NRA

and their use has been restricted. Although you may hear and occasionally see ORVs, you'll never have to share a trail with them or encounter them popping over the top of a dune. For example, a short strip of Horsfall Beach is closed to ORVs from May through September so that swimmers and beachcombers may enjoy the shore. Other beaches and dune areas are off-limits year-round. If you want to hike where the roar of ORVs doesn't drown out the ocean, consult the recreation area maps that show when and where ORVs are allowed in the area.

Umpqua Dunes

About 10 miles north of the Horsfall turnoff, you'll come to the parking lot for the **Umpqua Dunes Trail.** This 5-mile loop leads to the most stunning dunes in the whole recreation area. After a nice half-mile stroll through the coastal evergreen forest, you'll suddenly emerge into the **Umpqua Dunes**—several square miles of open sand. Start by getting barefoot, then ascend the nearest and highest dune you see; all the huffing and puffing is a small price to pay for the panoramic view of this sea of sand from atop a 200-foot mountain of the stuff. For a descent that's quicker and more fun, you can bound down the steep sides of the dune or, as some people do, bring a flat-bottomed snow toy and slide down the slope. That mammoth dune and its brethren represent a type of dune termed "oblique," referring to the angle at which both winter and summer winds strike. Because oblique dunes are constantly on

the move, no vegetation grows on them. But that doesn't mean they're lifeless. Look closely at the fine sand and you may see animal tracks, perhaps from a coyote or a deer, but more likely the faint traces of beetles (see sidebar p. 41) and rodents. Take time, too, to appreciate the intricate curves and ripples sculpted by the wind. Winter visitors may see sand sculpture on a huge scale: Southwesterly winds sometimes carve free-standing yardangs—keel-shaped formations—as tall as 15 feet.

Though it's not the stuff of movie drama, quicksand can develop in Oregon Dunes during the winter and early spring. The rising water table in some low, unvegetated areas between dunes creates standing water several feet deep that is disguised by a film of sand. Such quicksand is more of a danger to ORVs than to hikers, but it is best to avoid these areas.

Many people frolic for a while in that first series of high dunes and then loop back to their cars, but if you have the time, you can hike on another mile to the beach. The route through the open sand is unmarked and it is easy to get disoriented, but you can quickly regain your bearings by climbing to the top of a tall dune and looking around. Beyond the beach you will spot several distinct tree islands. After walking briefly north on the beach, the trail markers will lead you back through the deflation plain, a broad strip of low-lying land just east of the beach. Water-loving plants thrive in this wet sand, creating freshwater marshes favored by birds and small mammals.

After a short, northward jog, the trail slices through the fore-dune and deposits you on a lightly visited beach. You can walk miles north or south, every step increasing the odds that you'll have the place all to yourself. Kick a pile of washed-up seaweed and watch the beach hoppers explode from their hideaway. Look near the water's edge and watch sanderlings scurrying through the backwash of the surf. Sometimes in the spring you'll encounter a stretch of purple beach. The unexpected color derives from washed-up purple jellyfish. Called "by-the-wind sailors," these jellies have a triangular flap atop their oval bodies that stands up like a sail to catch the wind; it can propel them for great distances across the sea. You may even come across a beached whale. In 1979 dozens of sperm whales mysteriously stranded themselves on an Oregon Dunes beach.

About 10 miles north of the Umpqua Dunes Trail parking lot is the town of Reedsport, home of the recently renovated **Oregon Dunes Visitor Center** *(open late May-early Sept.; Mon.-Sat. rest of*

ORV enthusiast kicks up his wheels

Hiking in Oregon Dunes National Recreation Area

the year). It's small, but a few displays and a short introductory video effectively describe the area's natural, cultural, and geological history. The helpful staff can provide plenty of literature and maps to the recreation area.

Tahkenitch Dunes and Vicinity

The finest hiking in Oregon Dunes awaits you 7 miles north of the visitor center, on the **Tahkenitch Dunes Trail** and the network of routes with which it connects. Park your car at the south end of the Tahkenitch Campground and start out on the trail that serves both Tahkenitch Dunes and Threemile Lake. After a quarter mile the trails split. Take the Tahkenitch Dunes Trail west 2 miles to the beach. The first third passes through fern-fringed conifer forest blessed by an understory of huckleberry and rhododendron. In May, when the rhododendrons are in flower, their white blossoms fill the forest with a mild citrus scent. The second third of the trail crosses open sand dunes, providing glimpses of the ocean. The last third cuts through the deflation plain to the beach. Between mid-March and mid-September you may encounter signs asking you to avoid certain areas in which imperiled western snowy plovers are nesting.

Allow ample time to explore the little estuary of the creek and the area where it runs into the ocean. In the sand along the creek you're likely to see the tracks of many animals, such as bear, mink, river otter, and alligator lizard—and occasionally the animals themselves. Killdeer, sandpipers, black-bellied plover, and other shorebirds often hunt for food along the margins of the estuary. The beach is a graveyard of forest bones: driftwood half buried in the sand or piled up at odd angles. Terns and gulls patrol the shore, occasionally joined by ospreys. To extend this hike, you can branch off north onto the **Tahkenitch Creek Trail** or south for 1.5 miles along the beach or along the eastern edge of the deflation plain to join the **Threemile Lake Trail** and loop back to your car.

A 2-mile drive north from the Tahkenitch Campground brings travelers to the **Oregon Dunes Overlook,** the most accessible site from which to see a representative sample of the dunes ecosystem. From a couple of viewing structures and from the walkway that runs next to the parking lot, you can sweep your gaze across open sand dunes, forest, tree islands, deflation plain, foredune, and beach. Informative signs help explain what you're seeing, and during the summer, guides host

walks and talks here. A 1-mile trail leads out to the beach.

The **Siltcoos Recreation Area,** about 3 miles north of the dunes overlook, offers two appealing trails: the Lagoon Trail and the Waxmyrtle Trail. Park at the lot labeled "Stagecoach Trailhead"— there is no Stagecoach Trail—and walk a quarter mile east, back to the bridge across the Siltcoos River and the entrance to Waxmyrtle Campground. The **Waxmyrtle Trail** crosses the bridge, then turns west and follows the south bank of the Siltcoos to the beach, about 1.5 miles. The river soon widens into a lush estuary, home to herons, egrets, bitterns, and ospreys, which often nest in the tall conifers along the riverbanks. At the mouth of the Siltcoos, you'll encounter more wildlife in marshes and along the driftwood-littered beach. The **Lagoon Trail,** a 1-mile loop, strikes north from the bridge. Move quietly along the boardwalk and be on the lookout for kingfishers, ospreys, wood ducks, frogs, and herons. ■

Tracking Dune Beetles

Sand dunes, particularly when slightly damp, register the tracks of even the lightest animals. Explore away from the tramplings of human visitors, and you'll encounter the traces of many sorts of critters. Among them, you'll often see a curving, circling line that looks as if it were left behind by a wayward strand of cooked spaghetti. This odd track marks the slow passage of a ciliated sand beetle. These quarter-inch dwellers of the dunes spend the day under the sand and make those tracks at night as they crawl about in search of food. Another little track you may find looks like the herringbone marks left by a skier walking up a slope, with a dashed line running down the middle. Follow this trail and you may catch up to the shiny, black, 1-inch-long insect known as a stink beetle. Beware, if it tilts its hind end in your direction it may be about to demonstrate the aptness of its name.

Cobra lilies at Darlingtonia State Natural Site

Darlingtonia State Natural Site

■ 18 acres ■ Central Oregon coast, north of Florence 8 miles , off US 101
■ Peak blooms May-June ■ Walking, plant viewing ■ Contact Honeyman State
Park, 84505 US 101 S, Florence, OR 97439; phone 541-997-3851 or 800-551-
6949. www.prd.state.or.us

DARLINGTONIA. This plant's Latin name evokes images of a sweet flower
praised by poets. Reality is reflected in the species' common name: cobra
lily. The cobra lily is a carnivore. Its leaves form a 2-foot-high tube—
think of it as a gullet—topped by an inwardly curving hood that looks
like the business end of a puffed-up cobra. However, *Darlingtonia* doesn't
strike its prey like a snake; its methods are more subtle.

Nectar glands near the gullet's opening lure insects into the tube. The
inner surface of the tube is slick and crawling bugs can't find a good
foothold. Flying bugs are fooled by translucent spots in the sides of the
tube that look like holes. The bugs exhaust themselves by repeatedly
buzzing into these closed windows. When victims slip farther down the
tube, angled hairs that act like barbs allow only downward passage.

At the tube's bottom, a pool of water drowns the bugs. The carcasses
decompose and provide the cobra lily with nutrients, notably nitrogen.
In fact, cobra lilies and nearly all other carnivorous plants evolved their
meat-eating ways mainly to obtain the nitrogen their boggy habitats lack.

Cobra lilies grow only in a few bogs in southern Oregon and northern
California, and this small site is the best spot to see them. A 100-yard trail
leads to a bog that bristles with thousands of hearty specimens. ■

Cape Perpetua Scenic Area

■ 2,700 acres ■ Central Oregon coast, south of Yachats 3 miles ■ Season year-round ■ Camping, hiking, guided walks, whale-watching, tide-pooling ■ Adm. fee ■ Contact the interpretive center, 2400 US 101 S, Yachats, OR 97498; phone 541-547-3289. www.newportnet.com/capeperpetua

THE CAPE PERPETUA Scenic Area has a dual personality. Along US 101, you'll see the scenic area's coastal character—one of the most dramatic meetings of land and sea on the Oregon coast. Inland from the highway, the bulk of the 2,700-acre preserve stretches back into the Coast Ranges, where the forest character of Cape Perpetua awaits. Put them together, and you've got a compact, accessible site that blends Oregon's two most renowned natural environments.

What to See and Do

For an overview par excellence, drive up to the **Cape Perpetua Overlook.** Situated atop the hulking cape that gave the scenic area its name, this 800-foot lookout is the highest viewpoint directly on the Oregon coast. You can gaze out to sea, back at the Coast Ranges, or almost straight down on the shoreline. This is a great place from which to watch for migrating gray whales in spring and winter.

The **Cape Perpetua Interpretive Center** (*open Memorial Day-Labor Day; Wed.-Sun. in May and Sept.; weekends only rest of year*) makes a logical second stop. Check out the exhibits, interactive displays, and videos on the area's natural and cultural history. From the center, trails fan out in all directions to coast and forest. You also can sign up for guided walks.

To explore the shore, take the half-mile **Captain Cook Trail** under the highway and down to **Cooks Chasm,** at the southernmost end of the scenic area's coastal strip. The chasm is a long, narrow channel through the rough volcanic rock. As waves surge up the chasm, they shatter into white spray and geyser up through a blowhole named the Spouting Horn. At low tide, nearby tide pools beckon the curious. Follow the shoreline trail north a few hundred yards to **Cape Cove,** where you can walk down to the beach. Another couple of hundred yards brings you to **Devils Churn,** a larger version of Cooks Chasm.

Several trails, ranging from 2 to 10 miles round-trip, head inland from the interpretive center into the coastal forest. The easiest and most popular is the **Giant Spruce Trail,** a flat 1-mile route that goes up Cape Creek through the spruce and ferns of the lush old-growth forest to a gigantic dead Sitka spruce. From the interpretive brochures, learn about nurse logs, canopy critters, mycorrhiza fungi, and other aspects of this complex ecosystem. If you can stay overnight, the campground along Cape Creek is lovely—and very popular during summer, so you'll need to reserve well ahead. ■

Following pages: Breaking waves at Cape Kiwanda

Yaquina Head Lighthouse, near Newport

Yaquina Head Outstanding Natural Area

■ 100 acres ■ Central Oregon coast; north of Newport 3 miles, west of US 101 ■ Best months March–June for bird-watching; late Dec.–early Jan. and mid-March–mid-April for whale-watching ■ Hiking, bird-watching, whale-watching, wildlife viewing, wildflower viewing, tide-pooling ■ Adm. fee ■ Contact the natural area, P.O. Box 936, Newport, OR 97365; phone 541-574-3100. www.or.blm.gov/salem/html/yaquina

THIS NATURAL AREA's official designation as "outstanding" may sound like bureaucratic hyperbole, but in this case the term is deserved. Yaquina Head is a 100-acre finger of volcanic rock that juts a mile into the ocean. Its high ground yields panoramic views, its shoreline offers some of the best tide-pooling in Oregon, its offshore rocks are home to a sprawling seabird colony, and it has a new interpretive center.

What to See and Do

The **interpretive center,** opened in 1997, contains a variety of exhibits, reflecting the varied nature of Yaquina Head itself. Some of the displays focus on the human aspects of the area, particularly the Yaquina Head Lighthouse and the Native Americans who lived here as long ago as 4,000 years, but many others delve into the headland's natural history. One exhibit shows the bones of various birds and challenges you to match them to the correct bird species. Nearby you can listen to recordings of seabird calls, most of which are less than musical; those cute tufted puffins sound like a cross between a bullfrog and a rusty door hinge. At another display, you'll learn that sunflower stars (sea stars) are the dominant predators of the lowest tide-pool zone. Measuring as much as 3 feet across and traveling on more than 15,000 tube feet, these tigers of the intertidal zone race along at 3 feet per minute. And outside, behind the interpretive center, check out the basalt cliff face that has been turned into a geology exhibit.

To start your exploration of the real world at Yaquina Head, hike or drive about half a mile to the tip of the headland, by the lighthouse. To see the lay of the land—and water—take the steep but short **Salal Hill Trail** to the top of **Salal Hill.** In the spring, enjoy the wildflowers, such as wild rose and false lily-of-the-valley.

When you return to the parking area, go to the other side of the lot and take the **Cobble Beach Stairway.** Platforms along the stairway yield fine views of **Seal Island,** perhaps 100 yards distant, and the harbor seals that often hang out there. You'll probably see them during their inactive stage, draped motionless over the rocks like plump, 5-foot-long, mottled gray sausages. When they're busy hunting—they consume fish, mainly—they spend most of their time underwater.

If you've come at low tide—and you should—continue to the bottom of the stairs and across the smooth, fist-sized stones that give **Cobble Beach** its name. When waves roll these cobbles around they produce a surprisingly light sound akin to the tinkling of glass wind chimes. Beyond the cobbles lies the excellent tide-pooling area, often staffed by a BLM employee who informs visitors about intertidal life. (A wheelchair-accessible tide pool area is located back up the road at **Quarry Cove,** just east of the interpretive center.)

The tide pools teem with chitons, sculpins, hermit crabs, sea cucumbers, and many other critters, but most people immediately head for the nearest sea stars, arguably the most famous residents of the rocky intertidal area. Along the Pacific coast and at Cobble Beach, ocher stars—which, for reasons not yet understood, come in purple, brown, red, orange, and tan as well as ocher—are by far the most common of the sea stars. You'll see them clinging to rocks, but what you don't see is what happens after the returning tide covers the rocks and the ocher stars go to work. These fearsome predators move into mussel beds, where they attach their thousands

Whale-Watching

Each year, more than 20,000 gray whales migrate along the Pacific coast between their feeding grounds in the Bering Sea and their breeding and calving grounds in Mexico. Southbound whales pass close along the Northwest coast from early December to early February, peaking at about 30 whales an hour from late December to early January. When they head back north during March, April, and May, they pass even closer to shore; mid-March to mid-April is the best whale-watching time. For more on whale-watching, including sites, contact the Oregon Parks and Recreation office in Waldport at 541-563-2002.

of suction-cup tube feet to the shell of an unfortunate victim and force the mussel to open slightly—even a millimeter will do. Then the ocher star pushes its stomach out of its body and slips part of it through the shell opening. Powerful enzymes begin digesting the bivalve, including the muscles that clamp its shell shut, so that it eventually gapes wide open, allowing the sea star to fully insert its stomach and devour the mussel.

Another common Cobble Beach tide-pool resident is an animal that looks like a plant: the giant green anemone. Robust specimens measure a strapping 6 inches in diameter, not counting the inch-long tentacles that protrude from the rim like petals on a flower. You'll also see much smaller cousins, only an inch across, called aggregating anemones. What they lack in size they make up for in numbers. A single progenitor will reproduce asexually and populate a section of rock with dozens, even hundreds, of its clones, packed tightly to-gether. The narrow strips of bare rock that wind through mats of aggregating anemones serve as demilitarized zones, separating the warring clans.

The last stop at Yaquina Head is the deck just beyond the lighthouse, on the very end of the headland. This excellent **whale-watching station** offers great views of migrating gray whales heading south during the peak season from early December to early February and moving north from March through May. You may also get an occasional look at the resident grays who linger around Yaquina Head from May through October.

And then there's **Colony Rock**, a steep little island just a few dozen yards from the viewing deck. From roughly March through June, some 25,000 seabirds nest there. You can watch thousands of common murres, gulls, cormorants, pigeon guillemots, and occasional tufted puffins and black oystercatchers as they go about their daily business. You may see murres diving for food to bring back to their baby chicks, cormorants intertwining their necks in a courtship display, or uncertain fledgings flapping at the edge of the precipice as they prepare to take their first flight. ■

Exploring tide pools at Yaquina Head Outstanding Natural Area

Enjoying the view from Cape Lookout overlook

Three Capes Scenic Drive

■ Northern Oregon coast, between Nestucca Bay and Tillamook ■ Camping, hiking, kayaking, fishing, bird-watching, wildlife viewing, auto tour ■ Day-use fee for Cape Lookout State Park ■ Contact Tillamook Chamber of Commerce, 3705 US 101 N, Tillamook, OR 97141; phone 503-842-7525. www.tillamookchamber.org

FOR ALMOST THE ENTIRE LENGTH of Oregon, US 101 sticks close to the ocean, but from Nestucca Bay to just north of Tillamook the highway deviates from its coastal course. No problem. The Three Capes drive takes motorists from US 101 back to the Pacific for 40 miles on back roads between Nestucca Bay and Tillamook—just follow the signs. Even on this route, however, the rugged coastline sometimes forces the road slightly inland, out of sight of the water. To see the best of the shore, you'll have to take some short spur roads and some short (or long) hikes. The three capes themselves—Cape Kiwanda, Cape Lookout, and Cape Meares—are indeed the highlights of the tour and deserve better than a quick drive-by. Start by taking the route south to north.

Cape Kiwanda

The well-marked route heads west from US 101 on Brooten Road, about a mile north of the bridge across the Little Nestucca River. You'll follow the north shore of Nestucca Bay and the estuary of the **Nestucca River,** famed for its salmon and steelhead fishing. After a couple of miles the drive enters Pacific City, where, as the town's name promises, you'll once again meet up with the ocean. About 2 miles to the south, on the spit that protects Nestucca Bay from the sea, lies **Robert W. Straub State Park** *(800-551-6949),* 483 acres of grassy sand dunes and little-used beach. But the scenic drive turns north here on Cape Kiwanda Drive, drawn by the allure of **Cape Kiwanda,** about 2 miles beyond downtown Pacific City. From the parking lot, walk about a quarter mile north along the beach and you'll reach the cape.

The sandstone cliffs of this small headland are said to be the most photographed subject on the Oregon coast. The curving layers of tan, red, and gold sandstone nearly burst into flame in the setting sun. The relentless Pacific breakers would have reduced the soft rock of Cape Kiwanda to sand long ago but for the looming presence of **Haystack Rock,** a broad 327-foot sea stack just offshore that to some degree shields the cliffs from waves.

After admiring the cape from the beach, you can reach the top of the cliffs by laboring up the steep sand dune just behind the headland. Once there, follow the network of informal trails that lead across the top of the cape toward the ocean. Some are easy, some require scrambling and climbing. You can decide what level of challenge you want, but for safety's sake always stay back from the crumbling edges of the sandstone cliffs.

Sea kyaker at Haystack Rock, Cape Kiwanda

Some trails lead through unexpected patches of wildflowers, salal, and wind-stunted conifers. Most end with breathtaking vistas of the sea and shore. In places you'll encounter sculpture gardens of sandstone hoodoos, knobs, pillars, and pancake stacks. Below the bluffs a rocky shelf forms a marine garden of tide pools, where gulls and oystercatchers screech and squabble as they forage for food.

Cape Lookout

A little north of Cape Kiwanda, the drive veers inland on Sandlake Road and winds through forest, sand dunes, and pastures for about 10 miles. It rejoins the coast via Cape Lookout Road at **Cape Lookout State Park** *(Cape Lookout visitor center. 503-842-4981),* which includes the headquarters, campground, and day-use area. However, about 2 miles before the road hits the coast, you'll come to the trailhead for three hikes. (The highway signs don't name the trails; they just bear the symbols for state park, hiking, and wildlife viewing.) The trails begin together but branch shortly after leaving the parking lot. One switchbacks 2 miles down to a broad sandy beach. A second winds north 2.5 miles to the day-use area. The third, the easiest and the one you don't want to miss, forges straight ahead 2.5 miles out to the tip of the cape.

The **Cape Lookout trail** starts in old-growth coastal forest, passing beneath 200-foot Sitka spruce and western redcedar and brushing by a thronged understory of ferns and evergreen huckleberry. Steller's jays and downy woodpeckers flit amid the trees and Douglas' squirrels scold passersby. After half a mile or so you'll begin catching glimpses of the sea.

Soon the trail breaks out into the open along the south flank of the headland, providing a gull's-eye view of the surf far below and distant vistas south to Cape Kiwanda, Cascade Head, and clear down to Cape Foulweather, 40 miles away. Temperatures rise on this south-facing slope and you'll often encounter snakes sunning themselves. They aren't poisonous, and they'll slither out of your way. The trail ends at an observation area, which offers more terrific views.

Back on the scenic drive, continue north to **Cape Lookout's day-use area.** Some beautifully sited picnic tables are scattered amid the coastal scrub on the short bluff above the shoreline. Interpretive signs and a nature trail relate the park's natural and human history. You can hike 5 miles north along the driftwood-littered sand spit that separates the ocean from Netarts Bay.

From Cape Lookout, the route hugs the shoreline of **Netarts Bay** for about 5 miles until you reach the town of Netarts, at the mouth of the bay. Watch for great blue herons in the shallows and harbor seals hauled out on sandbars in the bay's protected waters. Beyond the bay you're back to open ocean and thundering surf as the road curves the 3 miles to the little resort town of Oceanside. About a quarter mile offshore the trio of huge sea stacks known as **Three Arch Rocks** juts from the sea. One of North America's largest seabird colonies, this sanctuary hosts about a quarter-million murres, puffins, and cormorants during spring and early summer. Look for sea lions on the lower ledges.

Surf fishing, Cape Lookout State Park

Cape Meares

A couple of miles north of Oceanside you'll come to Cape Meares, home to both a state park *(800-551-6949)* and a national wildlife refuge *(541-867-4550)*. A 30-second stroll from the parking lot puts you at the edge of a sheer cliff, 200 feet above a cove. You can look far out to sea or scan the cliff faces for seabirds and the peregrine falcon that has favored this spot in recent years. About 200 yards from the parking lot is the **Octopus Tree,** a giant Sitka spruce with a diameter that exceeds 10 feet and limbs as thick as 5 feet that branch out nearly horizontally.

The centerpiece of Cape Meares is the paved, nearly flat, half-mile trail that runs along the northern rim of the headland to the tip of the promontory and then back along the southern rim to the parking lot. The path is lined with excellent interpretive signs, many regarding seabirds. Tufted puffins, you'll learn, have barbed tongues, enabling them to hold one fish while opening their jaws to snatch another. And common murres work diligently to protect their eggs: On sunny days they shade the eggs with their bodies and on cold days they cradle them in their webbed feet, which are warm due to an abundance of blood vessels.

The reason for the interpretive emphasis on seabirds becomes apparent once you reach the lighthouse area at the tip of the cape, especially if it's spring or early summer. Murres, cormorants, pelicans, puffins, pigeon guillemots, and other ocean-oriented birds throng the waters, bobbing on the swell, skimming low over the water, and flying underwater in pursuit of fish. **Pillar** and **Pyramid Rocks,** located just north of the lighthouse, give visitors a close look at life in a seabird colony. Social skills are at a premium under these crowded conditions. Though they're the size of a duck, murres pack up to seven nests on a square foot of rock. To protect their tiny territories, which they return to every year, murres use a threat display, drawing their wings back like a rooster about to crow.

From Cape Meares the route cuts inland a couple of miles to **Tillamook Bay.** There it turns southeast and edges right along the water for a few miles until the road enters the town of Tillamook and ends downtown at the junction with US 101. ∎

Brown pelicans on sea stacks

Seaweed in pounding surf

Oswald West State Park

■ 2,474 acres ■ Northern Oregon coast, south of Cannon Beach 10 miles on US 101 ■ Best months March-Oct. ■ Camping, hiking, wildlife viewing ■ Contact Nehalem Bay State Park, P.O. Box 366, Nehalem, OR 97131; phone 503-368-5154. www.prd.state.or.us

WHEN OSWALD WEST, the governor of Oregon in 1911-15, signed the law making all of Oregon's beaches public, he had no idea his name would become attached to the glorious stretch of undeveloped shoreline and old-growth coastal rain forest that is now Oswald West State Park.

For the quintessential Oswald West experience, leave your car in the lot on the east side of US 101 near the park's southern boundary and take the trail that goes under the highway. As you amble down this paved path alongside **Short Sands Creek,** take your time. Observe the immense trees and watch for American dippers twitching their tail feathers on streamside rocks. In about 15 minutes you'll emerge onto **Short Sands Beach** at **Smuggler's Cove.** This sandy quarter-mile curve of beach is backed by steep bluffs thick with conifers. You can stroll this beach quickly, but you may feel compelled to stay for hours to hunt shells or watch the waves.

A section of the **Oregon Coast Trail** (see sidebar p. 19) runs just behind the beach. You can follow it either north or south, but if your time is limited try to hike the moderately difficult trail north at least a couple of miles. You'll slip through some grand old-growth Sitka spruce forest, where moss drapes the tree branches and the forest floor is a spongy green carpet. After about an hour you'll come to an unmarked trail that branches west to **Cape Falcon.** About 10 minutes of negotiating the maze of trails that cut through the head-high scrub brings you into an open grassy area with superb ocean views. ■

Ecola State Park

Ecola State Park

■ 1,303 acres ■ Northern Oregon coast, north of Cannon Beach 2 miles
■ Hiking, swimming, wildlife viewing, beachcombing ■ Adm. fee ■ Contact
Nehalem Bay State Park, P.O. Box 366, Nehalem, OR 97131; phone 503-368-
5154. www.prd.state.or.us

ECOLA STATE PARK has been wowing visitors since 1806. That's when
William Clark, Sacagawea, and other members of the Lewis and Clark
Expedition passed through some of the 1,300 acres that today constitute
the park. Clark wrote glowingly of the magnificent coastline and the
views from what is now called Tillamook Head. You can enjoy much the
same experience—little has changed since Clark sang the praises of this
dramatic landscape.

What to See and Do

After entering the park and driving slowly through the forest for
about 10 minutes, you'll come to a
signed junction. Go west to **Ecola
Beach.** This rocky shore features a
grassy picnic area overlooking the
sea and numerous trails running
along the coastline. On the beach
to the south, weathered driftwood
has collected in piles, and a creek
cascades 15 or 20 feet from the
bluff onto the sand.

Ecola Beach's most popular
trail is a half-mile path that runs
out to the end of **Ecola Point,** a
short headland. From the tip you
get good views of **Sea Lion Rocks,**
home to—surprise—seals (especially from April to mid-July) and
seabirds (April to August). For
reasons not yet clarified, sea lions
have not been stopping at the
rocks for about 10 years now.
Sometimes you'll see the birds

gathering grass from the picnic area to take out to the rocks for their nests. Farther offshore juts **Tillamook Rock,** site of a historic lighthouse, thousands of common murres, and the remains of many deceased people: Part of the area has been turned into a columbarium, where ashes are laid to rest by a company called Eternity at Sea.

Return to the main road and continue winding north through the forest. In a couple of miles the road ends at **Indian Beach,** one of those cozy little coves that evokes daydreams of leaving the fast lane and leading a beachcombing life. The Indian Beach parking lot also serves as the trailhead for one of Oregon's premier hikes, the 6-mile **Tillamook Head Trail.** This fairly strenuous route stretches all the way to Seaside, so parties with two vehicles can arrange a shuttle if they want to avoid a 12-mile round-trip trek.

Soon after starting the gradual ascent from the sea-level lot at Indian Beach, the trail enters classic, cathedral-like old-growth forest. Grand Sitka spruces dominate, many of them 6 or 8 feet in diameter. Sitka spruce typically grow only within 4 miles of the ocean. You can identify them by their gray, jigsaw-puzzle bark and their prickly needles. Many of these forest patriarchs and matriarchs spread their arms wide, sending out massive horizontal branches big enough to be the trunks of lesser trees. Often miniature forests of thick moss and 3-foot-high ferns take up residence on the tops of these branches.

Despite the dense forest foliage, at various points you'll get tremendous views; the trail ranges as high as 1,000 feet as it crosses over **Tillamook Head.** At one viewpoint, perhaps 600 feet above the ocean, you can look down upon a black cobble beach and, if it's quiet enough, you can hear the music of the cobbles as they jostle in the surf. You'll soon understand why, when hiking over Tillamook Head on January 8, 1806, Clark wrote, "I beheld the grandest and most pleasing prospects which my eyes ever surveyed." ■

Going Bananas

The banana slug is a Northwest icon. Six, eight, even ten inches long; yellowish with black stripes; gloriously slimy: What's not to admire? Banana slugs are commonly encountered on damp forest trails in the Coast Ranges and on the west side of the Cascades. Look for them when it's rainy or very humid; they use up lots of water producing the slime that enables them to ooze across the forest floor. One might think that these slow creatures would be easy pickings for any small predator, but banana slugs know how to defend themselves. Just ask any of the many Northwest children who has licked a banana slug—it's something of a rite of passage in the region—and they will tell you how their tongue went numb and felt weird for most of the day. Evidentially, predators find the sensation offputting too.

Saddle Mountain State Park

■ 2,921 acres ■ Northwest Oregon; northeast of Cannon Beach 20 miles, off US 26 ■ Best months for wildflowers are May-Aug ■ Hiking, camping, wildlife viewing, wildflower viewing ■ Contact Nehalem Bay State Park, P.O. Box 366, Nehalem, OR 97131; phone 503-368-5154. www.prd.state.or.us

THOUGH SADDLE MOUNTAIN STATE PARK encompasses nearly 3,000 acres of the Coast Ranges, its considerable fame stems from a single trail and the summit to which that trail leads. The hike is demanding—an elevation gain of more than 1,600 feet in 2.5 miles, plus some sections that get slippery during rainy weather—but the rewards merit the effort.

The **Saddle Mountain Trail** begins at the parking lot and campground. At first the climb is gradual as the path cuts through heavy forest up the south flank of the mountain. Listen to the ravens and jays as their calls reverberate among the big trees and watch for elk, which frequent both the forested areas and the open slopes farther up.

About halfway up, the trail emerges from the dark forest into the sunny, open meadows that characterize the higher elevations. During the spring and summer, blooms of red, white, yellow, blue, purple, and pink are sprinkled through the green of the meadows. The trail grows steeper after this halfway point, but you'll want to stop often to look at the wildflowers and the increasingly fine views anyway.

For another half mile or so, the trail weaves back and forth between forest and meadow, though the forest shrinks in stature as you get higher until it's eventually reduced to krummholz—the bent, stunted trees near

Clear-cuts, Saddle Mountain State Park

timberline that are barely coping. Just past the 2-mile point, the trail crosses a bridge that spans a saddle, providing long views to the east and the west. A little way beyond the bridge the grade becomes steeper still and covered with loose rock; there's a cable strung between poles that you can hold onto for assistance. It's slow going, but don't give up now. The muscular hump of the summit looms close ahead; you're only a few hundred wheezes and gasps from the top.

While you're resting, savor the alpine meadows that surround you. And don't just soak in the big picture of the flower-bedecked slopes. Look closely. You'll see ground-hugging succulents and pin-cushion plants wearing tiny pink blossoms. There are alpine lilies, Saddle Mountain saxifrage, pink fawn-lilies, Saddle Mountain bittercress, and hairy-stemmed sidalcea, some of which are rare and endangered plants. This mountaintop, the highest Coast Ranges peak for miles around, serves as a wet, cool refuge for many species more commonly found in Canada and Alaska. The ice age enabled them to spread south into Oregon, but after the glaciers and cold retreated the plants died off at lower elevations.

At last, you'll reach the summit, 3,283 feet above sea level. The 360-degree view includes hundreds of square miles of the Pacific and dozens of miles of shoreline; the mouth of the Columbia and much of the lower river; and a vast swath of the Cascades, including Mount Hood, Mount St. Helens, Mount Rainier, and other volcanic peaks. Only the plethora of clear-cuts sully this otherwise marvelous panorama. You also get a grand view of Saddle Mountain itself, including its knife-edge ridges, sheer cliffs, and sharp promontories. ■

South Cascades

Mount Hood, reflected in Mirror Lake

THE SOUTH CASCADES owe their existence to titanic forces at work deep within the planet. For tens of millions of years, two tectonic plates—the Juan de Fuca and Blanco—bearing the floor of the Pacific Ocean have been sliding beneath the North American plate, producing a volcanic arc. As the seafloor descends into the earth's fiery bowels, it heats up. The presence of seawater allows the rock to melt more easily than dry rocks at the same depth and temperature. This molten rock is less dense than the surrounding rocks and it is fluid, so it rises toward the earth's surface and erupts through volcanoes.

The South Cascades of Oregon actually consist of two sections that date from different volcanic episodes: the Old Cascades and the High Cascades. The Old Cascades lie in the southwestern part of the range. They erupted into being between 50 million and 12 million years ago. Today these rounded and slumped mountains, all of which long ago became extinct, hardly fit the image of volcanoes. The younger, more robust High Cascades, on the other hand, include some classic volcanic peaks, many of which are still active—some emphatically so, such as Mount St. Helens (see p. 103).

The High Cascades began forming just to the east of the Old Cascades several million years ago. This volcanic episode has yet to end, as was demonstrated 7,700 years ago when Mount Mazama—located where Crater Lake is today—blew, blasting hundreds of square miles of the neighboring landscape and dumping ash over most of the Pacific Northwest. Even more recently, in 1980, volcanic forces inside Mount St. Helens crumpled the top 1,300 feet of its conical peak and released a tremendous lateral blast that flattened 150,000 acres of forest, reminding people in the region that the Cascades are indeed still active.

Between south-central Oregon and south-central Washington, at least 13 major volcanic centers jut from the South Cascades. Many are located above tree line. Fortunately, though, the area consists of more than erupting volcanoes, or even extinct volcanoes. Most of the range is much lower in elevation and heavily forested, and it receives plenty of precipitation. These vast green seas of towering conifers have no equal in the contiguous 48 states, though logging has reduced much of the old-growth forest to clear-cuts or tree plantations. Many roads and trails in the South Cascades wind through quiet groves of ancient trees that rise 150, 200, even 250 feet above an understory alive with ferns, moss-covered fallen giants, mushrooms, and rhododendrons. This is the province of elk, spotted owls, voles, flying squirrels, pileated woodpeckers, and pine martens—though animals can be difficult to spot in this verdant habitat. In addition to their intrinsic worth, beauty, and recreational offerings, these old-growth forests provide practical services to humans. Arguments about logging versus conservation often tend to overlook the immense but difficult-to-calculate economic value of the old-growth ecosystem, which includes such factors as flood control, the cleansing of airborne pollutants, healthy fisheries, the moderation of climate, and the protection of water supplies.

As all that vegetation suggests, the South Cascades receive a great deal of precipitation, though much less on the leeward east side of the crest than on the windward west. Residents of the area must contend with 40, 60, perhaps 80 inches of rain a year in some places, but little of that falls during the exceedingly pleasant summers. However, snow often lingers on high-country roads and trails well into the summer months, so be sure to talk to park officials before you visit and plan accordingly. ■

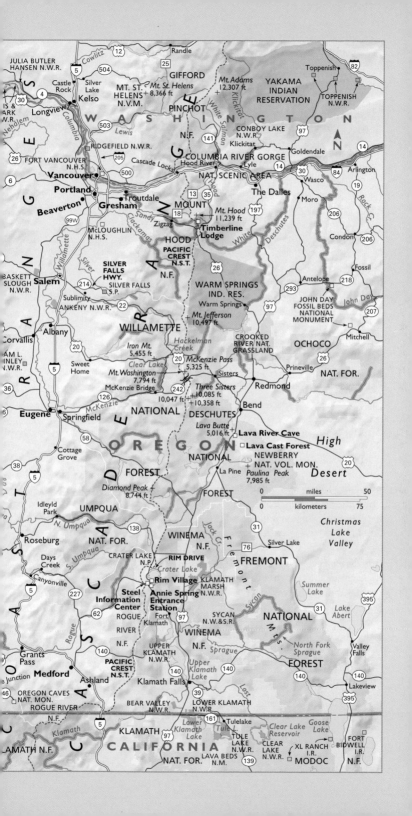

American white pelicans, Klamath Basin NWR

Klamath Basin National Wildlife Refuges

■ 185,000 acres ■ South-central Oregon, north-central California, off US 97
■ Best seasons vary with wildlife; check with NWR headquarters ■ Hiking,
canoeing, bird-watching, wildlife viewing, self-guided auto tours ■ Contact the
refuges, Route 1, Box 74, Tulelake, CA 96143; phone 530-667-2231.
www.klamathnwr.org

FIRST YOU HEAR THEM. As dawn restores color to the marshes and fields,
murmurings, faint squawks, and coos tease your ears. Slowly the decibel
level grows as the great flocks of geese, ducks, and swans warm to the day.
Suddenly they take to the sky, heading to the fields to feed or resuming
their migration. The uprising usually starts with a few birds, quickly followed by dozens, then hundreds, then thousands more. The low-angled
light flickers as the waterfowl swirl in front of the rising sun, their feathers flashing white and black and red and green. The thump of their
wingbeats pummels you, and the resonant cacophony of their squabbling
strands you somewhere between wanting to whoop with them and wanting to cover your ears. You're momentarily transported to an earlier time,
an era when vast bison herds roamed the plains, salmon choked the
rivers, and the howls of wolves filled the night.

This primeval experience awaits you at the Klamath Basin National
Wildlife Refuges. The six units in this 185,000-acre complex of federal
lands straddle the Oregon-California border, on the southeast edge of the
Cascades. One refuge, Clear Lake, is closed to the public except for a brief
hunting season and offers nothing for the casual visitor. Another, Bear
Valley, also is closed, but draws many visitors to its perimeter to view the
hundreds of bald eagles that roost there in winter. But the other four

refuges—Tule Lake, Lower Klamath, Upper Klamath, and Klamath Marsh—welcome visitors and can be explored via auto tour routes, hiking trails, and canoe trips. What you see depends on the time of year, but there is always wildlife to be enjoyed.

The Klamath Basin refuges are renowned for the waterfowl that migrate through here—one million to two million birds twice a year, which constitutes about three-quarters of all the geese, ducks, and swans that migrate up and down the Pacific flyway. That's the largest concentration in North America. But this basin is far more than just a giant duck pond, thanks to the variety of habitats, which includes grasslands, conifer forests, meadows, rocky cliffs, and farmlands, in addition to the marshes, lakes, and ponds favored by waterfowl. For example, the Klamath Basin boasts the largest concentration of bald eagles in the lower 48 states. The eagles are joined by thousands of other raptors, including rough-legged hawks, American kestrels, northern harriers, and red-tailed hawks. During the spring and fall, large numbers of shorebirds migrate through here. American white pelicans, sandhill cranes, and white-faced ibises occupy a bird list that numbers 263 species, an alluring diversity that brings birders and wildlife lovers here from the world over. The refuges also shelter many animals that can't fly, such as pronghorn, western pond turtles, river otters, white sturgeon, elk, kangaroo rats, and long-toed salamanders.

Still, the Klamath Basin is not the wildlife haven it once was. In the early 1900s the government and farmers began building dams, dikes, canals, ditches, and pumping plants in the basin. Eventually they drained nearly 80 percent of the original wetlands and began growing barley, wheat, and potatoes where tundra swans, beavers, and trout once flourished. Waterfowl numbers dropped from six million to the present level of one million to two million. Farmers also grow crops on thousands of

Roost Sweet Roost

When we size up a hotel, we consider numerous factors. Is it close to restaurants? Will it provide a quiet night's rest? Does it have convenient parking? Is it warm and comfortable? The bald eagles that winter in the Klamath Basin make a similar analysis when they pick a roost for the night. Is it close to the waterfowl and rodents on which the eagles generally feed? Is it far from human disturbance? Does it offer trees that can hold the weight of a number of eagles? Are there bare branches for easy landing and takeoff? Is it protected from the prevailing winds? Important factors all, since a poor choice of roosts can decrease a bald eagle's chances of surviving a winter.

Eagles must shift roosts through the winter, too, much as travelers change lodgings. As the waterfowl and other food sources move about, so must the eagles. This transience means that we must protect good roosting sites in order to protect the eagles.

acres inside the refuges. On some of this land they raise grains, some of which is left behind for waterfowl. However, recent research indicates that native aquatic plants are likely to be more nutritious than grains.

Predictably, pesticides and fertilizers from farms wash into the refuges, compromising their water quality and harming aquatic life. The pollution in turn harms the birds and other animals that rely on the aquatic environment for food and shelter. In time the situation may improve, however: The U.S. Fish and Wildlife Service and local farmers are taking steps to cut down on the amount of chemical pesticides that drain into the refuges.

Water quantity appears to be a more intractable problem. In dry years refuge wetlands don't get sufficiently wet, even with contaminated water; the vast majority of the basin's water goes to farms. In 1998, refuge managers asserted that on refuge lands, the water requirements of wildlife would come before those of irrigated agriculture. This policy has angered many farmers, who fear their crops will suffer during dry years. It remains to be seen whether a workable compromise can be found.

Great egret

Deer in velvet

What to See and Do

Tule Lake and Lower Klamath Refuges

Start at the **Tule Lake refuge,** off Calif. 161. At the **visitor center** and refuge headquarters located there you can pick up brochures, wildlife lists, and interpretive guides for the auto tour routes, hiking trails, and canoe trips. You also can start wildlife-watching immediately. Behind the building to the west rise the rocky cliffs of **Sheepy Ridge,** a favorite spot of prairie falcons, barn owls, and great-horned owls. Look for the mud nests of cliff swallows plastered to the rocks and scout for mule deer on the ridge's upper slopes. Near the center, hike up the steep, quarter-mile interpretive trail and look out over a vast expanse of the basin. The short, level interpretive path near the center provides a close-up look at **Discovery Marsh.**

After you've exhausted the area around the visitor center, drive south on Hill Road. Some consider this the start of the auto tour, but the 9.6-mile route described in the "Wildlife Tour Route" booklet begins about 5 miles south of the center, on the gravel road that strikes out east into the heart of the refuge. However, about a mile before you reach that road, stop at the wildlife overlook and look east into the refuge. If it's spring, fall, or winter, the shallow lake stretching out in front of you probably will be dotted with many different species of geese and ducks, with a sprinkling of tundra swans. Even in the summer you'll often see Canada geese, cinnamon teal, northern shovelers, and other waterfowl that nest on the refuge.

Once you've turned east on the gravel road, you'll be driving between Sump 1-A and the

Evening bike ride along Klamath wetlands

Southwest Sump; those unprepossessing names remind one that these wetland complexes have been drastically altered by development, Tule Lake most of all. But don't let that keep you from enjoying the sight of preening white-fronted geese or yellow-headed blackbirds hanging from the cattails. As you slowly motor along, remember that your car serves as a wildlife blind; getting out is likely to scare the animals away. In winter, you can watch in comfort the spectacle that occurs when the lakes freeze over, except for those areas kept open by huge flocks of ducks. Bald eagles and hawks, sometimes by the hundreds, come to feed on the vulnerable waterfowl.

As you pass from Sump 1-A to Sump 1-B, you'll drive along the west bank of the **English Channel.** Its relatively deep water attracts diving ducks, such as canvasback and common goldeneye. In spring watch for western grebes, famed for their courtship ritual, which

includes the so-called rushing display: The courting pair runs across the water flapping madly. Another member of this bird family, the eared grebe, usually forms summer colonies in Sump 1-B. They construct floating nests out of algae and reeds, anchored to rooted plants. Look closely at the grebes' backs and you may spot a little fluff ball with a bill—grebe chicks hitching a ride on the adults.

Just west of Tule Lake on Calif. 161 lies the **Lower Klamath refuge,** the country's first waterfowl refuge. Established in 1908, it is the largest of the six units. The Lower Klamath is less developed than Tule Lake (though hardly unscathed), and it encompasses a greater variety of marshes and other habitats. Given these attributes, it's not surprising that Lower Klamath hosts the highest numbers of migrating waterfowl in the basin. If you want to overwhelm your senses with masses of geese and ducks flapping, honking, feeding, and quacking, take a spring or fall drive on the 10-mile auto tour route, which loops right through the middle of Lower Klamath. In the spring you'll also spot stately sandhill cranes stalking about the refuge like wise elders lost in thought. Migrating shorebirds, including svelte avocets and stilts, mince around in the shallow water on spindly legs and big feet. For a summer treat take in the nesting white-faced ibis—more than 900 pairs in 1999. Two feet tall with a long downward-curving bill and dark iridescent plumage, the ibises are handsome creatures. Summer visitors may assume that male ibises hatch their young, but that's only because they typically sit on the nest during the day. Females sit on the nests at night.

Bear Valley, Upper Klamath, and Klamath Marsh Refuges

Except for early fall deer hunters, the general public may not enter **Bear Valley refuge,** located 15 miles south of Klamath Falls on US 97. Yet this small unit is one of the most popular places in the Klamath Basin among wildlife-watchers. To discover the answer to this mystery, get up before dawn sometime between December and mid-March and drive out on the short dirt road that comes within about half a mile of the southeast corner of the refuge. Park the car and train your binoculars on the old-growth conifers to the west just as the rising sun gilds them. Soon a bald eagle will fly out into the golden light. Eventually as many as 300 will have flown from the trees, leaving their roost to begin the day's hunt. In some years more than a thousand bald eagles winter at the Klamath Basin.

During the day you'll spot the eagles and other raptors patrolling the skies throughout the Klamath Basin. One place you might see bald eagles and ospreys fishing is in **Upper Klamath refuge.** But the only way into these 15,000 acres of marsh and open water is via the canoe trail. If you don't have your own craft, you can rent a canoe at the start of the route *(Rocky Point Resort, 541-356-2287)*. Paddle quietly and keep your voices down, and you'll likely encounter all manner of wildlife, including a cluster of American white pelicans swimming and dipping their bills as they feed in unison. Watch for the wriggling wake of a snake slithering through the rushes, and the sleek heads of curious river otters popping up to check you out.

The finest and most extensive natural marshes in the Klamath Basin are located in **Klamath Marsh Refuge** *(off US 97, near Crater Lake National Park)*, the northernmost of the six units. The basin's ubiquitous waterfowl show up here, of course, along with herons, pelicans, snipes, muskrats, phalaropes, ospreys, avocets, mule deer, and hundreds of other species that thrive in this relative-ly undisturbed wetland complex. The pine forests of the refuge even harbor Rocky Mountain elk. A 10-mile loop trail makes this the one refuge that can be explored in part on foot. You also can slowly drive across the main marsh on Silver Lake Road. **Wocus Bay,** a marshy area in the extreme southeast portion of the refuge, is open to canoes during summer. ∎

Crater Lake National Park

- 183,224 acres ■ South-central Oregon, 80 miles northeast of Medford
- Season year-round ■ Camping, hiking, boat tours, fishing, snowmobiling, cross-country skiing, snowshoeing, wildlife viewing, wildflower viewing ■ Adm. fee; backcountry use permits required for overnight stays ■ Contact the park, P.O. Box 7, Crater Lake, OR 97604; phone 541-594-2211. www.nps.gov/crla or www.crater.lake.national-park.com

GAZING DOWN on Crater Lake, it's hard to imagine the violence that created this serene mountain scene. It all started about 420,000 years ago, when massive volcanic eruptions began forming what became known as Mount Mazama, one of the string of volcanoes that anchors the crest of the Cascades. Over the millennia lava flows from enormous cracks in the earth and eruptions of ash, pumice, and cinders built Mount Mazama into an awesome 12,000-foot peak. Then, about 7,700 years ago, the volcano erupted as it had never erupted before. Scientists estimate that the force of the outburst was 50 to 100 times greater than that of Mount St. Helens in 1980. Hot gas, pumice, and ash blew high into the air, and ash spread across an area that now includes eight states and three Canadian provinces. As the magma chamber beneath Mazama's peak emptied, the mountain collapsed, forming the caldera that today holds Crater Lake.

The word caldera derives from the Spanish for "kettle," and it is the term geologists use to describe a basin-shaped volcanic depression. Some scientific sticklers note that Crater Lake rightly should be called Caldera Lake, and a number of 19th-century visitors lobbied for the names Deep Blue Lake and Lake Majesty. But in 1869 a newspaper editor demonstrated the power of the press when he wrote an article calling this body of water Crater Lake. The name stuck.

By any other name, Crater Lake still would be grand. It is the deepest lake in the United States and the seventh deepest in the world, plunging

1,932 feet. The cliffs that cup the lake rise on average 1,000 feet from the surface of the water, and in some places the rim looms 2,000 feet above. Crater Lake's water is remarkably clear, owing to the fact that there is no current volcanic activity in the caldera; also, no streams flow into the lake from outside. (The lake is fed by rain and snow melt.) Most striking of all, however, is the color of the lake—a deep, luminous blue. As the perhaps apocryphal story goes, when Kodak first processed photographs of Crater Lake, the company apologized to its customers; the lab technicians could only assume that the unbelievable blue in the pictures had resulted from bungled processing.

Though many visitors leave the park once they've enjoyed the lake, the park does offer other worthwhile features. You can drive out to a cluster of dramatic formations of fused pumice and ash called the Pinnacles. Hiking trails and roads provide access to pine and fir forests, wildflower meadows, an artistically eroded canyon, a pumice desert, and to several mountaintops. Observant visitors may spot deer, coyotes, red foxes, yellow-bellied marmots, and occasionally some of the more elusive of the park's 50-plus mammal species, such as martens, elk, and black bears.

What to See and Do

Most visitors simply want to see the lake. They'll pass peaks, creeks, canyons, desert, hiking trails, and more in their rush to get there. If you come in from the west or south on Oreg. 62, as most visitors do, consider pausing at the **Steel Information Center** to watch the 18-minute film about the park. Then drive the last 3 miles to the lake, turn right into the Rim Village area, park, and hustle over to the **Sinnot Memorial** on the east rim of the lake. From the viewpoint atop the 900-foot cliff, that first unobstructed view of Crater Lake's shocking blueness and its magnificent caldera setting is a moment to be relished, like the first time you see a grizzly or a shooting star. It is also a good time in which to remember this caution: Much of the rock near the crater's rim is crumbly, so stay well back from the edge unless you are at an established viewpoint.

It is the lake's depth and clarity that creates the storied shade of blue. In 1997 scientists conducted a standard measurement of water clarity by lowering an 8-inch disk into the lake and watching to see when it would disappear. It remained visible from the surface for an incredible 142 feet. As light passes through water, different colors of the spectrum are absorbed. Red is absorbed first, then orange, then yellow, and, by 350 feet, green vanishes, too. Only the blues remain unabsorbed, and at depths greater than 350 feet they constitute the only illumination, which is what scatters back to your admiring eyes on the rim.

From the unobstructed vista at Sinnott Memorial a moderate 7.5-mile pathway leads along the rim in either direction. Or you can explore the **Rim Village** itself, which consists of a restaurant, gift shop, the Rim Village Visitor

Center, and the grand **Crater Lake Lodge** *(541-830-8700),* with its outstanding views of the caldera.

Outside the lodge, you can pick up the rather steep 1.7-mile **Garfield Peak Trail,** which leads east to the top of Garfield Peak. The elevation gain of 1,000 feet will leave you panting, but so will the view from the 8,060-foot summit. Along the way stop to appreciate the Indian paintbrush, phlox, and penstemon. Rim Village visitors who prefer a flatter experience can take the gently undulating **Discovery Point Trail** 1.3 miles northwest along the rim. It leads to the point from which a trio of gold miners saw the lake in 1853, the first non-native people known to have encountered Crater Lake.

Rim Drive

Another option from Rim Village is the Rim Drive, which loops around the caldera. This 33-mile drive is the route to most of the park's sights and activities. It also provides more than 20 overlooks from which to contemplate the lake. For further exploring, a number of trails and a side road branch off from Rim Drive.

One historic and scenic overlook, atop the 8,013-foot peak called **The Watchman,** is located on the west side of the caldera, barely 4 miles up Rim Drive from Rim Village. Starting from the overlook's parking area, a steep, three-quarter-mile path switchbacks 650 feet up to the summit, which nearly hangs over the lake. The peak earned its name when it was used as a reference point for sounding the lake in 1886 and lived up to it as the site of a fire

lookout during the 1930s. Not only is the sturdy lava-boulder-and-wooden-beam lookout still standing, it is scheduled to be thoroughly rehabilitated by the end of summer 2000, so that it can continue to mark The Watchman's history and also be used as a modern fire lookout station. Note the old wooden stool with glass insulators on the ends of its legs; in bygone days that is where the fire spotter would sit, probably a bit uneasily, during lightning storms.

As one would expect, the views from the fire lookout are fantastic. You can gaze right down on the lake; on Wizard Island, located in the middle of the lake; or across hundreds of square miles of the Cascades. Experience a sunrise here if you can. As the pre-dawn sky brightens, the surrounding mountains emerge, then the forests, and finally the lake. Next, the sharp light of the still unseen sun ignites the tops of the peaks one by one until it shines in your eyes. Soon the rich, ruddy early morning light brings the cliffs to life. Then, maybe 20 minutes after sliding above the horizon, the sun shines directly on the lake, sparking the first glimmer of that incomparable blue.

Continuing clockwise a couple of miles on Rim Drive, you'll come to the **North Entrance Road,** the only other access to the Rim Drive. Even if you're not leaving, you may want to drive 15 minutes north to take a look at the **Pumice Desert.** Here the eruption of Mount Mazama dumped more than 50 feet of ash, creating a porous soil that holds little water. Only bunchgrasses, dwarf lupine, and a few

View from Rim Drive, which circles Crater Lake

Winter at the Lake

For nearly nine months of the year snow covers Crater Lake National Park. The road from the south entrance to the rim is cleared, however, and from Rim Village you can tour established lookout sites. At unofficial stops, stay back from the rim; snow can obscure the edge, and ice makes slipping all too easy. On weekend days interpreters lead winter ecology walks; they even provide snowshoes.

other scraggly plants survive here.

Back on Rim Drive going east, proceed 4.5 miles to the **Cleetwood Cove Trail.** This 2.2-mile round-trip path descends 750 feet into the caldera. It offers nothing of note in the way of scenery or wildlife, and it inflicts a relentless 11 percent grade on hikers. Even so, it remains one of the most popular trails in the park because it's the only trail that descends from the rim to the lake and it is the landing from which boat tours depart. *(Purchase tickets in parking lot on Rim Drive.)* The tours, which run from July through Labor Day, last 1 hour and 45 minutes and are narrated by National Park Service interpreters.

The water-level perspective justifies the steep climb that awaits at the end of the boat tour. Gaze down into that lucid water or look up at the cliffs as the ranger explains the horizontal striping that defines the different layers of lava that have been deposited there. Sometimes boat tours

encounter the **Old Man of the Lake,** a 35-foot barkless tree that has been bobbing about the lake since at least 1929. Perhaps you'll cruise through one of the yellow swirls that can be seen from the rim. The ranger will explain that it's not pollution but pine pollen that has blown in from the surrounding forests. Scientists love pollen because old grains can be accurately dated. By examining pollen buried in the deepest sediments at the bottom of the lake, researchers determined that Crater Lake began to fill immediately after the collapse of Mount Mazama and that it took about 300 years for the water to reach its present level. Given that the lake has no outlets, you may wonder why the water level doesn't continue to rise until it spills over the rim. The answer is that for now the lake has achieved an equilibrium in which evaporation and seepage maintain a balance with rain and snowmelt.

A highlight of the boat tour is a quick stop at **Wizard Island.** The island is a cinder cone that erupted out of the caldera's floor after Mount Mazama's big blowup, pushing 764 feet above the lake surface. You can debark and hike to Funeral Bay, or take the 0.9-mile **Wizard Island Trail** to the peak's summit and stare down into the crater that gave this park its name. Return boats stop at Wizard Island every 60 to 90 minutes, but afternoon boats are often full. The wait for a space may be several hours.

If your legs aren't too wobbly from hiking The Watchman, Cleetwood Cove, and Wizard Island, drive another 7 miles on Rim

Drive and pull over at the **Mount Scott Trail.** This strenuous, 5-mile round-trip route climbs almost 1,500 vertical feet to the 8,929-foot summit of Mount Scott, the highest point in the park. Bring plenty of water and determination. The reward will be superb views: of the lake, the rest of the park, the Cascades, and even Klamath Basin far to the south. If Mount Scott seems a bit daunting, opt for the spur road across Rim Drive from the trailhead, which goes out to **Cloudcap Overlook,** one of the finest vantage points you can reach by car.

About 3.5 miles beyond Cloudcap and Mount Scott, you'll arrive at **Kerr Notch,** also known as the Phantom Ship Overlook. Just offshore, about a mile west of the overlook, a rock formation that vaguely resembles a ship juts from the lake. Whether or not the Phantom Ship fires your imagination, you may want to linger at this viewpoint—it's the last one on the Rim Drive that can be reached without hiking. After this stop,

Rim Drive descends into the forests and winds back to the visitor center. From Kerr Notch you also can choose to follow a 7-mile spur road south to **Pinnacles Overlook,** the site of some photogenic pumice spires.

Before bidding the lake adieu, take a moment to consider its future. At the moment it is nearly pristine, but researchers worry that it could be harmed by global climate change, air pollution, boat and auto traffic, and, most of all, by alien fish. To people who aren't aware of the far-reaching dangers posed by invasive species, this comes as a surprise, but park scientists have long known that non-native fish may constitute a serious threat to the lake's health. From 1888 to 1941 people placed a variety of fish in these naturally fishless waters. Two species, kokanee salmon and rainbow trout, have survived and multiplied; hundreds of thousands of kokanee and a fair number of trout now inhabit the lake. These intruders could trigger a ripple effect that

Meadow wildflowers, Castle Crest Wildflower Trail

might alter the lake's food web, primary production, water chemistry, and other vital properties. Researchers are studying the ways in which the alien fish cause damage and what might be done to deal with them.

Other Park Trails

Although many visitors leave after glimpsing the lake from Rim Village or motoring along Rim Drive, the 170,000 non-lake acres of the park offer sites well worth seeing. The easiest place to sample these other attributes is in the area between the visitor center at Rim Village and the Annie Spring Entrance Station. Three easy hikes will make you forget about the lake, at least momentarily.

Starting from Rim Drive a quarter mile east of the Steel Information Center, stroll the nearly flat, 0.4-mile **Castle Crest Wildflower Trail.** It features a classic babbling brook and plenty of the wildflowers promised by the trail's name, including Lewis monkey flower, scarlet paintbrush, and

Columbia monkshood. Remember, in this snow-ridden realm— the area receives an average of 45 feet of snow a year—spring doesn't come until the summer months, so the flowers are blooming in late July and early August. The 1-mile **Godfrey Glen Trail,** another level loop, starts about 2.5 miles from the information center on the road to the Annie Spring Entrance Station. It winds through an old-growth forest and in a few places overlooks **Annie Creek Canyon,** your next stop.

To reach the **Annie Creek Canyon Trail,** turn east on the spur road to Mazama Village just before the Annie Spring Entrance Station. The trail begins near the amphitheater behind the Mazama Campground. Pick up one of the excellent trail guides at the trailhead. The path winds along the canyon rim and then descends 200 feet to Annie Creek. This canyon used to be a broad, U-shaped glacial valley, but the big eruption of Mount Mazama filled it with pumice and other rock fragments, which the creek later carved into a V-shaped canyon. In places along the trail you'll see contorted pumice spires fashioned by rain and wind, reminders of the eruption. Most of the canyon, however, is lushly vegetated by old-growth red firs and mountain hemlocks and a verdant understory, sprinkled with occasional meadows full of buttercups, Indian paintbrush, and monkey flowers. Watch for animals, too, such as marmots, Steller's jays, and chipmunks. When the huckleberries ripen, you might even encounter a black bear with a purple-stained mouth. ■

Vidae Falls, Crater Lake Rim Drive

Hikers on Newberry's Big Obsidian Flow Trail

Newberry National Volcanic Monument

■ 55,000 acres ■ Central Oregon, just south of Bend on US 97 ■ Best months mid-June–Sept. ■ Camping, hiking, boating (hand-powered only), fishing, snowmobiling, cross-country skiing, wildlife viewing, lava tube cave ■ Snow typically closes the higher elevations Nov.-May ■ Adm. fee ■ Contact the Lava Lands center, 58201 S. Hwy. 97, Bend, OR 97707, phone 541-593-2421; or Deschutes National Forest, 1645 Hwy. 20 E, Bend, OR 97701, phone 541-388-2715. www.fs.fed.us/r6/deschutes/monument/monument.html

NEWBERRY VOLCANO covers more than 500 square miles, making it one of the largest recent shield-type volcanoes in the United States. Yet you can drive right past it without even noticing it's there. Unlike the tall, proud cone of a classic composite volcano, a shield volcano is a nondescript, flattened dome. But looks can be deceiving. Newberry has erupted powerfully and often during the last million years, leaving volcanic features over a section of central Oregon informally referred to as the "Lava Lands." Despite its slumped form, it is an active volcano, having erupted as recently as 1,300 years ago.

Newberry Volcano and many of the geologic features it spawned make up the Newberry National Volcanic Monument, established by Congress in 1990. The monument includes lava tubes, cinder cones, mountain-size obsidian flows, an eerie forest of lava casts, and vast fields of stubbly lava. Visitors also will enjoy many nonvolcanic attractions within the monument's 55,000 acres, which are squeezed between the Cascade Range to the west and the high desert to the east and share elements of each. When you tire of looking at the distinct lava features, shift your gaze to the waterfalls, ponderosa pines, sagebrush, larkspur, coyotes, black bears, and ospreys found thoughout the volcanic monument.

What to See and Do

Start at the north end of the monument at **Lava Lands Visitor Center** *(June-Labor Day),* off US 97 about 15 minutes south of Bend. The center has exhibits on the area's wildlife, archaeology, and, especially, geology. If you wander onto the back patio, you'll soon notice a 500-foot cinder cone looming above you just a few hundred yards to the north. That's **Lava Butte.** It formed 7,000 years ago when gas-charged magma blew up through the ground and spewed ash and cinders high into the sky. The cinders drifted back down into the crater, and the prevailing wind smoothed them into a cone. Liquid lava also gushed from the base of the butte and spilled across the countryside, eventually hardening into more than 9 square miles of edgy, *aa* lava—a Hawaiian term for a type of lava flow that develops an uneven, jagged surface as it hardens.

If you tried to scramble across this jumble of razor-blade rocks, it would take you about three days to go a mile, and you'd shred your shoes in the process. Fortunately, you can explore the lava flow on the easy **Trail of the Molten Lands,** a paved, three-quarter-mile loop dotted with interpretive signs. At one point the trail crosses the basalt lava flow, and at another it rises to a viewpoint that looks out across the lava to the west. Here you'll see the Cascade forests backed by the horizon-hogging, 10,000-foot-plus tips of the **Three Sisters** mountains, part of the volcanic Cascade chain. In various places along the trail you'll encounter pines—sometimes as bonsai miniatures, sometimes reaching 50 feet high—seemingly growing right out of bare rock. Actually, the roots of the trees find their way to soil pockets that the wind has blown into the lava field over the years, or they take hold in fertile patches created by the process of lichens breaking down rock.

Lava Butte

If you'd like to see the view from above, you can walk up the 1.75-mile road that winds from the visitor center up to the summit of Lava Butte. Most people either take the shuttle bus, which leaves every half hour from the visitor center and runs from late May through Labor Day, or drive up in their own vehicle from early April to late May and from Labor Day to mid-October *(the road is closed to private vehicles during peak season, shuttle bus from center; fare).* When you see the views of the Cascades to the west and the juniper woodlands and high desert to the east,

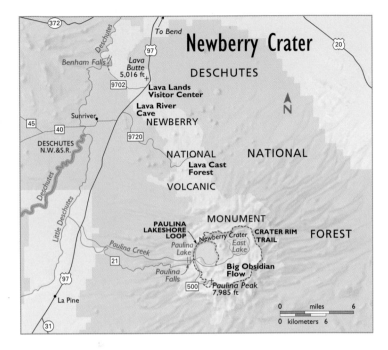

you'll understand why there's an active fire lookout atop the butte. A quarter-mile interpretive loop takes you around the cinder cone, which is 180 feet deep in places. Notice that some of the cinders are black and some are red. There's a simple explanation—simple, that is, if you've read "Volcanic Vistas," the excellent publication on the Lava Lands put out by the Deschutes National Forest. When the cinders erupt from the crater, they are black. Some simply remain black when they fall to the ground, but others repeatedly fall back into the crater and get blown out again, which oxidizes them and turns them a rusty red color.

From the entrance to the visitor center, take Forest Road 9702 west 4 miles to the **Benham Falls Trail.** This easy path crosses the Deschutes River on a footbridge

and then follows this pretty wild and scenic river for three-quarters of a mile to **Benham Falls,** which is more a series of cascading rapids than a classic, plunging waterfall. Watch for ospreys fishing in the quiet parts of the river and American dippers braving the lesser rapids in their pursuit of crawfish, caddis fly larvae, and the like. These songbirds actually plunge beneath the surface and hunt by walking along the bottom or by flying underwater.

Lava River Cave

If it's a hot summer day and you'd like to cool off, drive a mile south on US 97 from the visitor center to Lava River Cave, where the temperature is a constant 42°F deep inside. Even if it's 90°F up top, you'd better bring a coat. And always bring at least two light

Paulina Falls, Newberry National Volcanic Monument

sources. Lava River Cave is a 1-mile-long lava tube, the longest known uncollapsed tube in Oregon. It formed from a channel of fluid *pahoehoe* lava—a Hawaiian term for a lava flow with a ropey or gently folded surface—flowing down from Newberry Volcano. A crust of hardened lava began arching over the channel until eventually it formed a thin roof above the torrent of molten rock. When lava occasionally escaped through a hole and spread across the top of the tube, the roof thickened. When the eruptions stopped, the flowing lava drained away and the empty tube remained.

As you start down into the lava tube, note the unusual plants. Roses, strawberry, false Solomon's seal, and other species not typical of the surrounding ponderosa pine and bitterbrush community grow at the tube's mouth, where the cool breath of the cave produces condensation when it meets the warm air outside. If you're in the cave before summer has really hit, look for stalactites and stalagmites of ice near the entrance and in the first big chamber.

After about 1,000 feet you walk into the main section of the tunnel, called **Echo Hall.** Here the tube is about 50 feet wide and the ceiling as high as 58 feet, creating a vast stone tunnel in which voices and sounds reverberate eerily. When you see the post marking the 1,500-foot point, US 97 is about 80 feet directly above you. At about this same point, the cave ceiling dips down, and for 500 feet or so anyone taller than 5-foot-6 inches will spend some time ducking. While you're in this stretch,

called **Low Bridge Lane,** the variously shaped rock stalactites you've been admiring become hazards, so watch your head. (Beyond Low Bridge Lane the ceiling rises a bit, and you no longer need to stoop.) Soon you'll come to **Two Tube Tunnel,** where there's a second, smaller lava tube within the main tube. At about the 3,200-foot mark pause to admire the **Sand Gardens,** where over hundreds of years dripping water has sculptured a garden of sand figures. Continue another 1,000 feet and the cave begins narrowing, until the sandy floor and the ceiling meet and it's time to turn around.

Lava Cast Forest

To view another unusual volcanic feature, drive 2.5 miles south on US 97 from the Lava River Cave to Forest Road 9720 and take it southeast to Lava Cast Forest. You'll curve through a ponderosa and lodgepole-pine forest for a few miles then emerge into the openness of a 5-square-mile pahoehoe lava field. An easy, 1-mile interpretive trail loops through this field, which formed during a series of Newberry eruptions about 6,000 years ago. The distinguishing trait of this old lava flow is the abundance of lava casts of trees. Six millennia ago a fiery, sulphurous tide of lava surged over an old-growth ponderosa pine forest. The molten rock surrounded the trees and cooled rapidly, hardening around the tree trunks. When the trees eventually burned, molds in their shapes—a ghost forest—were left behind in the rock. As you stroll the trail you can see living pines, shrubs, and grasses slowly

Amateur spelunkers, Lava River Cave

reclaiming the ground their ancestors lost to the lava long ago.

Newberry Crater

Back on US 97, it's time to move
on to the last stop, Newberry
Crater, the centerpiece of the Lava
Lands. Just under 9 miles south of
the turnoff to the Lava Cast Forest,
head east on Forest Road 021
(Paulina Lake Road). In about a

dozen miles you'll enter the
crater—actually, it's a caldera,
since it's much wider than it is
deep. About a half-mile before you
reach Paulina Lake, you'll come to
the half-mile loop trail to **Paulina
Falls,** where Paulina Creek takes
an 80-foot dive over dark volcanic
rock cliffs into a canyon. Just a few
hundred yards east, **Paulina Lake**
shimmers in the sun, and the

Paulina Visitor Center awaits travelers. The center is the starting point for naturalist-led walks and the site of traditional arrowhead-making demonstrations.

If you'd like an overview of the crater and then some, continue east on Forest Road 021 a quarter of a mile and then turn south on the 4-mile side road that climbs to the summit of **Paulina Peak**. At 7,985 feet, it is the highest point in the monument and the 360-degree view reveals the layout of the caldera, the volcano, and the rest of central Oregon's Lava Lands. On a clear day you can see north along the Cascades to Washington and south to California.

From the visitor center, hardy hikers can climb up to Paulina Peak on the 3.5-mile (one way) **Paulina Peak Trail**—the trail gains 1,600 feet in elevation—but many less vertical trails invite visitors to amble through other parts of the caldera. The **Crater Rim Trail** circles around the edge of the whole basin, passing through forest, desert, and mountains on its 20-mile circuit. The 7.5-mile **Paulina Lakeshore Loop** rounds the lake, encountering an obsidian flow and a beach where the icy lake water is warmed by an underwater hot springs. Whatever the trail, watch for critters; the caldera is a state game refuge. On Paulina Lake and neighboring East Lake look for birds, including tundra swans, ospreys, and a pair of bald eagles that nests on the shore of East Lake. In the forest you may sight elk, black bears, deer, and, on occasion, badgers or pine martens.

Some day Newberry National Volcanic Monument may also be home to a geothermal project. About 3,000 feet below the caldera's surface, temperatures exceed 500°F—good potential for geothermal energy production. Exploratory wells drilled just outside the monument in 1995 didn't find a commercially viable resource, but some scientists feel confident that further exploration is warranted. Monument managers must be careful, however, that any such development does not disrupt the volcano's internal workings.

Big Obsidian Flow

Arguably the most fascinating feature of the caldera is the Big Obsidian Flow. A mere 1,300 years ago, a vent in the side of Newberry Volcano disgorged tens of millions of cubic yards of molten glass, which hardened into the mountain of obsidian you'll find just south of Forest Road 021 between Paulina and East Lakes. **The Big Obsidian Flow Trail,** a 0.3-mile loop, is dotted with interpretive signs that lead you up and around a small section of this massive flow, stained black by a small amount of iron mixed with the molten glass. The obsidian on the surface has broken into fragments that range from huge boulders to slivers.

The early inhabitants of the Northwest prized obsidian as a material for making arrowheads, knives, and other tools. Due to its atomic structure, obsidian can be honed to a sharper edge than can other rocks and metals. High-quality Newberry obsidian was traded throughout the Pacific Northwest. A 1994 dig near Paulina Visitor Center unearthed a 9,000-year-old obsidian spearpoint. ∎

Exploring Deschutes National Forest by car

McKenzie Pass

■ 38 miles long ■ North-central Oregon, on Oreg. 242 between Oreg. 126 and Sisters ■ Peak season summer. Oreg. 242 closed by snow Nov.–early July ■ Camping, hiking, wildflower viewing ■ Vehicles more than 35 feet long prohibited ■ Contact Sisters Area Chamber of Commerce, 164 N. Elm St., Sisters, OR 97759; phone 541-549-0251

OREG. 242 CUTS THROUGH the middle of the Oregon Cascades for 38 miles, between Oreg. 126 and the town of Sisters. This deliciously slow, meandering road bridges the crest at McKenzie Pass, providing a taste of both the east and west sides of the range. Pick up the west end of Oreg. 242 at the intersection with Oreg. 126, about 4 miles east of the little town of McKenzie Bridge. After you've passed through a mix of old-growth and managed forest for nearly 7 miles, you enter a long section of the historic old highway. At just over 9 miles from Oreg. 126, pull off at the trail to **Proxy Falls.** This easy 1.3-mile loop takes you through a 3,000-year-old lava field that is being overgrown by forest to a pair of cool, moss-and-fern-draped waterfalls. **Upper Falls** cascades into a pool that has no visible outlet; it simply soaks into the porous lava field.

For the next 5 miles or so, the road climbs steeply through a series of hairpin turns and sharp bends. As it attains the high country, the road flattens and straightens out a bit. Near Mile 17 you can take a half-mile spur road to **Scott Lake,** a pleasant, conifer-ringed lake where you can camp or picnic. From the end of the spur road, a 1.4-mile trail leads up to **Benson Lake,** deep blue and backed by cliffs. Back on Oreg. 242, travel a mile farther to the **Hand Lake Trail,** where a flat, half-mile path leads to another lake and extensive meadows that bloom madly in early summer.

About 1.5 miles east from the Hand Lake Trailhead on Oreg. 242, you'll see a lava field, an expansive tumult of broken rock leading the eye up to Belknap Crater. Soon seas of lava lap at both sides of the road as you leave the forest behind and enter the realm of volcanoes. As you rise through the lava fields, you'll reach **McKenzie Pass,** elevation 5,325 feet, and **Dee Wright Observatory** at about Mile 23.

This historic observatory has no telescopes for viewing the heavens. Rather, the handcrafted, multistoried tower made of lava rocks provides an outstanding vantage point from which to observe the surrounding landscape. And what a landscape it is: aa lava beds, craters, forests, glaciers, and mountains. Mount the stone stairs to the observatory's open deck and use the direction arrows of the peak finder to locate and identify the landmarks of the Cascades. The sharp spire of Mount Washington is just 5 miles away. About 28 miles north is 10,495-foot Mount Jefferson. Almost filling the horizon to the south are two of the Three Sisters, both over 10,000 feet and only 7 and 8 miles away. Mount Hood, too, is visible 78 miles north. Below the observatory, a paved, half-mile trail enhanced by interpretive signs loops through the lava bed.

From Dee Wright and McKenzie Pass, the road gradually descends the east side of the Cascades, curving through lava fields and forest. Just over 3 miles beyond the pass, you can pull over at **Windy Point** for one last look. After that the road flows through ponderosa forests to Sisters. ■

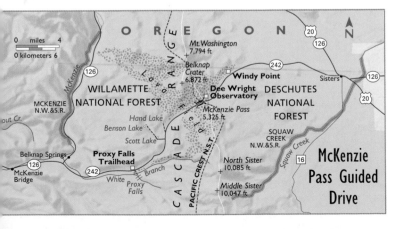

Boating and fishing, Willamette's Clear Lake

Willamette National Forest

■ 1.7 million acres ■ North-central Oregon, 30 miles west of Sisters, near US 20 and Oreg. 126 ■ Best season summer ■ Camping, hiking ■ Contact the Willamette National Forest, Federal Building, 211 E. 7th Ave., Eugene, OR 97440; phone 541-465-6521. www.fs.fed.us/r6/willamette/index.htm

MOST AMERICANS have never set foot in an old-growth forest. Even people who regularly hike and camp in the woods nearly always do so in forests that have been substantially altered by development, such as grazing, mining, and logging. In fact, more than 90 percent of the nation's original forest has been cut at least once, and most Northwest old growth has been logged, too. But substantial amounts of old-growth forest remain, and some of the finest stands can be found in the 1.7 million-acre Willamette National Forest, in the central Oregon Cascades. A number of the Willamette's accessible old-growth areas are located near the junction of US 20 and Oreg. 126, west of Santiam Pass. *(For a guide/map to the forest, request "50 Old-Growth Hikes in the Willamette National Forest" from Old-Growth Day Hikes, P.O. Box 5651, Eugene, OR 97405.)*

The **Hackleman Creek Trail,** on US 20 just over 5 miles west of the junction with Oreg. 126, is an excellent place to start. The main 1.2-mile loop *(wheelchair accessible)* is keyed to an interpretive brochure that you can obtain from Sweet Home Ranger District *(3225 Hwy. 20, Sweet Home, OR 97386. 541-367-5168)*. The brochure and trail cover the basic elements that characterize old growth, the importance of fungi, and the ways in which native cutthroat trout have adapted to the creek over thousands of years. Before you get caught up in the area's history and geology, however, just walk among these 400-year-old Douglas-firs and western hemlocks and absorb the gestalt of the place. You can add another half mile to your hike by taking the spur trail that swings down by the creek. This trail is not wheelchair accessible.

A quarter mile east of the Hackleman Creek trailhead, turn north on Forest Road 055 and wind north a couple of miles to the **Echo Basin Trail,** also called the Echo Mountain Old Growth Trail. This 2.5-mile loop starts at around 3,700 feet and leads up, but not steeply, through a high-elevation old-growth forest that is distinctly different from the mid-elevation community found at Hackleman Creek. You'll see snow-resistant Pacific silver fir trees and towering Alaska cedars, a species uncommon in Oregon with a trunk diameter of 6 feet. The basin also features an expanse of wet meadows that sparkle in midsummer with such wildflowers as lupine, bunchberry, queen's cup, and camas.

To see a low-elevation old-growth forest, go to the junction of US 20 and Oreg. 126 and head south on Oreg 126. Go just over 2 miles and turn left at the sign for the **McKenzie River Trail.** Take the rutted dirt road about 100 yards to a parking area, where you'll pick up the trail. As you hike south across a narrow footbridge and amble through a lush forest of king-size Douglas-fir, be sure to watch for careening mountain bikers. Lucky visitors will avoid bicycle mishaps and in the bargain might see a flash of red, black, and white swoop through the shady understory and alight on a tree trunk. This would be a pileated woodpecker, the largest woodpecker species in North America.

After about a mile you'll come to a second footbridge and a fork in the trail; you've intersected the northern end of the 5-mile **Clear Lake Trail,** which circles the lake. If you don't have time for the whole loop, at least cross the footbridge and walk the short distance to **Clear Lake.** Look closely into the clear, blue-green water of this mountain lake, and you can see the bleached skeletons of dead trees on the bottom. These are relics from the forest that stood here 3,000 years ago, before a lava flow dammed the river and created the lake. Farther along the trail skirts a partly overgrown lava field with trees 5 and 6 feet in diameter. ∎

Divine Decadence

The crowns of deeply furrowed Douglas-fir and wide-bodied western redcedar form a green canopy 200 feet above the forest floor. Below the canopy spreads an understory of vine maple, western hemlock, Pacific yew, big-leaf maple, and the dead husks and live young of the taller tree species. At ground level it's a jungle of salal, aromatic rhododendrons, salmonberry, ferns, white-flowered trillium, mushrooms, and moss-cloaked fallen trees. Endangered spotted owls, pileated woodpeckers, and northern flying squirrels cruise through the trees while Roosevelt elk, Pacific giant salamanders, red-backed voles, and pine marten move about the forest floor. This is the classic low-elevation old-growth forest found on the west side of the Cascades.

Until just a couple of decades ago the timber industry commonly identified old-growth forests as decadent, meaning that the trees had reached the point where they no longer grew appreciably. But during the last 30 years some scientists have been taking a closer look and they've discovered that old-growth forests are among the most biologically rich places on earth.

Old-growth forests harbor significant numbers of old, large trees; a typical definition says these trees must be at least 3 feet in diameter—in fact, some are as large as 10 feet—and the trees must be at least 250 years old—some have seen more than 1,000 years pass. Other essential old-growth traits are the presence of many layers of canopy and understory; a structural variety created by gaps; a variety of tree species; and trees of different ages. Snags—standing dead trees that are vital to so many plants and animals—also must be present. Finally, fallen logs must litter the forest floor. The vast majority of the nation's forestlands, which have been and continue to be logged, replanted, and managed in the traditional industrial way, lack these essential elements.

The roles these elements play are complex, but as an example briefly consider those fallen logs. They jumble the forest floor like giant pickup sticks, as much as 150 tons per acre. They also serve the forest roughly as long as live trees do; it can take 500 years for a large fallen tree to fully decompose. When you approach a rotting old log, a skunk or pine marten may emerge; one study in Oregon found that 178 vertebrate species use downed trees as habitat. Notice the saplings growing from those prostrate trees. The fallen trees, called nurse logs, provide young trees with nutrients, water, and an elevated position in which to capture sunlight. Inside the log, swarms of beetles, carpenter ants, and mites breed and feed, while trying to avoid the centipedes, spiders, and salamanders that prey upon them. This complex food web loops outward all the way to black bears and spotted owls—and to people.

Humans may not be among the hundreds of species whose future depends almost exclusively on the presence of ample old-growth forests, but ancient forests certainly are of practical importance to us. They provide biodiversity, flood control, water quality, fish habitat, medicines, and other benefits. And this doesn't even take into account their tranquillity, mystery, and inspiring beauty.

Hikers on Hackleman Creek Trail, Willamette National Forest

Butterfly and wildflowers on the Iron Mountain Trail

Iron Mountain

■ 2,500 acres ■ West-central Oregon, east of Sweet Home, 34 miles off US 20 ■ Best months mid-June–July ■ Hiking, wildflower viewing ■ Contact Sweet Home Ranger Station, Willamette National Forest, 3225 Hwy. 20, Sweet Home, OR 97386; phone 541-367-5168

IRON MOUNTAIN OFFERS grand views of the Oregon Cascades, a short but invigorating hike, and a historic fire lookout—but that's not why most people come here. They come for the wildflowers. Nearly every wildflower species that grows in the western Cascades—more than 300—can be found along the steep, 1-mile **Iron Mountain Trail** during the prime season of mid-June through the end of July. You can reach the trail via a couple of other trails, but most people drive 34 miles east of Sweet Home on US 20, turn left onto Civil Road (near Milepost 62), and follow it about 3 miles to the parking lot below the mountain.

As you tramp up the switchbacking trail, you'll pass through 11 different habitats. Each of them varies slightly in the amount of shade, sunlight, soil moisture, elevation, and other factors that determine which plant species will thrive where. In the damp shade of Douglas-firs not far from the start, look for violets and coral-root orchids. A little farther there's a dry meadow that is devoid of trees due to lightning fires, grazing elk and deer, and seedling-munching squirrels, pocket gophers, and mountain beaver. Here fireweed, trillium, and other flowers prosper. Higher up, in a moist meadow, you'll spot thimbleberry and columbines and the butterflies and hummingbirds that favor them. When you reach the top of the trail, the expansive vista before you sweeps from Mount Hood in the north to Diamond Peak in the south, some 130 miles.

To add another mile (one way) and 1,000 feet of elevation to this hike, pick up the trail at the Iron Mountain Trailhead on Deer Creek Road, one-quarter mile from US 20. ■

Silver Falls State Park

■ 8,700 acres ■ North-central Oregon, east of Salem, 26 miles off Oreg. 22
■ Heaviest water flow occurs in spring or early summer ■ Camping, hiking,
swimming, fishing, biking, wildlife viewing, waterfalls ■ Contact the park,
20024 Silver Falls Hwy., SE, Sublimity, OR 97385; phone 503-873-8681.
www.prd.state.or.us

HUMANS LOVE WATER, perhaps because we can't live without it, perhaps for
reasons that have nothing to do with reason. We love ocean surf, a
sparkling lake, a spritely creek. We also love water when it thunders over
high cliffs, and that's why people love Silver Falls State Park. Over the
eons Cascades' volcanoes laid down beds of tough basalt interspersed

with beds of soft volcanic ash. As
water ran over the resistant basalt
but wore away the adjacent ash,
waterfalls developed. This natural
force continues today: Water tumbling over the lip of basalt erodes
the soft material below, with the
result that the waterfalls grow
higher and higher over time.

As visitors will see, the **North
Fork Silver Creek** and the **South
Fork Silver Creek** have had time
to create towering falls. The park's
ten cascades range in height from
27-foot **Drake Falls** to 178-foot
Double Falls. Five of the falls measure more than 100 feet high.

Stop by the **visitor center** for
interpretive information about
the geology and human history of
the area, plus tips on wildlife viewing. Then head for the falls. You
can see them from viewpoints
along the park road or by taking a
short walk from the South Falls
day-use area. But to get the full
experience, you need to hike the
easy 7.9-mile **Trail of Ten Falls.** At
four of the falls, the trail even goes
behind the plunging water. If time
is tight, a cutoff allows you to
shorten the hike by a couple of
miles. But somewhere along the
trail be sure to take a swim. ■

South Falls, Silver Falls State Park

Mount Hood and Vicinity

■ Northwest Oregon, east of Portland, 25 miles off US 26 ■ Season year-round ■ Camping, hiking, boating, fishing, downhill skiing, cross-country skiing, snowshoeing, wildlife viewing, berry picking ■ Day passes required for hiking ■ Contact Mount Hood Information Center, 65000 E. Hwy. 26, Welches, OR 97067; phone 503-622-7674. www.mthood.org

MOUNT HOOD AND THE AREA AROUND IT epitomize the South Cascades. The 11,239-foot mountain is the highest in Oregon, a photogenic volcano with a snowcapped cone for a peak. Visitors never seem to tire of driving or hiking to different vantage points from which to contemplate this leading light of the Pacific Rim's famed Ring of Fire. Additionally, the area around Mount Hood offers many of the features visitors seek in the South Cascades, such as old-growth forests, lakes, wild rivers, hundreds of miles of hiking trails, wildlife-watching, fishing, and waterfalls.

What to See and Do

Start your tour at the physical and spiritual heart of this area: **Mount Hood.** If you're so inclined, you can take it from the top. Every year some 10,000 climbers set out for the summit, but don't take Mount Hood lightly. Though the ascent is relatively easy, it's still a technical climb and the mountain generates notoriously volatile weather. Because people tend to underestimate it, Mount Hood has one of the highest climbing-accident rates in the United States.

For those who would rather view the mountain from a safe distance, your alternative to climbing is to drive up to **Timberline Lodge** *(503-272-3311)*. It's not a natural feature, but this finely crafted historic edifice comes as close as a building can. Its blend of large beams and stones and the spacious design make it seem as if it grew out of the mountainside. Situated at 6,000 feet amid the sparse trees at timberline, the lodge balconies

and windows provide great views. From the north side you get a close-up of the high reaches of Mount Hood since the summit is a mere 3.6 miles away. From the south side you look out over thousands of square miles of the South Cascades, from Trillium Lake in the foreground to the Three Sisters on the horizon. A mile away and a couple of thousand vertical feet above the lodge is the renowned **Palmer Snowfield,** which offers skiing even during the summer. For a higher lookout, take the **Magic Mile Super Express** *(fare),* a ski lift from the lodge up to the Silcox Hut at the 7,000-foot level.

Hikers can go behind the lodge and walk up the mountain a couple hundred feet to the **Timberline Trail.** (At this point the Pacific Crest National Scenic Trail—see p. 95—shares the path.) This 41-mile trail circles the entire mountain. For something a bit more manageable, head west on the

Hikers above Timberline Lodge

Timberline Trail 2.2 miles and use the overlook above Zigzag Canyon as a turnaround point. You pass through meadows of penstemon, Cascade aster, and partridge foot, with a sprinkling of gnarled whitebark pines and subalpine firs.

The Lakes

On US 26 just 1.5 miles east of the road up to Timberline, a short spur road leads down to one of the area's most popular destinations: **Trillium Lake.** To quickly grasp its appeal, park in the day-use lot and walk to the shore just left of the boat ramp. Go out on the wooden platform that juts into the lake and look due north. Mount Hood fills the sky and is reflected in the deep blue surface of the water. The bench on this platform has got to be one of the finest places to sit in the Northwest. With a good pair of binoculars you can make out architectural details on the Timberline Lodge building, skiers schussing down the Palmer Snowfield above, the alpine meadows, and the aqua radiance of some of the mountain's 11 glaciers. An easy 2-mile trail loops around Trillium

Newts on Parade

Full of purpose, rough-skinned newts move across the forest floor in slow motion, seemingly oblivious to everything but the mission they must complete. Often mistaken for lizards, these 7-inch-long amphibians are migrating from the moist litter of the forest to their breeding sites in backwaters and shallow ponds. They make this annual pilgrimage sometime during the spring or summer, depending on the area's climate. You may encounter dozens of them marching intently down a trail or see a cluster of them in the mating waters. In the fall you may witness the parade again, in reverse.

Newts are by far the most commonly seen species of salamander in the Northwest; they are found in all moist forestlands west of the Cascade crest. You'll know them by their reddish-brown topsides and bright orange undersides. In nature, bright orange often says "I'm poison; don't eat me or we'll both be sorry," and that's the case with the rough-skinned newt. In fact, the toxin they secrete from glands on their skin is identical to the noxious poison produced by puffer fishes. If you ate a newt you would probably die. If your kids handle one—and children find these slow, gentle creatures irresistible—they'll most likely be fine because the poison doesn't penetrate the skin. But they could get sick if they handle a newt and then touch their hands to their mouths. Immediate and thorough hand-washing following a close encounter with these creatures is advised.

Lake, providing a closer look at the forest and the lily pads, great blue herons, and skunk cabbage that inhabit the marshy margin.

Another deservedly popular body of water is **Mirror Lake,** located just a few miles northwest of Trillium. The easy, 2-mile trail to Mirror Lake starts from a parking lot on the south side of US 26 a mile west of the town of Government Camp. You'll get excellent views of Mount Hood—mirrored in the lake, of course—and of the Zigzag Valley. And if you've timed your visit to occur between the middle of August and late September, you also will find excellent huckleberries growing along the sunny stretches of the trail. Numerous huckleberry hot spots exist in the Mount Hood area; the Mount Hood Forest Service office in Welches even offers a brochure on these delectable, dark blue berries. Picking huckleberries for muffins, jam, or immediate, mouth-staining consumption is a Northwest tradition.

Old-Growth Forests

Most motorists skirt Mount Hood to the south on US 26 or to the east on Oreg. 35, but a back road leads around the mountain on the west and north sides. From US 26 at Zigzag, head northeast on Forest Road 018 (East Lolo Pass Road), which quickly enters the national forest. This route climbs through clear-cuts and young forest until it meets Forest Road 1810, where the pavement ends, about 10 miles northeast of Zigzag.

The **Pacific Crest National Scenic Trail,** which leads toward Bald Mountain, intersects Forest Road 018 at this junction. Park on the side of the road and hike several miles south on the Pacific Crest National Scenic Trail; the obscure trailhead begins next to a Forest Service information sign. For maybe 10 minutes you'll walk through a clear-cut, with fine views of Mount Hood, and then you'll enter an old-growth forest. In summer, the forest floor is absolutely chockablock with strapping rhododendrons. If you continue 2 or 3 miles, you'll walk along a ridgeline flanked with old growth; here you can get wonderful views of Mount Hood from Bald Mountain.

Back in the car, turn east on gravel-topped Forest Road 1810 (do not proceed straight on Forest Road 018, which rapidly degenerates into a jeep track) and drive for about 6 miles through a mix of clear-cuts and older forest; this takes you back to Forest Road 018. Continue north on Forest Road 018 along a creek thick with red alder to Forest Road 013. Before taking this route northeast to Hood River, take it southwest about 6 miles to **Lost Lake.** You may want to pitch a tent at the fine campground there or at least stroll the old-growth interpretive trail that runs through it. Down at the lake, one of the prettiest in the region, the rustic Lost Lake Resort *(541-386-6366)* rents canoes, rowboats, and paddleboats. You can also hike the easy, 3.5-mile trail that loops around the lake to pass through stands of old-growth western redcedar and western hemlock. Or take a break and relax on a bench on the lake's north end for grand views of Mount Hood. ■

Columbia River Gorge National Scenic Area

■ 80 miles long ■ Northwest Oregon, east of Portland about 20 miles ■ Best months mid-July–early Oct. in the west, June–early Oct. in the east ■ Hiking, white-water rafting, bird-watching, wildflower viewing ■ Adm. fee; Trail Park Day Passes required on some trails ■ Contact the national scenic area, 902 Wasco Ave., Suite 200, Hood River, OR 97031; phone 541-308-1700. www.fs.fed.us/r6/columbia

DURING THE LAST ICE AGE a lobe of the continental ice sheet moved down into what is now northwestern Montana, damming the waters flowing west from the Rockies. The waters built up to form the Glacial Lake Missoula, a lake 4,200 feet deep that covered more than 100,000 square miles. It was only a matter of time until the dam broke, sending water hundreds of feet deep roaring westward down the channel of the Columbia River. The thundering tide gouged the channel, the only sea-level corridor through the Cascades, carving it much deeper and wider. In ensuing years similar conditions created more massive floods, and when the water finally subsided, the Columbia River Gorge—roughly as it appears today—was revealed: a magnificent realm of dramatic waterfalls cascading from basalt cliffs, some of which soar to a height of 4,000 feet.

No wonder this 80-mile gorge, which runs east to west on both sides of the Oregon-Washington border, was declared a National Scenic Area in 1986. Such a designation does not confer anything like wilderness or park status—after all, tens of thousands of people live in the small towns and rural enclaves inside the national scenic area and rail lines, barge traffic, and highways pass through it. The intent is to protect the scenic character of the gorge by managing its development. So far, so good.

What to See and Do

Washington Side

The gorge can be explored in any number of ways. One rewarding route starts at the west end of the scenic area on the Washington side and heads east on Wash. 14 along the Columbia River. Within a minute you will come to the **Steigerwald Lake National Wildlife Refuge** (NWR Complex, 509-427-5208; call ahead before visiting), where you might spot great blue herons or Canada geese. Within the next 20 miles you'll

pass two more refuges. Soon you'll come to **Beacon Rock State Park** (509-427-8265), where the volcanic core called Beacon Rock thrusts 848 feet into the air. Needless to say, the 1.1-mile (one way) trail up this pinnacle is steep, but the views are worth the sweat.

A few miles past the park, you will approach the town of Stevenson. Make a stop at the **Columbia Gorge Interpretive Center** (900 S.W. Rock Creek Dr. 509-427-8211; Adm. fee), which is on Wash. 14.

Vista House, Crown Point State Park

From the indoor waterfall to the soaring 40-foot ceiling, this facility captures a sense of the Columbia River Gorge. It features exhibits on natural and human history.

About 9 miles east of Stevenson, stop at the **Dog Mountain Trail,** one of the top hikes in the scenic area. Three routes of varying difficulty (none easy) climb through forest up to the steeply slanting meadows that make Dog Mountain famous. In spring and summer balsamroot, lupine, phlox, and other wildflowers bloom here. After climbing about 3 miles, you'll arrive at the summit and views that will make resting even more of a pleasure.

About 10 miles east of Dog Mountain, the **White Salmon Wild and Scenic River** flows into the Columbia. Drive a few miles north on Wash. 141 along the White Salmon's east bank to a section of the river that has been designated wild and scenic. If you'd like to see the vertical basalt walls of the narrow canyon up close,

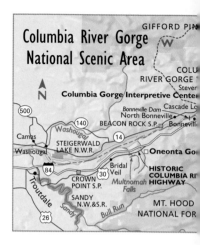

local outfitters run raft trips down this challenging white-water reach. On the west side of Lyle—about 12 miles east of the White Salmon River on Wash. 14—there is another wild and scenic river, the **Klickitat,** whose designated reach runs right down to the Columbia River. Drive about 2 miles along the cliffs on Wash. 142 to the scenic area boundary and turn west across the bridge. Park on the other side and carefully walk out onto the rocks; from here you can gaze weak-kneed into the depths of a gorge that is nearly 70 feet deep in places and less than 10 feet wide. From the bridge you can see the scaffolds from which Yakama Indians dipnet salmon with their long-handled nets. However, it is considered impolite to watch them.

To view a seldom visited corner of the gorge, go just under a mile past the US 197 junction on Wash. 14 and turn northeast on Dalles Mountain Road. About 3.5 miles later, turn uphill onto a bumpy service road that takes you into the **Columbia Hills natural area preserve.** This hot, south-facing slope

One More for the Road
If you're driving west from Vista House, turn left after about a mile onto Larch Mountain Highway and head up into the mountains. For about 14 miles the paved road wanders through forestlands until it ends in the parking lot atop Larch Mountain. From there a quarter-mile trail takes you to the summit, which, at 4,056 feet, yields a panorama that will take your breath away.

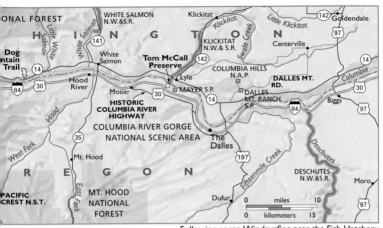

Following pages: Windsurfing near the Fish Hatchery

covered with nondescript grasses will strike most visitors as barren. But the 3,000-acre preserve shelters numerous rare native plants, such as the hot-rock penstemon and obscure buttercup, as well as imperiled native plant communities that invasive weeds, agriculture, and livestock grazing have largely eliminated elsewhere. You can drive or hike up the preserve's 1.5-mile road to a parking lot at a locked gate, but do not leave the road. Look for deer and birds in the oak groves that line the draws and enjoy the views of Mount Hood, Mount Jefferson, the Columbia River, and the rolling hills of eastern Washington and Oregon. This preserve dramatically illustrates the contrast between the dry east side and the wet west side of the gorge.

Oregon Side

Return to US 197 and go south across the bridge into Oregon, where you can head back west along the Columbia on I-84. Near Mayer State Park, turn off onto a short remnant of the **Historic**

Columbia River Highway, built with great skill and imagination in the early 1900s. Ascend the wildly meandering **Rowena Loops road** to the top of Rowena Plateau and stop at **Rowena Crest Viewpoint.** From this 800-foot aerie, visitors enjoy a vast panorama of the east end of the scenic area. During the catastrophic ice age floods, water washed over this plateau, scouring away the topsoil and exposing the dark basalt you see today.

Opposite the entrance to Rowena Crest Viewpoint sprawls the 230-acre **Tom McCall Preserve,** a Nature Conservancy property. A nearly flat 2-mile trail loops through the preserve, which is known for its native plant diversity. Some of the species are endemics, found only in the gorge. In spring the preserve bursts into bloom as shooting star, yellow bell, broad-leaf lupine, balsamroot, and other wildflowers bask in the sun.

Eagle Creek Recreation Area and Oneonta Gorge

Back on I-84, drive about half an hour west to the **Eagle Creek Trail,**

one of the finest easy hikes in the South Cascades. (It may not be suitable for children, however, due to steep drop-offs without guard rails.) The hardest part for west-bound travelers is getting to the trailhead; there's no exit from the highway. You have to go past Eagle Creek to the Bonneville Dam exit and backtrack east on I-84 to the Eagle Creek Recreation Area exit. Once in the Eagle Creek Recreation Area (541-308-1700), find your way past the hatchery and the lovely old picnic area to a creek-side spur road that goes a quarter-mile to the trail's start.

The trail is well worth the effort to find it. Passing a number of waterfalls, it follows old-growth-bordered Eagle Creek up a steep-walled canyon. The entire route covers more than 13 miles one way, but there are several convenient turn-around points for day-hikers. Just 1.5 miles up the trail you'll reach 150-foot **Metlako Falls;** at 2 miles it's **Punchbowl Falls;** at 3.3 miles you'll cross a deep chasm on **High Bridge;** at 6 miles the trail cuts into the basalt cliff and goes behind **Tunnel Falls.**

About 6 miles west from Eagle Creek on I-84, follow the signs to another section of the **Historic Columbia River Highway.** Along this 22-mile stretch of road, basalt cliffs spout tumbling waterfalls and icy creeks slice through side canyons graced by old-growth conifer forests.

Oneonta Gorge and Crown Point State Park

A couple of miles along the highway lands you at the narrow, winding Oneonta Gorge. For the full effect, hike 100 yards up the gorge; you'll have to do a bit of rock hopping and usually some shallow wading. Here the 100-foot, vertical basalt walls squeeze to within about 15 or 20 feet of each other. Even in summer, Oneonta is cool and moist, and this habitat shelters numerous rare plants.

Back in the car, another couple of miles on the Columbia River Gorge Scenic Highway brings you to **Multnomah Falls.** The most famous natural feature in the gorge, it has a visitor center, gift shop, and restaurant all housed in a converted historic stone lodge, and its own exit off I-84. The object of all this attention is the 620-foot dive that Multnomah Creek takes from a looming basalt cliff, making this the nation's second-highest year-round waterfall. An outstanding view awaits five minutes up the paved pathway to Benson Bridge, which crosses the creek between the upper and lower parts of the falls. Another mile of hiking and you attain a vantage point at the top of the falls.

Obviously, waterfalls are a big attraction in this area. In fact, there are 77 substantial falls along this 42-mile stretch, the greatest concentration in North America. As you continue down the old highway you'll encounter one waterfall after another until you near the west end of the scenic area and begin climbing the cliffs.

Soon you'll top out at **Crown Point State Park,** 733 feet above the Columbia River. For the perfect vista, go to **Vista House** (503-695-2230), a 1918 multistory, circular edifice on the point. Enjoy the view from the upper deck. ■

Wildflowers amid the debris near Lava Canyon

Mount St. Helens National Volcanic Monument

■ 110,000 acres ■ Southern Washington, northeast of Portland 50 miles
■ Best months May-Oct. ■ Hiking, fishing, wildlife viewing ■ Visitors pass
required for most sites ■ Contact the monument, 44218 NE Yale Bridge Road,
Amboy, WA 98601; phone 360-247-3900. www.fs.fed.US/gpnf/wshnvm/

THERE'S NOTHING LIKE a good volcanic eruption to cure—however temporarily—a people's myopia. As a nation, we seldom see beyond the now; with fading memories of human history a generation ago, let alone geologic history dating back millions of years. This lack of hindsight can result in a lack of foresight. In order to accept how much change will occur in the future—a future that starts tomorrow—we must acknowledge how much change occurred in the past.

For people in the Northwest, complacency about the natural order of their world evaporated with the explosion of Mount St. Helens on May 18, 1980. No doubt most people in the area got out of bed that Sunday morning assuming that the top 1,300 feet of this beloved Cascade peak would still be there when they went to bed that night. But Mother Nature had other ideas.

At 8:30 a.m. a pilot and two geologists were flying in a small plane above Mount St. Helens. For months the volcano had been giving signs of an impending event, so the watch was on. But no one had anticipated what happened next. At 8:32 a.m. the excited pilot radioed that the whole north side of the mountain "just went." Its collapse released a pent-up brew of steam, ash, and hot gas in a lateral, 300-mile-an-hour blast that leveled everything in its path. People as far away as Canada and Montana heard the explosion. Climbers on Mount Adams, 34 miles east, saw the eruption; ten minutes later a heat wave washed over them, raising the air temperature by an astounding 30 to 40 degrees. Pyroclastic flows surged down rivers and creeks, smashing bridges, leveling forests, and flooding the surrounding landscape. Debris from this giant landslide filled the North Fork Toutle River, its drainage area, and the Spirit Lake Basin. A mushroom cloud of ash billowed more than a dozen miles into the sky and blew east and north, turning day into twilight over thousands of square miles and laying a blanket of gray ash over vast expanses of eastern Washington.

So much for complacency. Towering old-growth forests were suddenly flattened. Sparkling creeks were buried beneath hundreds of feet of mud. The lives of 57 people—campers, loggers, scientists—ended in an instant. But devastation is no more permanent than tranquillity; life soon began returning to the area. Animals that burrow underground, including pocket gophers, peeked out; fish in nearby lakes survived; elk eventually returned; and within weeks flowers resprouted and hummingbirds returned. Now, 20 years later, you can see beginnings of a future forest. In another 300 years vaulting Douglas-fir trees, crystalline creeks, and pileated woodpeckers may once again grace this landscape. Unless, of course, the mountain blows once more.

What to See and Do

Because the monument lies just east of I-5, most visitors approach Mount St. Helens from the west on Wash. 504, from the town of Castle Rock. Five miles from town you'll come to the **Mount St. Helens visitor center** on the shores of **Silver Lake.** Under the center's glass-walled, 50-foot ceiling you'll find a museumlike range of exhibits. One walk-through exhibit allows you to enter the interior of a simulated volcano and see how the earth's forces produce an eruption.

From the Mount St. Helens visitor center, Wash. 504 continues about 40 miles east through private forestlands before it skirts along the northwest border of the monument. Stop at the **Weyerhauser Forest Learning Center** (*Milepost 42. 360-274-2131*) to see a display on sound waves that

explains why people 700 miles away heard the mountain's blowout while others 10 miles away did not. From a viewpoint there look down on the **North Fork Toutle River,** where evidence of the debris avalanche and massive mudflows can be seen. Look, too, for a large elk herd that roams this valley.

West Side Crater

Soon after reaching the monument's border, the road turns south into the monument itself; about 1 mile ahead is the **Coldwater Ridge Visitor Center,** overlooking Coldwater Lake. From the center, where you can browse interactive exhibits, you have a good view of the mountain. You may even see a little steam rising from vents inside the crater, but

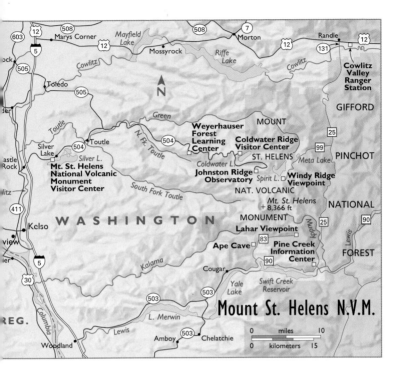

Mount St. Helens N.V.M.

don't worry, that doesn't mean an eruption is imminent. This visitor center focuses mainly on the rebirth of the mountain after the eruption, as do the interpretive and guided walks on the adjacent quarter-mile **Winds of Change Trail.** For example, you'll learn that lupine was able to recolonize two years after the devastation because it produces numerous seeds that germinate easily, and the compact structure of the plant traps windborne material to help build soil. It is also a nitrogen fixer (it converts nitrogen from the air into a usuable nutrient), which helped ready the earth so that other plants could return.

Continue to the end of the road, just 5 miles from the crater. There you'll come to the newest of the monument's facilities:

Johnston Ridge Observatory.
From here you get a fantastic view of the gaping crater that was left when the north side of peak collapsed. You'll see the blast zone, the pumice plain, the landslide deposit, and the 1,000-foot lava dome that bulges up in the middle of the crater. Inside, the state-of-the-art interactive exhibits show how the 1980 eruption came to pass and how scientists are monitoring Mount St. Helens and making predictions about future volcanic activity. You may have to wait a bit to see the excellent 16-minute film, but it is well worth it.

East Side Crater

For another view of the crater from the less developed east side of the monument, head east from I-5 on US 12 about 50 miles to the

Cowlitz Valley Ranger Station, a mile east of Randle. You can also get information and a monument pass here. Then head south maybe 20 minutes on Forest Road 025, turn southwest on Forest Road 099 for 10 minutes, and you're in the monument proper. Forest Road 099 leads to Windy Ridge, but stop at some of the viewpoints and interpretive trails along the way. From one of the viewpoints at the blast edge, you stand at the eerie dividing line between trees that were scorched yet left standing and those mowed down. Beyond this point you drive through the landscape of downed trees, all lying in the same direction as if slicked down by a giant comb. During the summer an interpreter at nearby **Meta Lake** can explain how the plants and animals in this emerald lake survived the blast. The road ends at **Windy Ridge,** some 4 miles from the crater. In the outdoor amphitheater you can sit and gaze at the crater while a forest interpreter explains the eruption.

South Side Crater

To enter the south side of the monument, continue south on Forest Road 025, turn west on Forest Road 090, and then north on Forest Road 083. Stop in at the **Pine Creek Information Station** (*Jct. of FR 025 and FR 090*) for a monument pass and information.

The prime attraction on the south side is **Ape Cave,** a 2,000-year-old lava tube that you can explore on a 45-minute walk on your own or with a monument guide. The temperatures in the cave hover around 40°F so bring warm clothes. Seven miles farther up Forest Road 83 you'll come to **Lahar Viewpoint.** Looming behind the lahar—a broad floodplain formed by a river of hot mud, water, and ash—is the mountain responsible for that mud and ash. Half a mile east of the viewpoint is **Lava Canyon**, where 1980 mudflows scoured off all the vegetation, revealing old lava flows that speak of geologic events 2,000 years ago. ∎

Will It Blow Again?

Will Mount St. Helens erupt again? Yes. The only question is when, and that's difficult to predict. An eruption will occur when molten rock gushes up from the magma chamber that lies between 1 and 4 miles beneath the volcano. In 1998 increased seismic activity once more got the attention of volcano watchers. As the magma under the lava domes cools, gas pressure builds and causes many very small earthquakes; about 60 a month is average. But in May 1998 seismologists counted 165 small quakes. They also detected carbon dioxide coming out of cracks in the dome and the volcano floor, a sign that new magma was flowing into the magma chamber. In June 1998, 318 earthquakes tweaked the mountain. That number rose to 445 in July, and the quakes also grew stronger. But then, underscoring the fickleness of volcanoes, the earthquake pattern rapidly returned to normal. When will Mount St. Helens erupt again? Maybe—probably—sometime in this millennium.

Johnson Ridge, Mount St. Helens

High Desert

Hikers, Mount Howard, Wallowa-Whitman National Forest

A DESERT IN THE Pacific Northwest? The notion of a high desert here surprises people who think of the Northwest as a land of lush valleys, scenic coastlines, big rivers, and densely forested mountains. These classic calendar vistas do make up much of the Northwest landmass, but tucked in the region's southeastern quadrant is an area of more subtle beauty.

A continuation of the Great Basin, Oregon's high desert lies just southwest of the state's plateau country,

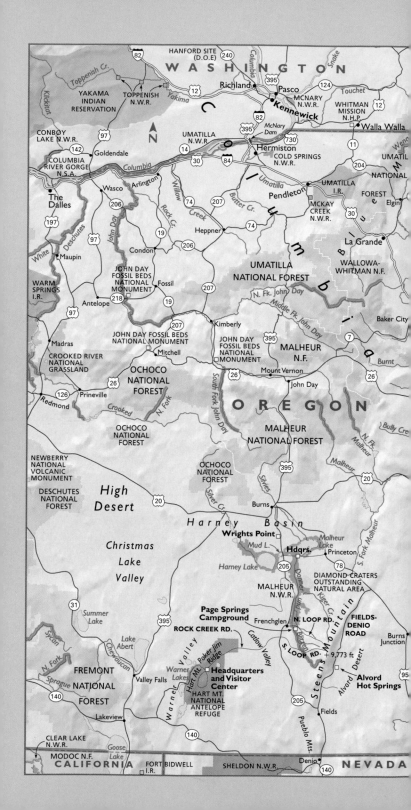

bordered on the east by Idaho and on the south by Nevada. But it is the border to the west, where the land meets the Cascade Range, that largely accounts for this region's desert character. The high mountains wring nearly all the moisture from the clouds, leaving only enough rainfall to support a sagebrush grassland or perhaps a pinyon pine-juniper community. And because of the high desert's northern latitude and base elevation of some 4,000 feet, most of the precipitation that manages to slip by the Cascades in winter arrives in the form of snow, making the area the only so-called cold desert among the nation's four deserts. Of course, this fact may slip your mind in summer, when temperatures often climb into the 90s.

Oregon's high desert is one of the least populated regions in the United States, with only a few thousand residents occupying an area roughly the size of South Carolina. The land is not as wild as the scarcity of people might imply, since what the desert lacks in people, it makes up in livestock: Cattle and sheep graze nearly every acre of the region. Arid habitat is easily damaged by overgrazing, but a few places remain in good condition, a testament to the surprising charms of the natural high desert.

Granted, there are some stark stretches here, where sagebrush and dried grass are all you see as your gaze sweeps from horizon to horizon. But even in the stretches that appear most desolate, treasures await those who are patient. Perhaps you'll spy a black-tailed jackrabbit hiding in the shade of a sagebrush thicket. Look closely at the large, translucent ears that serve as the creature's natural cooling system, ventilating blood in veins near the skin's surface. You might also see the predators that hunt jackrabbits: the golden eagle coasting high above or the coyote trotting along the desert floor. And you may come to appreciate the minimalist landscape itself, with its seemingly infinite open space and a quiet that nearly over-whelms urbanized senses.

But there is much more to the high desert than an uninterrupted expanse of sagebrush flats. You can drive to the top of a mountain that thrusts nearly 10,000 feet into the sky and look out over terrain that is laced with deep canyons cut by rivers or gouged out thousands of years ago by glaciers. On some of the higher slopes you can amble through cool groves of aspens, their leaves trembling in the breeze, or enjoy alpine terrain splashed with spring wildflowers. Dramatic views—sometimes punctuated by a sighting of elk, pronghorn, or bighorn sheep—unfold before you. Prairie falcons and red-tailed hawks soar through winding canyons, rising on the thermals. Blindingly white alkali flats coruscate in the sunlight. Vast wetlands create an oasis beloved by sandhill cranes, trumpeter swans, deer, porcupines, and a multitude of other wildlife. Whether you choose to hike, bike, run the river, or simply pull your car off the road and watch out your window, spend some time here. You'll soon learn that the seemingly parched, barren desert that stretches before you is actually a vital world unto itself. ■

Wildflowers at Steens Mountain

Hart Mountain National Antelope Refuge

■ 275,000 acres ■ South-central Oregon, 65 miles northeast of Lakeview
■ Season year-round, with best weather mid–May–Oct. ■ This is a remote,
primitive area without food or gasoline. Trails through the refuge are unmaintained, and all roads are unpaved. Visitor center open 24 hours a day year-
round, but staffed only sporadically. Even for travel during the best weather,
always inquire ahead about road conditions. ■ Camping, hiking, bird-watching,
wildlife viewing ■ Contact the refuge, P.O. Box 111, Lakeview, OR 97630;
phone 541-947-3315

YOU WON'T SEE AN ANTELOPE at this refuge. But you will likely see a pronghorn, the fastest land animal in North America and the only animal with
branched horns, as distinct from antlers. Commonly—but erroneously—
called antelope, pronghorn dwindled to dangerously low numbers early
in the 20th century, from an estimated 40 million in the early 1800s to an
ebb of some 30,000 in 1924. At one point, thousands of pronghorn were
killed and used as poison bait for coyotes and wolves. It was to protect a
herd that spent much of the year in the vicinity of Hart Mountain that
this refuge was established in 1936. Although pronghorn are still scarce
compared to historic levels, conservation measures have brought them
back to more than 500,000 nationwide. The numbers at Hart Mountain
fluctuate, but in a given year some 1,500 to 2,000 of these fleet-footed
beasts race across the refuge.

The 275,000 acres that make up the refuge shelter more than pronghorn.
Particularly since the removal of livestock in the early 1990s and the use of
prescribed fire—controlled burns designed to mimic the natural fires that
remove soil-covering litter, release nutrients, and stimulate the growth of
native grasses—the high-desert habitat has been evolving into a haven for
native flora and fauna, such as bighorn sheep and golden eagles.

Speed

Pronghorn are the swiftest runners in North America and, in a sense, are the finest runners in the world. Cheetahs achieve a slightly faster top speed, but they tire in seconds; pronghorn can maintain their 60 miles an hour sprint for three or four minutes and can bound along at more than 40 miles an hour for several miles. Their legs and feet are long and thin, allowing them to take very long strides. And their bodies excel in delivering oxygen to their muscles, a primary requirement for fast distance running. Research comparing pronghorn with goats—probably their closest living relative—revealed that pronghorn have a larger windpipe and more hemoglobin in their blood. They also possess a heart that is three times larger than that of goats and lungs with five times the capacity.

Pronghorn

But the dramatic landscape itself also deserves attention. Travelers approaching on Hart Mountain Road encounter a 25-mile-long tidal wave of basalt that rears more than 3,500 feet above the valley floor. This escarpment, shot through with rough canyons, constitutes the western rampart of the refuge. A switchbacking road takes you up this fault-block ridge to the rest of the refuge, delivering you to a sloping sagebrush and bitterbrush plain broken by rounded hills and rocky draws. The plain is also dotted with creeks, a few small lakes, a pocket of conifer forest in the south, and a smattering of mountains that rise as high as 8,065 feet.

This is a wild and remote place. The visitor center is tiny and often unstaffed, all the roads are unpaved, and the two campgrounds are rudimentary. Although the open terrain invites cross-country rambles, there are few established hiking trails. But if you can bring yourself to brave the primitive conditions, you'll be richly rewarded.

What to See and Do

First things first. While in the nation's one and only pronghorn refuge, you must see some pronghorn. Although these animals are sometimes called pronghorn antelope, true antelope live only in Africa, Asia, and Europe. Pronghorn belong to the genus *Antilocapra americana,* which is native only to North America. Other members of this family used to roam the continent during the ice ages and earlier, but all are extinct except the pronghorn.

You might spot pronghorn in any of the open, flatter stretches of the refuge. Your best bet is to drive slowly along the gravel road from the west entrance to the headquarters compound and then south along Blue Sky Road to **Blue Sky,** a pleasant stand of aspen and ponderosa pine. Scan the ridge for a silhouette, then, as you get closer, look for a tan-and-white mammal of approximately 120 pounds that stands about 3 feet high at the shoulder. Pronghorn have comely black-and-white markings coloring

their throat and face, and although both males and females can sport horns, females sometimes lack them. While the horns of the female seldom exceed a few inches in length, those of the male are typically one and a half feet long. Usually only the males exhibit branching—the distinctive "prong."

Infrequently will you see a pronghorn running, but you may get lucky. More likely, though, you'll spot one a few hundred feet from the road munching on grass. With its keen eyesight adapted to the wide open terrain of the desert, however, it's a safe bet the pronghorn will spot you first. Their protruding eyes enable these sturdy beasts to see both forward and backward, and to detect small moving objects up to 4 miles away. If a pronghorn is standing alone, it might be an adult male guarding his territory, which can be as large as 1 square mile. Occasionally, when males can't settle territorial matters by staring and vocalizing, a fierce battle will ensue, sometimes resulting in injury or death to an animal. If you see a group of males, it's most likely a young bachelor herd. During May and June, the birthing months, you may encounter herds of females with gangly fawns in tow. These little fawns aren't as helpless as they look, however: By the time they're four days old, they can run like the wind.

Pronghorn are not the only remarkable wildlife in the refuge. Nearly 400 bighorn sheep climb about on the steep western escarpment. They're generally hard to spot, but as you approach the refuge from the west and the paved road ends, look for an interpretive sign indicating bighorn. Between that sign and the point at which the road starts climbing the basalt wall, pull over and scan the cliffs with binoculars; this is considered one of the best areas in Oregon for viewing these aptly named creatures.

Birds of Prey

Watch the cliffs for birds of prey, too. Golden eagles and prairie falcons nest along the rim and on some of the stone towers. During courtship, the male prairie falcon arcs through the sky at high speed and calls to the object of his affections, who sometimes rockets up to join him. Other birds of note include mountain bluebirds, the melodious western meadowlarks, green-tailed towhees, pygmy nuthatches, and sage grouse, which conduct their flamboyant courtship rituals at dawn from late March to early May.

If you'll be hiking, try the path that tightropes along **Poker Jim Ridge.** You'll have excellent views of the **Warner Lakes** below and far beyond. From the campground, follow the easy trail that winds along **Rock Creek.** Reed-rimmed ponds sparkle behind beaver dams, and beaver meadows brim with wild irises and crimson-red columbines. Though such streamside areas are rare in the high desert—they constitute only a fraction of the acreage in Hart Mountain refuge—they're essential: A large majority of the wildlife species make extensive use of these oases for food and shelter.

Surprisingly, those forbidding western cliffs harbor some trails that are reasonably undemanding, such as the track that leads up the north side of **DeGarmo Canyon.** Although finding the start can be a bit tricky, once there you'll walk along the green tangle of alder, willow, aspen, and dogwood that borders **DeGarmo Creek.** Listen for the descending trill of a canyon wren and keep watch for the sensuous lavender blossoms of mariposa lilies. Higher up you'll see basalt pinnacles where prairie falcons often nest; higher still you may encounter bighorn sheep.

While you're at Hart Mountain, try to venture out at night at least once. If you drive slowly along one of the roads, you may spot a shambling porcupine or a slinky coyote stalking rodents or other small mammals. Almost certainly you'll see jackrabbits bounding across the road. At some point, be sure to look up at the sky. You've probably never seen so many stars nor stars that shine so sharp and clear. Listen while you look and you may hear the hoot of an owl or the howl of a hunting coyote. ∎

Steens Mountain

■ Elevation 9,733 feet ■ Southeast Oregon, about 60 miles south of Burns and 50 miles east of Hart Mountain National Antelope Refuge. ■ Steens Mountain loop road opens in increments as the snow melts. Typically open July-Oct.. Road unpaved and rutted in places, particularly on one southern stretch. Passenger cars can make it at 10 to 25 mph. Potable drinking water available at Page Springs and Fish Lake campgrounds. ■ Summer thunderstorms often pummel the mountain; leave the rim area or take cover in car if you see lightning strike. ■ Camping, hiking, fishing, bird-watching, wildlife viewing, auto tour ■ Camping fee ■ Contact Burns District, Bureau of Land Management, HC 74, 12533 US 20, Hines, OR 97738; phone 541-573-4400. www.or.blm.gov

YOUR FIRST IMPRESSION of Steens Mountain will depend on how you approach it. While that sounds like a metaphor for life, in this case it's a hard geological fact. Drive up its western flank on the Steens Mountain National Back Country Byway, and the rise is so gradual you'll hardly know you're climbing a mountain. But approach it from the east on Fields-Denio Road, and you'll come face-to-rock-face with a steep wall of dark basalt that rises nearly a mile above you, up to a peak that reaches 9,733 feet. The Steens, as the locals call it, is a fault-block mountain. Picture a gigantic wedge lying on its side, with the sharp edge pointing west. About 15 million years ago massive pressure caused by the earth's cooling and contracting raised the mountain along a fault line and tilted it as the land below sank. The slanting of the fault block to the west created the rugged eastern face rising up to the escarpment, marking a stark contrast with the western slope, which gradually descends into the Blitzen and Catlow Valleys.

Steens Mountain towers above the high desert in southeast Oregon. Covering about a 30-mile area from north to south and about half that from east to west, the Steens is not a defined preserve, such as a national park or monument, although many private citizens are working toward that goal. It lies on Bureau of Land Management lands, and has been battered by years of mining, grazing, invading exotic weeds, off-road vehicle use, fire suppression, and geothermal energy exploration. But some measures have been taken to address these issues, and the Steens remains the high point—literally and figuratively—of this part of Oregon.

Because the mountain gets more precipitation than the surrounding land, including a healthy dose of snow in winter, it is something of an oasis in the desert—a wildlife haven of trees and creeks, and 17 miles of wild and scenic river. The Steens is largely undeveloped, but a single unpaved road wriggles up the mountain, along the rim, and back down, creating a 66-mile loop that provides access to aspen groves, lakes, glacial valleys, and the lofty summit.

What to See and Do

Officially known as the **Steens Mountain National Back Country Byway**, the 66-mile loop begins and ends in Frenchglen, a town whose population could fit around a large dining room table. Drive several miles northeast on the **North Loop Road** across the southern tip of Malheur National Wildlife Refuge (see p. 125)— watch for sandhill cranes, waterfowl, and deer—to Page Springs Campground, one of the area's five camping sites. It sits beside the **Donner und Blitzen River**, German for "thunder and lightning." The river was named by an army captain in 1864 when he and his troops crossed the river during a thunderstorm. In 1988 the upper 17 miles of the Donner und Blitzen, from about Page Springs to its headwaters atop the Steens, was designated a Wild and Scenic River. From the campground you can take a short hike up the river

corridor. On your walk, look very closely at the low branches of the juniper trees and you may spot a motionless, robin-size bird. These masters of camouflage are common nighthawks. So confident are they of their hiding skills you can walk to within 5 feet of one and it won't fly away. At dusk during the nesting season, the male nighthawks soar perhaps 100 feet above their intended mate then swoop down, vibrating their wing feathers to produce a loud, hollow booming sound.

Back in your car at Page Springs, head up the North Loop Road, which climbs the long western slope of the Steens. The gradual, 5,600-foot ascent from the campground to the summit passes through numerous habitat zones, which are determined by factors such as soil type, wind patterns, and elevation. You'll start in the arid sagebrush zone, a spare land

Following pages: Sunrise from Steens Mountain

of sagebrush and bunchgrasses, and end at the snow-cover zone, which includes the summit. (Don't worry, it's not always covered with snow.) At about 5,000 feet, you'll grade into the western juniper zone, a dark green belt of these aromatic trees.

About midway up the Steens, you'll enter the quaking aspen zone. Groves of 40-foot trees, with their smooth white bark and quivering leaves, provide a pleasant respite from the heat and meager vegetation of the flatlands. Pull off at **Lily Lake** or, a few miles up the road, at **Fish Lake,** which formed during the Pleistocene epoch when water pooled behind a dam of rocks and soil deposited by a glacier. As you stroll amid the aspens, look for waterfowl nests, boreal toads, and Pacific tree frogs. Also examine the dark scars that lace the bark of the older trees. Most of these cuts are natural, but you may spot an image of a wine glass, a coffeepot, or a ship, carved decades ago by Basque and Irish sheepherders. If you're interested in fishing, Fish Lake is stocked with rainbow and Eastern brook trout.

Just shy of the rim you'll come to half-mile-deep **Kiger Gorge.** Formed by a glacier that bulldozed its way down the mountain, scouring out soil and vegetation until it hit bedrock, Kiger Gorge is said to present the nation's clearest picture of a classic, U-shaped glacial valley. When you get to the viewpoint, use your binoculars to scan the bottom of the gorge for beaver ponds in the creek and for deer grazing in the meadows.

From Kiger Gorge, the road turns south and skirts along the rim. Pull off at the **East Rim Viewpoint** and gaze over the precipice to the Alvord Desert (see p. 124) nearly a mile below. On a clear day—and they're not uncommon —you can see Nevada, California, and Idaho, in addition to a vast spread of the Oregon high desert. Watch the sky for golden eagles, prairie falcons, and red-tailed hawks soaring and gliding on the thermals that sweep up the cliffs. And survey the steep, gullied mountainsides for bighorn sheep. Once native to the area, bighorns have been reestablished on the Steens by the Oregon Department of Fish & Wildlife. The actual summit of the mountain lies several miles up the road, but it's only 3 feet higher than the East Rim Viewpoint, requires a steep, quarter-mile hike, and has poorer views because of nearby ridges.

From the summit the road heads down the mountain's western slope. About 6 miles into the descent, you'll ease along a ridge that bisects the **Little Blitzen Gorge** and the **Big Indian Gorge.** Stop at one of the several viewpoints for panoramic views of these picturesque canyons, or take one of the trails that allow short walks out along the rims. Birders should be sure to keep their binoculars handy.

A few miles farther along the road, you'll recross the Donner und Blitzen River. From here down to where the loop rejoins the highway in the Catlow Valley, keep on the lookout for some of the wild horses of the south Steens herd; they are descendants of horses that escaped from Indians, early explorers, and settlers. ■

Northern sweet broom

The Desert Trail

The Desert Trail is an ambitious effort launched by a group led by the Bureau of Land Management and the Desert Trail Association. The group is working to create a national trail that will largely follow the arid lands just east of the Sierra Nevada and the Casacade Mountain Range. When it is completed, the Desert Trail will run from the Mexican border to Canada through California, Nevada, Oregon, Idaho, and Montana.

So far about 1,000 miles of trail have been established, many of them in southeast Oregon. Visitors to the Northwest can hike along the trail from Denio, on the Oregon-Nevada border, up through the Pueblo Mountains, the Alvord Desert, Steens Mountain, Diamond Craters, and Malheur National Wildlife Refuge. Unlike trails such as the Pacific Crest Trail, which are laid out more formally, the Desert Trail route will be minimally marked with rock cairns. By allowing hikers to choose their own routes through the area, this informal system will minimize damage to the soil and vegetation.

Hikers along the Desert Trail can expect to encounter sagebrush flats, rolling dunes, and stark canyons as well as volcanic craters, herds of pronghorn, and shallow lakes fluttering with birds. The trail also passes by waterfalls, mountain meadows bright with wildflowers, and marshes inhabited by beavers, swans, deer, and eagles. For more information and trail guides to the existing sections, contact Desert Trail Association, P.O. Box 34, Madras, OR 97741; phone 541-475-637.

Alvord Desert

■ 27,000 acres ■ Southeast Oregon, 20 miles north of Fields on the Fields-Denio Rd. Watch for the access road down to the Alvord. If you pass the shed at Alvord Hot Springs, turn around and go back 2.5 miles. ■ Ultralight flying, land-sailing ■ Contact Burns District, Bureau of Land Management, HC 74, 12533 US 20 West, Hines, OR 97738; phone 541-573-4400

THE STEENS DID IT. When the 9,733-foot fault-block mountain (see pp. 118-122) buckled upward, it created a rain shadow—blocking the passage of moisture-laden clouds from the west and parching the land below and to the east of it. At ground zero in that rain shadow sits the Alvord Desert, a 5-by-10-mile alkali expanse that resides in southeast Oregon but seems to belong on a planet closer to the sun. It is essentially lifeless: There are no birds, mammals, or insects, and no vegetation. There is only the utterly flat, cracked white-gray surface of dried mud.

This barren flatness makes Alvord a favorite site of hobbyists, including pilots of ultralight planes and land-sailors who captain sailboats on wheels. People also love to drive on the Alvord, provided their vehicle can negotiate the short access road off the Fields-Denio Road. (You can make it down this rough track in a passenger car, but it's a challenge.) Because there's nothing here to crash into—except perhaps other joyriders—motorists have been known to sit in the back seat while their cars pilot

Lake bed, Alvord Desert

themselves or to put thrilled eight-year-olds behind the wheel. However, don't venture out here if the desert is wet; the parched surface can become so slick that vehicles get stranded. And avoid the northern end, which tends to be soggy.

For visual relief, be sure to check out the dunes at the southern and eastern edges of the desert. Or just step out of your car, cut the engine, and enjoy a visit to another planet. Look to the west a couple of miles to Steens Mountain, which rises nearly a mile above the Alvord. In the afternoon nature may cook up a special treat by sending a thunderstorm over the Steens. Just remember to get back to the Fields-Denio Road before watching the booming, echoing, flashing spectacle. ■

Mule deer swimming, Malheur National Wildlife Refuge

Malheur National Wildlife Refuge

■ 187,000 acres ■ Southeast Oregon, about 32 miles south of Burns and just northwest of Steens Mountain ■ Visitor center open Mon.-Fri. year-round, weekends spring and summer ■ Hiking, bird-watching, wildlife viewing, auto tour ■ Contact the refuge, HC 72, Box 245, Princeton, OR, 97721; phone 541-493-2612. www.r1.fws.gov/malheur

IT MAY LACK DATE PALMS, but Malheur National Wildlife Refuge is an oasis nevertheless. While traveling through the sagebrush grasslands of southeast Oregon, it's something of a shock to come across a nearly 187,000-acre preserve dominated by wetlands and lakes, one of the largest freshwater marsh systems in the West. Malheur is greened by two primary rivers—the Donner und Blitzen and the Silvies—and numerous creeks that flow down from Steens Mountain to the south and from high country to the north.

Because the landscape is so open and the wildlife so abundant, you will see plenty of animals here. So far, at least 58 different types of mammals have been sighted. And your own list of wildlife sightings will grow rapidly if you get out early in the morning or late in the afternoon. Likely sightings include pronghorn, porcupines, garter snakes, deer, dragonflies, coyotes, ground squirrels, lizards, and butterflies.

And many, many birds. Birds are Malheur's pièce de résistance. More than 320 species have been spotted here, an incredible display of diversity. And some species, such as snow geese, congregate in flocks so large that in flight they can eclipse the sun. The reason for this astonishing wealth of wildlife is that the refuge is the only big, green, wet place around. Famed birdman Roger Tory Peterson declared the refuge, established by executive order of President Theodore Roosevelt in 1908, one of the nation's dozen best places for birdwatching, prompting people to come from all over the country—indeed, the world—to scan Malheur with their binoculars. At overlooks you'll catch odd snatches of conversation in birderspeak, such as "Have you gotten the veery?" or "Are the Ross's in yet?" And you'll encounter birders on refuge roads. You'll recognize them: They're the ones stopping and starting and weaving, paying more attention to the marsh than to their driving. Fortunately, they're usually going only about 5 mph.

Arrive in March or early April to view large flocks of waterfowl. For the sandhill cranes, come in March through April or August through mid-October, when they gather in large numbers prior to migration. However, from May through July, the cranes are nesting and raising their young and are very secretive. For maximum avian diversity, consider May. Winter is quiet, but you will still see ducks, geese, ravens, a variety of raptors, bald eagles, great horned owls, and black-billed magpies.

You needn't be a birder to appreciate Malheur and its winged creatures, however. Someone who wouldn't look twice—or even once— at a scruffy sparrow is apt to gaze admiringly at a mountain bluebird coursing against a sky the same color as its feathers, a black-necked stilt delicately picking its way through the water on its absurdly long legs, or a trumpeter swan sounding its resonant call.

Nearly all the wildlife viewing in Malheur should be done from your vehicle. This seems odd to most nature lovers, but cars serve as good blinds. If you get out, it often scares the animals away.

What to See and Do

The wildlife watching begins before you even get to the refuge proper, assuming you're heading south from Burns on Oreg. 205, as nearly every visitor does. Just outside this little high-desert town you'll start passing ranches and farms in the **Silvies Floodplain.** In spring, particularly in March and early April, the flooded meadows beside the highway and adjacent local roads brim with waterfowl. In fact, during this peak migration time you'll see far more waterfowl in the Silvies Floodplain than you will in the refuge itself, which lies just outside the main migration

corridor. Pull over and watch as thousands of tundra swans, northern pintail, snow geese, Ross's geese, and Canada geese waddle and swim about the meadows consuming food to fuel their long journey. Roll down your window and a blast of frantic squabbling will fill your car.

For an experience even more overwhelming, ask someone which fields the birds have been roosting in, then go to one before sunset and wait. Shortly before dark you may find yourself at the eye of a hurricane of thousands of swirling waterfowl, honking and flapping

Common snipe

as they search out a place to settle for the night.

About 10 miles south of Burns, the highway climbs from the flats onto **Wrights Point,** a basalt rampart several hundred feet high. Just before you reach the crest, you'll get long views north over the Silvies Floodplain and beyond to the mountains of the **Ochoco** and **Malheur National Forests.** Once over the top of the point, all of the wildlife refuge and Steens Mountain will be laid out in front of you. Soon you'll be back on level land, crossing the remaining 8 miles of sagebrush flat before you reach the refuge. Watch for pronghorn along the way. In fact, you may witness birds and unwitting pronghorn interacting. Sometimes a killdeer will put on a broken-wing display to lure a pronghorn away from the killdeer's nest, though the grazing pronghorn is probably oblivious to both the bird and the nest.

The Refuge

At the end of the sagebrush flat you enter the Malheur National Wildlife Refuge itself. The highway lifts onto a causeway and crosses an area called **The Narrows,** which separates **Malheur Lake** to the east from **Mud** and **Harney Lakes** to the west. In recent years, The Narrows usually has been flooded, but historically water levels have fluctuated drastically and you could find yourself driving above an expanse of dried mud. It's more likely, though, that you'll be surrounded by water and birds as you cruise the 2-mile causeway. Watch for northern shovelers stirring the water with their long bills; western grebes, famed for their

Yellow-headed blackbird

walk-on-water courtship dashes; and American white pelicans, enormous birds that dip and feed in unison with a grace that belies their size. In the reeds at the water's margin look for boisterous flocks of 20, 50, or even 100 yellow-headed blackbirds.

Just south of The Narrows the Princeton-Narrows Road takes visitors east a few miles to **refuge headquarters**. There, avid birders leap from their cars into the groves of big trees, a rarity on the refuge and a magnet for birds—including some seldom seen in this region, such as the indigo bunting and the yellow-billed cuckoo. Those who are less avid may want to start at the visitor center. The staff there happily provides tips on locating the wildlife. A powerful scope on the deck allows you to closely scan **Malheur Lake,** a marshy body of water that starts just below the headquarters and sprawls north and east. At the turn of the 20th century, plume hunters pillaged the lake to harvest swans, egrets, herons, and grebes for the millinery trade in New York and France, where an ounce of feathers was worth more than an ounce of gold. It was the imminent extermination of these birds that prompted President Roosevelt to establish the refuge. Today, hundreds of herons and egrets nest on islands in the lake.

Closer at hand, Belding ground squirrels, which have made the headquarters' lawns into their colony, scurry about as you stroll down to the small but excellent **bird museum.** The collection ranges widely, from dozens of stuffed specimens to a display on

Why Migrate North?

The tendency is to think of birds heading south for the winter to avoid the cold and snow. So why would a western sandpiper, for example, leave the equatorial ease of its wintering grounds in South America and labor thousands of miles north to spend the summer breeding on the Arctic tundra? In general birds head north to make better use of resources. If they stayed in one place they might exhaust the habitat. And up north the birds have long Arctic days in which to gather food for themselves and their young; they may encounter less competition for that food; and they can take advantage of the bountiful outburst of plants, bugs, and rodents that occurs during the brief Arctic summer.

broken bird eggs that tells you how to determine from the remains what cracked open an egg. If you join the birders outside, scrutinize the cottonwoods and you may spy great horned owls, most likely babes still round with fluffy down.

The Blitzen Valley, defined by the Donner und Blitzen River and its floodplain, lies south of headquarters. Along with Malheur Lake, this marshy valley constitutes the heart of the refuge and is its most accessible section. Malheur's main wildlife viewing route starts from headquarters and consists primarily of the Center Patrol Road, known locally as CPR.

Guided Drive on Center Patrol Road

CPR is the north-south dirt road that runs through the middle of the refuge. The official name was recently changed to "Auto Tour Route," which is somewhat more accurate since motorists taking the grand tour must briefly use a few other roads. Start at the refuge headquarters and drive southwest on the road toward Frenchglen. After just a few hundred yards you'll crest a low rise that yields expansive vistas of the grasslands, mesas, and mountains of the high desert. Here in the sagebrush uplands you'll often see hawks and jackrabbits. After 2 miles of gradual descent you'll cross the Donner und Blitzen River and enter the wetlands complex. Soon you'll be skirting **Wrights Pond,** a popular nesting area for geese and ducks. About 4 miles from head-quarters you'll intersect the CPR proper. In the evening or early morning short-eared owls often flutter about here, flying with erratic, stuttering wingbeats as they prowl for rodents.

Turn south onto the CPR and proceed slowly, windows down and binoculars poised. Sometimes it takes an hour to go 1 mile as you tarry at this marsh and that meadow. Depending on the season, you'll likely see cinnamon teal so close you can look right into their red eyes. Northern harriers—formerly called marsh hawks—are common, cruising slowly just above the vegetation, and you may hear yellow-breasted Western mead-owlarks belting out their sunny songs. Dozens of other species will have you flipping through your

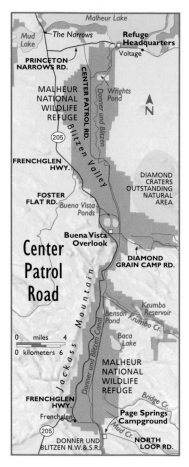

field guide. On the furry side, deer and beavers can be found here too, though the latter seldom appear.

After about 16 miles, the northern portion of the CPR ends at the road to Buena Vista. Turn west and you'll edge along the northern boundary of **Buena Vista Ponds,** home to white-faced ibises, with their long, curving bills and glossy plummage; stocky little snipes; elusive soras and rail stalk-ing through the reeds; deer; and an abundance of waterfowl. Sandhill cranes, perhaps the most famous of the species on the refuge, also favor this area. Three-and-a-half feet tall, with a red crown and orange-red eyes, the cranes emit a trumpeting rattle that can be heard for more than a mile. About 250 pairs of these increasingly imperiled birds nest on the refuge; up to 3,000 gather in fall before migrating to their winter haunts.

At the end of the ponds you'll come to a 1-mile side road that leads to the **Buena Vista Overlook,** where raptors float by the basalt rim on thermals. With luck you may also spot nests of once-rare trumpeter swans. The swans are now part of a conservation program begun in 1991 and aimed at transplanting swans to Malheur from Montana's Red Rock Lakes National Wildlife Refuge, and teaching them to migrate to a more hospitable wintering area.

Back on Oreg. 205 for the next 8.5 miles south, you'll see wetlands to the east and sagebrush grasslands to the west. At the end of this run, turn east on the dirt road to Krumbo Lake. Shortly you'll cross the Donner und Blitzen; immediately east of the river turn south to pick up the CPR again. Go a mile, then stop at **Benson Pond.** Again, look for trumpeter swans, and examine the big cottonwoods on the north end where you're almost sure to find great horned owls. You may also spot porcupines, which sometimes munch shrubs so close to your car that you can hear them chewing. As you continue south the wildlife parade rolls on, including coyotes sniffing through meadows, hundreds of swallows swarming over ponds, and vultures by the dozen hunched atop the tower at the P Ranch.

Several spurs branch off the CPR and Oreg. 205, such as Krumbo Lane, which leads a few miles up Krumbo Creek to **Krumbo Lake.** A pond along the road often attracts a notable variety of ducks and during the summer a colony of eared grebes usually hangs out at the reservoir. Nearby, a rimrock area hosts deer, quail, and chukar. Oreg. 205 follows a much grander rimrock canyon for several miles near the north-south midpoint of the refuge. Focus your binoculars on the bas-relief basalt walls and survey for prairie falcons and golden eagles.

Sage Grouse Show

Visitors willing to get up very early and park along **Foster Flat Road** before sunup will be treated to a wildlife show that is legendary in the West. Between March and May, male sage grouse strut their stuff at traditional display sites, or leks, along this road that the birds have been using for generations. (Ask the refuge for directions to the most active sites.) For about an hour after sunrise, these heavy, 2-foot-long birds gather at the lek and show off for prospective mates. The males puff up their chests by inflating yellowish air sacs and march about like pompous little generals, tail feathers fanned and wings held rigid and almost touching the ground. Then the males deflate their air sacs, making a loud popping-gurgling sound. Sage grouse populations are declining across the West as they lose their habitat to farming and ranching, but lucky visitors to Malheur can still catch one of the greatest shows on earth. ■

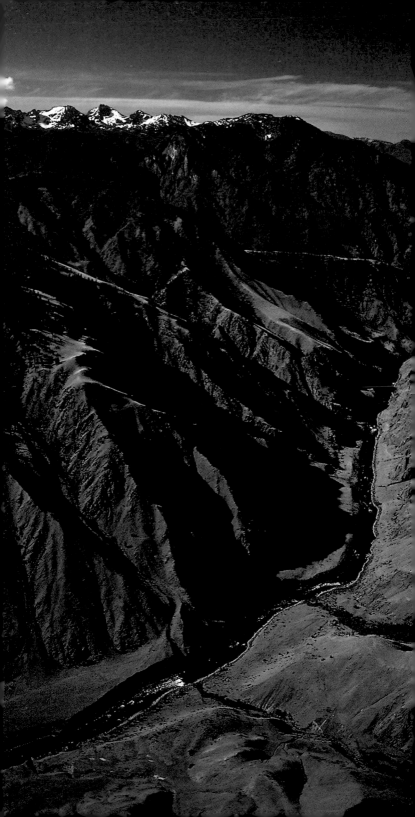

Hells Canyon National Recreation Area

■ 650,000 acres ■ At the conjunction of Oregon, Idaho, and Washington, 50 miles northeast of Enterprise ■ Open daily Mem. Day–Labor Day, Mon.-Fri. only the rest of year. ■ Snow up top Nov.–May or June; very hot in the canyon during the summer ■ Camping, hiking, boating, white-water rafting and kayaking, bird-watching, wildlife viewing ■ Parking fee at trailheads; permits required for river running ■ Contact NRA headquarters, 8401 Oreg. 82, Enterprise, OR 97828, phone 541-426-4978; or P.O. Box 699, Clarkston, WA 99403, phone 509-758-0616; or Riggins Administrative Site, P.O. Box 832, Riggins, ID 83549, phone 208-628-3916. www.fs.fed.us/r6/w-w/hcnra.htm

HELLS CANYON IS THE DEEPEST river gorge in North America—deeper even than the Grand Canyon, which measures a mere 4,000 feet from rim to river on the south side and 6,000 feet from top to bottom on the north. From the west rim of Hells Canyon the drop is 5,632 feet to the river below and from the east rim the canyon plummets an awesome 8,043 feet. But numbers and comparisons are beside the point. What's important—and what brings visitors flocking here—are the wildness, the remoteness, the biological wealth, and the dramatic scenery found in Hells Canyon and the adjacent lands that together constitute the Hells Canyon National Recreation Area.

This 650,000-acre site sprawls across northeast Oregon, includes a slice of west-central Idaho, and abuts southeastern Washington State. The Snake River curves through the bottom of the canyon, but it was not alone in carving this deep, 10-mile-wide gash in the earth. In fact, the Snake originally flowed south of what is now the canyon. About 13 million years ago, however, fault movement blocked the Snake and backed it up to form Lake Bonneville, which covered most of southern Idaho. When this ancient inland lake burst some 15,000 years ago, a flood of mammoth proportions gouged out much of what is now Hells Canyon, and the Snake flowed north through this new gorge.

Most of the Snake is shackled by dams, but the 70-odd miles flowing through the Hells Canyon NRA run free and are protected as a Wild and Scenic River. Every year thousands of people travel the canyon by raft or jet boat. At water level, where the elevation is perhaps 1,000 feet, you pass through an arid land of prickly pear cactus and rattlesnakes, a desert that receives less than 15 inches of rain a year and bakes in 100-degree-plus temperatures during the summer.

Thousands more people approach Hells Canyon from above, visiting the rims in Oregon or Idaho. This is a world entirely different from the canyon bottom. At rim level and above, visitors revel in cool subalpine forests, lush mountain meadows, old-growth ponderosa pine forests, and even snowfields.

Snake River, Hells Canyon

Whether you're on the river or at the rims, exploring Hells Canyon NRA presents a challenge. This is rough, isolated country. The Snake, particularly in spring, tests boaters with big water and serious rapids. But if you lack the skills and equipment to tackle such a river, outfitters can guide you through the canyon.

If you don't want to get your feet wet, 900 miles of hiking trails criss-cross the NRA. This vast trail system mostly follows old Forest Service access fire roads, and trails used by ranchers to move livestock to remote salting areas and watering holes. Many of these involve steep grades and daunting elevation gains. But moderate and accessible day hikes exist, and outfitters with packhorses or llamas can lead you on longer treks. Then there are the notorious roads. Disregarding the jeep tracks, several dirt roads that are barely passable to passenger cars lure visitors deep into the backcountry, offsetting the jarring ride with fantastic scenery and wildlife. Motorists also will enjoy long stretches of paved road and some good gravel roads that are part of the **Hells Canyon Scenic Byway,** which loops 150 miles from La Grande to Hells Canyon to Baker City.

What to See and Do

Let's take it from the top. Many travelers make the **Hells Canyon Overlook** on the Oregon side of the NRA their first stop. This perch sits at 5,400 feet on Forest Road 3965, a paved spur road 3 miles off the scenic byway. The overlook offers nice displays and

Feeder creek for Snake River

interpretive material, but ignore this when you first arrive. Just get over to the edge and look. Note the eroded mountainsides, all gullies and ridges, and how the slanting rays of early morning or late afternoon sun turn them into a dramatic landscape of shadow and light. Gazing into Idaho, note the snowy peaks, especially the towering **Seven Devils Mountains**—said to be named for a vision of seven dancing devils that appeared to an Indian lost in the area—about 10 miles to the northeast. For great views of the Snake River, continue along Forest Road 3965, which turns rough past the overlook.

More Views

To get to the highest and best views of the canyon from the Oregon side, you've got to pay the price. From the scenic byway, you must drive 23 miles on a single-lane gravel road (with turnouts) that is often steep and

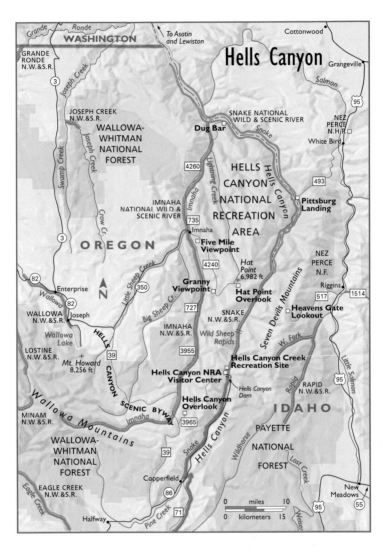

sometimes does a high-wire act along dizzying slopes. Cars can handle this road fine, but it's slow going; allow at least an hour one-way without stops. It's better to take more time, though, since there's plenty to see along the way. **Five Mile Viewpoint** provides your first look at the **Imnaha River Valley.** Another designated Wild and Scenic River, the Imnaha

splashes down from the Wallowa Mountains and runs north the length of the NRA before joining the Snake. At mile 17, **Granny View**—at 6,345 feet—provides an even better look at the Imnaha. This overlook also is notable for its spring wildflowers. Finally, ascend 6 miles more and you'll top out on the edge of Hells Canyon at **Hat Point,** more than

5,500 feet above the Snake River. After taking in the panoramic expanse, lower your sights and scan the slopes and benches below for deer and elk. If you're very lucky, you might spot an elusive bobcat or mountain lion. Golden eagles, peregrine falcons, and several species of hawks inhabit the canyon and are sometimes spotted from this and other overlooks. In fact, there are about 350 species of wildlife that reside either part- or full-time in the recreation area's habitats.

Idaho Viewpoints

On the Idaho side, three viewpoints worth stopping at can be reached by car. Perhaps the finest is **Heavens Gate Lookout**, which lies roughly across the river from Hat Point. At 8,600 feet, the view from here takes in a vast chunk of the canyon and hundreds of square miles beyond, plus the adjacent crags of the Seven Devils Mountains.

Raft and Kayak Trips

For those who want to explore the canyon at river level, there are several options. First is a trip down the Snake in a jet boat, raft, or kayak. Outfitters offer trips from various put-in points, the most popular of which is **Hells Canyon Creek Recreation Site**. This site is in Oregon but must be reached through Idaho on the paved 23-mile road from Copperfield (where Oreg. 86 bridges the Snake, just south of the NRA). When you reach Hells Canyon Dam, cross to Oregon and go north 1 mile to the end of the road. Jet boats leave from the recreation site, go downriver varying distances and return later that day (or the next day if you opt for the 220-mile round-trip journey to Lewiston).

Raft and kayak trips leaving from the recreation site are numerous and varied. Some last a couple of days and take out at Pittsburg Landing, 32 miles from the put-in. Others go for more than a week and take out 104 miles downriver at Asotin, Washington. If you'll want to explore, choose an outfitter that allows plenty of time at riverside camps for trekking into side canyons, investigating tributary creeks, and enjoying the arid-land flora and fauna. In spring, a short hike off the Snake might reveal a variety of song birds in courtship, or nesting in the brushy side canyons. There are two things boaters must remember,

Added Attractions

The stretch of the upper Imnaha River that lies just northwest of the spur road to the Hells Canyon Overlook holds some quiet beauty. Turn west off Forest Road 39 onto Forest Road 3960 and go along the north bank of the Imnaha. You'll pass through a forest of old-growth ponderosa pine, widely spaced trees that look as if they were planted in a park. Pick off a flake of the yellow-orange bark and sniff the underside—vanilla, without a doubt. The 9-mile spur road ends at Indian Crossing Campground. A trail continues up the river and into the Eagle Cap Wilderness.

Balsamroot blooming

however: One, bring a swim suit, because in summer the water can reach a balmy 70°F. Two, the first 17 miles below the dam are packed with white-water thrills—and potential spills. The monster diagonal waves at the end of **Wild Sheep Rapid** alone should sober up any cocky captains who are in over their heads, so to speak. You'll need a permit to run the river, so apply early to the NRA, or contact a professional outfitter *(for list of companies contact the NRA)*.

Other Activities

Even if you're a landlubber, you should take the drive to the recreation site. It hews to the reservoir behind the dam and gives you a water-level view of some of the canyon. As you head north, the landscape bordering the river changes from grassy hills to looming rock walls. From the boat launch, consider hiking the 1-mile trail north along the river. Other roads lead down to the Snake, but none is paved. An infamous track that bumps 27 miles north from Imnaha to Dug Bar is recommended only for high-clearance, four-wheel-drive vehicles. The road follows the Imnaha River most of the way to Dug Bar, the northern terminus of the 56-mile **Snake River Trail.** Venture a few miles down the path and savor this grand—with a small "g"—canyon. On the Idaho side, another Snake River Trail, this one 35-miles long, is much flatter and accessible via a decent, 19-mile gravel road from Whitebird. ■

Central Plateau

Painted Hills, John Day Fossil Beds National Monument

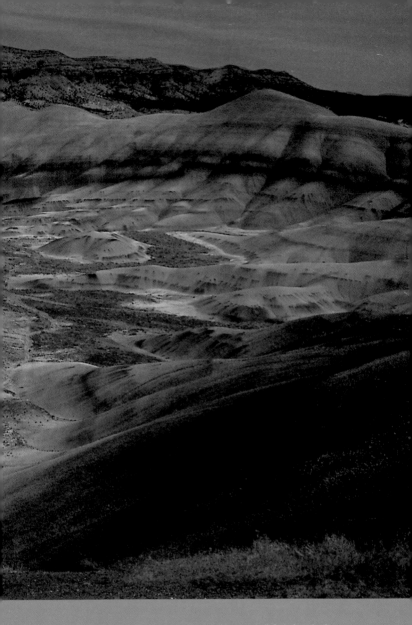

THIS LANDSCAPE BARES ITSELF to the world. Thick forests or
lush meadows are scarce on this semiarid plateau, which
sprawls from north-central Oregon across the Columbia
River into central and eastern Washington. You can see
the land—the scabs of volcanic rock, the rough-hewn
channels gouged in the earth by cataclysmic prehistoric
floods, waterfalls pouring over dark basalt cliffs, deep
river canyons framed by towering stone walls. Most of
the undeveloped land wears nothing more than a hardy

layer of rabbitbrush, bitterbrush, sagebrush, bunchgrasses, and other low-growing vegetation that can stand up to the harsh climate.

However, almost the entire region is developed and much of the area is farmed. In places the wheat fields turn the land golden as far as the eye can see. Most of what isn't farmed is grazed by livestock, even the scarce public lands. Visitors could whiz through this region on an interstate highway and never see any wild country. And that's just what most visitors do.

But the central plateau harbors a few pockets of raw land, and in these sanctuaries you can find plants and animals that have adapted to the harsh realm. Traces of some of these species' early ancestors exist, especially around the southeast margins of the region. Here, more than 40 million years ago, volcanic materials and heavy rain created massive mudflows that buried many of the plants and animals whose remains are being unearthed today in John Day Fossil Beds National Monument.

Two geological phenomena, in particular, shaped large expanses of the central plateau. The earliest began 17 million years ago when deep fissures in what is now southeast Washington began disgorging great flows of lava that blanketed much of the region. Some 200 flows over the course of 11 million years built up something akin to a gigantic layer cake of hardened basalt, forming what is known as Columbia Plateau basalt.

Then, around 17,000 to 12,500 years ago, a second geological phenomenon took place. As the ice age waned and the continental ice sheets retreated, melting glaciers formed vast lakes in present-day Montana and Idaho. These bodies of water were restrained only by ice dams, which inevitably weakened and collapsed. The largest ice age lake, Glacial Lake Missoula, covered some 500 cubic miles and was as much as 11,000 feet deep—nearly the depth of Lake Superior. When the dam broke, water poured out at a rate of nearly 400 million cubic feet per second—about 10 times the combined flow of all the rivers on earth. As this flood and others raged across the plateau, rushing waters scoured away flora, fauna, and soil and bulldozed deep channels in the rock. In the areas called channeled scablands, you'll see dramatic evidence of the terrible power of those monster floods, including giant boulders pushed miles downstream by the water.

Then, in a slow yet miraculous transformation, plants and animals reappeared in this desolate landscape; their descendants still inhabit the region. Deer, coyotes, hawks, kestrels, and other animals roam the sagebrush grasslands, and the scattered wetlands shelter sandhill cranes, great blue herons, avocets, Canada geese, beavers, muskrats, and many other water-loving species. And the sheer rock walls the volcanoes left in their wake, the fossil beds that quietly offer up clues to the plateau's past life, and the falls that thunder over a wall of hardened lava are now favored destinations for those who want not only to witness but to truly experience the enormous power of the natural forces that shape—and reshape—our world. ■

Grand Coulee formation

Smith Rock State Park

■ 640 acres ■ West-central Oregon, 25 miles north of Bend ■ Camping, hiking, climbing, fishing, mountain biking, horseback riding, bird-watching ■ Adm. fee ■ Contact the park, 9241 N.E. Crooked River Dr., Terrebonne, OR 97760; phone 541-548-7501

No, YOU DON'T NEED to bring a rope to visit Smith Rock State Park; even though a coil slung over the shoulder seems to be the accessory of choice of many folks in the parking lot. There is plenty to see and do here without scaling a rock, but the challenging walls and spires of Smith Rock induce climbers from around the country and the world to make pilgrimages here. Of the several thousand climbs in the 640-acre park, more than a thousand are bolted routes.

The sheer rock faces were carved about 28 million years ago, when a period of major volcanic activity laid down ash half a mile thick. Percolating groundwater caused the settled ash to harden while wind and water eroded it into the fantastic multihued shapes you see today. Then, less than half a million years ago, fluid basalt flows from the Horse Ridge area, 45 miles away, forced the ancestral Crooked River to change course and curve around the base of Smith Rock, creating the river gorge.

Even if you don't climb, you can watch as brightly clad figures inch their way up vertical rock faces that would scare a gecko. You also have the option of hiking amid the rocks and along the river. From the south end of the central day-use parking area, the quarter-mile **Memorial Bench Trail** leads to the **Rock Climbing Viewpoint** on the rim-rock above the south bank of the **Crooked River.** From here you can see many of the famed rock formations that quicken the pulses of climbers. If conditions for climbing are favorable, you'll probably also see people muscling up or down the big walls. Scan the tops of the rocks, preferably with binoculars, for other species that are drawn to high places—birds of prey, including red-tailed hawks, prairie falcons, golden eagles, and the occasional bald eagle.

Learning to Climb

Watching rock climbers slither up near-vertical cliffs can be a pleasant spectator sport. You can kick back in the shade, sip a cool drink, and raise your binoculars now and then to check on the progress of the hard-working figures high above you. If you find yourself saying, "Cool, I wish I could do that," you can—although you won't start out on those imposing vertical walls. A number of climbing schools offer courses for every level of student—make inquiries about nearby schools through the park administration. The instructors will help you learn the ropes and then take you out to some of the park's beginner sites—including a practice boulder called Rope de Dope.

Rock climbers, Smith Rock State Park

From the north end of the parking area, follow the main access trail to the **Geological Viewpoint**, where an informational panel explains the geology of the canyon. From there a path leads down to the river and the bridge that crosses to the north bank. As you come off the bridge, you're presented with the park's two choices for hiking: along the river (flat) or up and over the rocks (steep). If time and your legs allow, you can do both along the 5-mile **Misery Ridge Loop Trail**.

Start the loop dead ahead of the bridge by laboring up the hundreds of rough-cut steps that mount Misery Ridge. The name tells you all you need to know about the grade. But as you're panting up the steep slope, you'll see the cliffs and basalt pillars above; the juniper, sagebrush, and wildflowers at trail level; and the river and the horizon of rugged hills below and beyond. Ravens course overhead, their raucous calls echoing off the rock walls, the fluttering of their wings plainly audible from hundreds of feet away. About halfway up you'll pass beneath a raptor nesting area, where you might spy golden eagles coming or going as they tend to their young.

At 660 feet above the river, you'll reach level ground again at the 3,300-foot **Misery Ridge Summit**. Far from being a pinnacle, this broad summit includes many acres of juniper-dotted flats, which you can explore on a network of unnamed paths. Rest on a rock here and enjoy some fine views of the Cascades, from Mount Adams on the north end to Mount Bachelor on the south. On the summit the main loop trail mingles with the informal trails, so you may have to cast about a bit as you bear right to **Monkey Face,** perhaps the most renowned rock formation in the park. The top of this 350-foot monolith looks like a monkey's head—or so they say. Just east of Monkey Face, the trail switchbacks down a steep slope and joins the **River Trail.** Listen for the descending trill of canyon wrens.

Asters

Turn south on the River Trail and then follow the Crooked River around a couple of the bends that inspired its name. Often you'll see nesting Canada geese on the far bank. As you near the bridge and the end of the loop, you'll pass **The Dihedrals, Morning Glory Wall,** and some of the other popular climbing areas. Now you can watch the climbers from close up as they make their ascents. If you survey the cliff tops for prairie falcons, you might just spy a much larger bird atop the pinnacles. Look closely. It could be a golden eagle or a Canada goose aspiring to unaccustomed heights. ■

View from Sheep Rock Unit, John Day Fossil Beds NM

John Day Fossil Beds National Monument

■ 14,000 acres ■ North-central Oregon ■ Sheep Rock Unit visitor center open daily March-Oct.; closed weekends rest of year. Best season June-Aug. ■ Hiking, auto tour, fossil beds ■ Contact the monument, HCR 82, Box 126, Kimberly, OR 97848; phone 541-987-2333. www.nps.gov/joda

AT THIS NATIONAL MONUMENT, located in the Blue Mountains, it's what you can't see that matters most—the bits and pieces of prehistoric plants and animals, the faint impressions they made in rock. Mere whispers of ancient life, these tantalizing fragments of the past have lain buried for millions of years. No one knows how many fossils are embedded deep in the earth—millions, perhaps more—but as weather has eroded rock over time, some have made their way to the surface. Hundreds of fossils have been carefully extracted and put on display here in the monument museum and in other museums around the world. But it's safe to say that the vast majority still remain hidden beneath the juniper- and sagebrush-studded badlands of this preserve, holding close the secrets of the past.

John Day Fossil Beds National Monument—named for a Virginia explorer who came west in 1812—consists of 14,000 acres, divided into three units, scattered across a 50-mile stretch of north-central Oregon. Each unit offers visitors and paleontologists something different. But monument lands constitute just a small portion of the vast fossil beds that underlie this region. As of 1998 more than 640 fossil sites had been found spread across an area the size of New Jersey, and more are being discovered all the time.

But quantity alone is not the reason that paleontologists are excited by the John Day Fossil Beds. The biological diversity of the finds is tremendous—more than 2,100 species of prehistoric plants and animals have been identified so far. The fossils here are also well-preserved and many are complete. Moreover, they are interbedded with volcanic ashes and other vestiges of the contemporary landscape that serve as time markers, enabling scientists to date the fossils.

Perhaps most useful to researchers, the fossil record in the John Day area covers an extraordinarily long and nearly continuous span of time. Fossil beds that span as many as 5 million years are rare; the John Day beds are outstanding in that they cover a period of 50 million years. Such a remarkable span is analogous to showing scientists an epic movie instead of a single snapshot. It enables them to reconstruct how prehistoric animals and plants evolved over long periods of time, as well as how they related to one another, and how they were affected by floods and fires and by variations in climate. This piecing together of clues to form a coherent account of ancient life—and the dynamic processes that shaped it—is the essence of paleontology. Such an accounting gives us a better understanding not only of the earth today but also of how it might change in the future.

The promise of such knowledge has drawn scientists to the John Day region for well over a century. One famous early fossil hunter, Charles Sternberg, captured the excitement of this quest. Pondering his motivations, he wrote: "It is thus that I love creatures of other ages, and that I want to become acquainted with them in their natural environments. They are never dead to me; my imagination breathes life into 'the valley of dry bones,' and not only do the living forms of the animals stand before me, but the countries which they inhabited rise for me through the mists of the ages."

What to See and Do

Sheep Rock Unit

If your itinerary allows, start at the **Sheep Rock Unit,** north of US 26 midway between Redmond and Baker City, the farthest east of the three units that make up the monument. The **visitor center** at Sheep Rock showcases films, interpretive talks, and, most important, fossil exhibits. Careful browsing of the displays and discussions with monument staff will greatly enhance your visit. You'll learn how something as seemingly insignificant as a few fossilized grains of pollen can tell an important story, how fossils are preserved and studied in the laboratory, and how the fossil beds came to light in the 1860s due to the efforts of a young frontier minister named Thomas Condon. And, since most fossils remain hidden from sight or are in scientific collections not available to the public, the visitor center also

Hiking the Island in Time Trail

provides the best opportunity to view this evidence of past life.

The John Day Fossil Beds are considered the best in the world for studying the Tertiary period, the era when mammals became the dominant form of animal life and flowering plants became the dominant form of plant life. Dating from 54 million to 6 million years ago, fossils of ancient giant pigs, camels, mouse-deer, opossums, horses, elephants, bears, dogs, and hundreds of other mammalian species have been found here. Add in a few reptiles, birds, and amphibians, and it's quite a collection of fauna. On the flora side, there are lilies, dogwoods, magnolias, apples, and other flowering plants.

Although collecting fossils is prohibited, monument managers do encourage people to get out on established trails. Just 3 miles north of the visitor center on Oreg. 19 lies the **Blue Basin Area**. Here, on the **Island in Time Trail** (an easy 1-mile round-trip) you'll go back 20 million years as you walk through an amphitheater of volcanic ash that has turned to blue-green claystone. At trailside interpretive exhibits, you'll learn that fossils include more than preserved bones or impressions in rock. A burrow, a root trace, scat—any clue about past life preserved by geologic processes qualifies as a fossil. At other stops you'll see reproductions of fossils that were found here. If you prefer a more strenuous hike, you can pick up a 3-mile loop called the **Blue Basin Overlook Trail** from the same trailhead as the Island in Time. The 600-foot elevation gain lands you at an overlook that offers a grand view of the John Day River Valley.

Another interpretive trail, the **Story in Stone Trail,** loops for a quarter mile through the **Foree Area** of the Sheep Rock Unit, about 4 miles north of Blue Basin on Oreg. 19. At several of the trail stops you'll encounter simulations of fossils imbedded in claystone. Look closely and see if you can detect the mouse-deer teeth at one stop, the upper femur of an ancient rhinoceros at another, and the skull of a *Miohippus* (a small, three-toed horse) at a third.

Guided Drive from Sheep Rock to Painted Hills

Before you make the 45-mile drive west from the Sheep Rock Unit to the Painted Hills Unit (which lies off US 26), pick up a "Geology Road Log" at the visitor center and learn about the lay of the land. The log lists several dozen roadside sites at which to stop and provides geological details about each feature. It even tells you on which side of the road to pull off and exactly where to direct your eyes. This drive isn't for people in a hurry, however, since it eschews the 40-mile direct route in favor of a roundabout 75-mile meander.

The first stop tells you all you need to know about **Goose Rock Conglomerate,** a 100-million-year-old formation. A few miles later you'll stop at **Cathedral Rock,** distinguished by red- and buff-colored bands near its top. These stripes consist of Picture Gorge ignimbrite, a type of rock deposited during an immense volcanic explosion about 29 million years ago and named for an area of the Painted Hills where the rock is prominent. At Mile 22.5 the log directs you to the **Shady Grove Recreation Site,** which lies amid basalt flows dating from about 17 to 12 million years ago and covers most of the Columbia Plateau. You'll learn how the rate at which molten lava cools helps determine the shape and texture of the rock it forms. Near the end of the tour you'll stop at a site from which workers removed a 5-foot-long mammoth tusk, now on display at the BLM office in nearby Prineville *(541-416-6700)*.

Painted Hills Unit

Arguably the most scenic of the three monument units, the Painted Hills look like colorful layer cakes that have melted in the sun. The vivid horizontal stripes of pink, black, red, bronze, and tan get their color from the weathering of the volcanic ash that formed this landscape. For an easily won panorama, drive up to the **Painted Hills Overlook.** More views await those who hike out from the overlook on the easy, half-mile round-trip **Painted Hills Overlook Trail.** For the best views of all, however, take the moderately demanding **Carroll Rim Trail** (one and a half miles round- trip). From the rim you can see the rolling colored sea of the Painted Hills and beyond to Sutton Mountain. Back down to

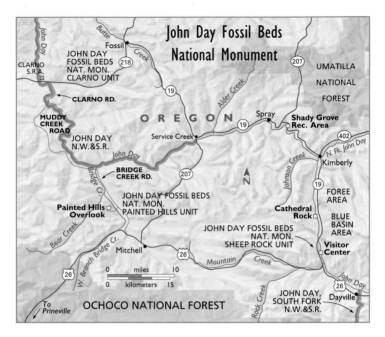

John Day Fossil Beds National Monument

earth, head south on the Painted Hills Overlook Trail to reach the 400-yard-long **Leaf Hill Trail.** Along the path you'll see exhibits showing some of the types of fossil leaves found in this hill, which contains the remains of a 33-million-year-old hardwood forest. Finally, wind around a crimson and ocher hill on the quarter-mile **Painted Cove Trail,** which permits a close-up view of popcorn-textured claystones that expand when wet.

Clarno Unit

From the Painted Hills, drive about two hours northwest on Oreg. 207 and Oreg. 218 to the Clarno Unit. This tract of the monument is anchored by the **Palisades,** a wall of dramatically eroded, castlelike cliffs that dates back 44 million years. The quarter-mile **Arch Trail** leads up to the base of the Palisades, where you can see birds of

prey, a fossil log, the mud nests of cliff-dwelling swallows, and the modest rock arch that gave the trail its name.

The highlight of the unit is the **Trail of the Fossils**—also a quarter mile long—where you get to see world-class deposits of fossilized nuts, seeds, wood, and leaves exposed in the rocks. The key to appreciating the wonder of the Trail of the Fossils is to use your imagination. In the trace of a sycamore leaf, visualize healthy green foliage on a tree in the lush, near-tropical forest that existed on this arid spot 44 million years ago. Imagine the 100 inches of rain storming down every year, saturating the new soils until the earth gave way and huge mud flows called lahars poured down the slopes. If you focus your mind's eye on the past, this trail—and this monument—come alive. ■

White-water rafting, Lower Deschutes

Lower Deschutes River

■ 100 miles long ■ Central Oregon, 10 miles northwest of Madras near Warm Springs ■ Peak flows in summer ■ Camping, hiking, boating, white-water rafting and kayaking, fishing, biking, horseback riding ■ Camping and boating fees ■ Lists of licensed river outfitters and fishing guides available ■ Contact Prineville District BLM, 3050 N.E. 3rd St., Prineville, OR 97754; phone 541-416-6700

IN 1988 CONGRESS BESTOWED the designation wild and scenic upon the Lower Deschutes River, acknowledging attributes the river has evinced since time immemorial—scenery, wildlife, fish, recreation, and historic, cultural, and geologic interest. Emerging from the central Oregon Cascades, the Deschutes winds north, passing through the central plateau to feed into the Columbia River. The Lower Deschutes consists of the last 100 miles of the 252-mile-long river. Much of this stretch flows through a massive canyon, with stone walls as high as 2,000 feet above river level, and cuts through a semiarid land of sagebrush, rattlesnakes, and coyotes.

While a boat provides the best opportunity to see the Lower Deschutes, you can explore it by other means as well. From **Deschutes State Recreation Area** *(89600 Biggs-Rufus Hwy., Wasco, 541-739-2322)*, at the confluence with the Columbia, three trails allow hikers to walk a couple of miles along the east bank and onto the uplands above. Bikers can pedal 32 miles on a trail adapted from a former railroad bed. If you take this route, be sure to bring along a patch kit. Those on horseback can ride the 22-mile equestrian trail along the river from March through June. But as enjoyable as these experiences are, they pale in comparison to a journey down the river by raft, kayak, or powerboat.

One of the most popular float trips runs 26 miles between **Macks Canyon** and Deschutes State Recreation Area. It's possible to make this a day trip, but most visitors take two days, spending the night at one of the primitive campsites along the way. For a longer run, start in Maupin and go 50 miles down to the Columbia. Numerous outfitters in the Maupin area and elsewhere guide trips along this stretch. You'll need their guidance, too, unless you're a highly skilled river runner. Though you'll encounter quiet stretches that can go on for as long as 34 miles, some parts of the run down to the Columbia bristle with white water, including perhaps a dozen major rapids. The rock garden known as **Washout Rapids,** for example, was created when a flash flood spewed boulders from a side canyon through a pair of ten-foot culverts into the river.

Another wild example is **Sherars Falls,** where the Lower Deschutes rages through a frothing channel of steep drops amid huge rocks. The falls are unrunnable, but boaters can put in at Buckhollow Boat Launch half a mile below the falls. Before setting out, take a moment to stop and appreciate this roller-coaster rapid, especially if you're visiting during the traditional fishing season for Native Americans from the Confederated Tribes of Warm Springs. Fishing in much the same way as their ancestors have done for centuries, they build wooden platforms that lean precariously out over the churning water. When the salmon are running, the fishermen pluck them up out of the river with long-handled dip nets.

The salmon runs in the waters of the Columbia Basin have been destroyed by development over the years, but some of the spawning runs up the Deschutes have done well recently. In 1998 an estimated 20,000 wild (not hatchery-born) fall chinook crowded up the river. Both salmon and steelhead draw a lot of fishermen to the Lower Deschutes. However, most visitors come to run the white water, float the slack water, admire the looming canyon walls, and watch for deer, elk, river otters, beavers, great blue herons, and other wildlife. This river is wild and scenic, indeed. ∎

No Substitute for Nature

With dams, logging, overgrazing, and development decimating the Columbia River system's fabled salmon runs, Northwest policymakers hatched a plot to compensate for the loss of wild salmon—by cultivating salmon in hatcheries. However, the number of salmon in the Columbia network has fallen dramatically since the days when nature reigned. Hatchery fish actually harm wild fish by spreading disease and competing for food. They also degrade wild populations by interbreeding with them, passing on the inferior genes of fish that have adapted to life in concrete raceways, not to the rough-and-tumble life of Northwest rivers and the ocean. If you see the thousands of wild fall chinook pushing up the Lower Deschutes, you're witnessing a marvelous and increasingly rare sight.

Trolling for salmon, Hanford Reach

Hanford Reach

■ 560 square miles ■ South-central Washington, running 51 miles north of Richland ■ Tour boat up the Hanford Reach runs May–mid-Oct. ■ Hiking, boating, boat tour, fishing, mountain biking, bird-watching, wildlife viewing ■ Contact Tri-Cities Visitor & Convention Bureau, P.O. Box 2241, Tri-Cities, WA 99302; phone 509-735-8486 or 800-254-5824. www.visittri-cities.com

IN JANUARY 1943 the U.S. Department of Defense claimed a chunk of sagebrush grassland that was one-half the size of Rhode Island in south-central Washington and called the area the Hanford Works. There, far from prying eyes, the government manufactured plutonium for atomic bombs. The site was chosen for its remoteness but also for its proximity to the Columbia River, since plutonium manufacturing requires vast quantities of water for cooling. The area was sealed off and patrolled by dogs, helicopters, and heavily armed guards. For decades the 560 square miles of the nuclear reservation remained apart from the world around it.

As the Cold War wound down in the late 1980s and the manufacture of nuclear bombs slowed, Hanford stopped producing plutonium. Gradually the veil of secrecy lifted and biologists discovered something marvelous about the site. The tight security measures had not only kept out spies, they had prevented the intrusion of freeways, malls, airports, golf courses, subdivisions, farm equipment, livestock, and all other forms of development. Only about 5 percent of the property had been built upon for the nuclear program, leaving 95 percent to the bluebunch wheatgrass, rabbitbrush, elk, coyotes, hawks, and owls.

While development has transformed almost all of the nation's and Washington's sagebrush habitat, Hanford shelters one of the last large blocks of unspoiled sagebrush grassland in the state. Through this nearly forgotten realm runs a 51-mile segment of the Columbia River known as the Hanford Reach. This water source is a key part of the pristine sagebrush grassland ecosystem, but the reach is special in its own right. As the last undammed nontidal stretch of the Columbia in the United States, it is the site of more than 90 percent of all fall chinook spawning. Dams drastically alter river habitat, greatly diminishing its ecological value. Although other salmon species still spawn elsewhere along the Columbia, chinook, for the most part, do not. The reach also has practical significance to visitors: The easiest way for the general public to get a good look at this sagebrush Shangri-la is to take a boat up or down the reach; security at Hanford may have relaxed but, except for an area called the North Slope, they still don't allow casual visitors to wander about.

What to See and Do

Even if you don't want to get out on the water, there is still one way you can see a bit of the Hanford Reach. It involves a twisting and turning back road's drive of 35 to 40 miles. From Pasco, take Taylor Road north to Ringhold Road. Go left on Ringhold Road, then left again at the fish hatchery. At Ringhold River Road, turn right and go north along the river for about 15 miles to the gate. Park there and continue on foot or mountain bike. You're now on the **Wahluke Slope,** the far northeast section of the nuclear reservation. You can hike up to a point above the 400-foot cliffs known as the White Bluffs, with the reach flowing far below. Watch for jackrabbits, hawks, coyotes, deer, and maybe even a golden eagle—and watch out for rattlesnakes.

The better way to see the Hanford Reach is from a tour boat floating on it. Catch the 26-passenger craft at the Columbia Park Marina in Richland. Columbia River Journeys (*509-943-0231. May–mid-Oct.*) offers a four-and-a-half-hour trip running some 38 miles upriver and back, penetrating deep into what is now called the **Hanford Site.** You won't see much evidence of development at Hanford, but you will see a vestige of the site's past—a tall siren that bears a sign reading "If you hear a steady 3-minute siren, leave this area immediately." Some of the tour commentary concerns the human history of the area and especially of the reservation, but much of the it focuses on the natural attributes of the reach.

The amount and diversity of the wildlife will surprise you. In this arid landscape coyotes are expected. You may even see a mom with her pups. Mule deer also come as no shock in the sagebrush grassland. They stick pretty close to the river and you'll probably see several. Pregnant does sometimes swim out to the river islands to bear their fawns in relative safety, then raise them out there until the leggy little critters are big enough to swim to shore.

But American white pelicans? On average about 75 of these huge birds with 9-foot wingspans are in residence on the reach. That's particularly impressive considering the state of Washington lists them as endangered. And how about ospreys? You'll see them on their nests or dive-bombing into the water after fish.

The list of the unexpected also includes bald eagles, gulls, hundreds of nesting Canada geese, a colony of black-crowned nightherons (looking ever grumpy), great egrets, cormorants, hovering Caspian terns scanning the reach for swimming snacks, western grebes, and leggy great blue herons. In between wildlife sightings, you can sit back and take in the wild sagebrush grasslands, the sand dunes, or the broad-shouldered **White Bluffs,** which constitute the east bank of the reach during the last few miles of the tour. Prairie falcons, red-tailed hawks, American kestrels, and other birds nest on the rugged bluffs, while inside the rock rest fossils of extinct species of bison, camel, and horse.

Below the White Bluffs and elsewhere, you may spot salmon traveling upriver. Several species swim up the reach, including fall chinook, a regal species that can weigh up to 60 pounds. In autumn, tens of thousands of fall chinook spawn in the Hanford Reach, the only significant spawning habitat left in the mainstem of the Columbia. This is one of the primary reasons that a group of local citizens, Native American tribes, conservation organizations, sportfishing groups, and others have banded together in an effort to persuade Congress to protect the reach by designating it as a Wild and Scenic River.

The fate of the reach remains uncertain, especially since it is inseparable from the fate of the North Slope. The biological value of the slope itself is immense, but what happens on the bordering

The Imperiled Sage Grouse

No one who has seen the mating display of a sage grouse will ever forget it: the inflated yellow air sacs ballooning from the proud male's breast; the gurgling-popping sound the bird makes when it deflates those sacs; and the strutting about with tail feathers erect and fanned out. This largest of all grouse is, indeed, a memorable icon of the West. Sadly, memories of the sage grouse are all people in most of the West have left. Throughout most of this creature's vast range, livestock grazing, conversion of sagebrush lands to farms, invasive weeds, and other factors have driven sage grouse to extinction or reduced them to dangerously low numbers.

Hanford is a case in point. David Douglas, a scientist who explored the area in 1826-27, reported prolific numbers of sage grouse along parts of the Hanford Reach. Today, sage grouse essentially are gone from Hanford, although government biologists hope to restore them. In all of Washington, only about a thousand sage grouse remain on lands that once supported hundreds of thousands of the birds. And it is not just the sage grouse that is in danger of vanishing; it is the entire community of plants and animals native to sagebrush country.

White-tailed deer, White Bluffs

uplands intimately influences the health of the reach. The White Bluffs provide a dramatic example. This long, tall wall of sand and clay has been crumbling into the reach at an accelerating pace for the last couple of decades. Geologists suspect that the increase in landslides is largely due to irrigated agriculture in the uplands behind the bluffs. The excess water seeps into the soil and loosens its hold. The debris slides into the river, burying salmon spawning habitat and changing the course of the chan-

nel, to the detriment of islands that are important to wildlife.

In 1998 the American Rivers conservation group ranked the Hanford Reach as the most endangered river segment in the nation. A small group of citizens and officials wants to place the land and water under county control so that it can be farmed and ranched. However, recent developments make it likely that the proponents of protection will be successful in safeguarding those biological treasures that had remained hidden for more than 50 years. ■

Palouse Falls State Park

■ 105 acres ■ Southeast Washington, 6 miles north of Lyons Ferry and 17 miles southeast of Washtucna. From Wash. 261, follow the gravel Palouse Falls Road two miles to the park ■ High flows occur spring–early summer
■ Camping, hiking, waterfalls ■ Contact the park, P.O. Box 157, Starbuck, WA 99359; phone 509-646-3252

AS YOU MOTOR THROUGH Palouse Falls State Park, it's as if you're driving through a minimalist painting. Gently rolling hills bristling with golden wheat fields, cloudless blue sky, the ribbon of a gravel road, and not much else. Almost this entire expanse of southeast Washington has been converted into this simple agricultural landscape. But the Palouse (which is contiguous with Lyons Ferry State Park) holds a grand surprise, and that is Palouse Falls.

Wheat fields have covered over most of the scars this land bears from the catastrophic Glacial Lake Missoula floods 15,000 years ago. The floods formed a series of waterfalls along the Palouse River, and the largest— Palouse Falls—remains a raw reminder of that ice age disaster. Next to the state park, at **Palouse Falls Natural Area,** you can still see the channeled scablands, the wounds in the dark basalt gouged by those berserking rivers of melted glacial ice. Here you will also encounter a remnant of the unplowed, ungrazed sagebrush grassland that once characterized this region.

The focus of the natural area is the 198-foot-high, 30-foot-wide waterfall where the Palouse River thunders over a wall of hardened lava that has resisted erosion these many years. But at the bottom, the falls have scoured out a big, rough amphitheater and a downstream canyon framed by brawny columnar basalt. You can look out on this scene from a shaded picnic area near the parking lot. For a different per- spective, take the informal trail, which doubles as a service road, that leads north from the picnic area parking lot up to the top of the falls. Listen for the call of canyon wrens and for the buzz of rattlesnakes. ■

Palouse Falls

The Scablands, Columbia NWR

Columbia National Wildlife Refuge

■ 23,200 acres ■ South-central Washington, 10 miles south of Moses Lake
■ Open to hiking and wildlife viewing March–Sept.; access restrictions fall and
winter ■ Hiking, canoeing, bird-watching, wildlife viewing, auto tour ■ Contact
the refuge, 735 E. Main St., Othello, WA 99344; phone 509-488-2668

SMACK IN THE RAINSHADOW of the Cascades, the Columbia National
Wildlife Refuge gets fewer than 8 inches of precipitation a year. At a
wildlife refuge in such a dry region you'd expect to find desert species,
such as mule deer, coyotes, lizards, ravens, and snakes. And so you do. But
in this south-central Washington sanctuary you'll also find a great many
other animals and plants, due to the construction of the monumental
Grand Coulee Dam on the Columbia River, 80 miles to the north.

When irrigation water from the dam's reservoir began flowing to
farmers' fields in 1955, the water table of the entire region rose. The rocky
channels and canyons of the refuge—the work of the massive glacial
floods that sculpted this landscape near the end of the ice age—became
lakes and ponds. Now the 23,200 acres that constitute the refuge feature
diverse habitats that serve a variety of wildlife. From rimrock overlooks
you can see other rugged rimrock areas, marshes, sagebrush hills, wet
meadows, canyons, and lakes.

Preeminent among the wildlife that seek shelter here are waterfowl,
including Canada geese, ringneck ducks, tundra swans, green-winged

teal, northern pintail, and tens of thousands of mallards. Waterfowl numbers peak during the fall and winter, and in order to protect the birds the public is kept away from the main concentration areas. However, the overlook at the south end of Byers Road gives you a look at thousands of ducks and geese on **Royal Lake.**

Many other water birds are found on the refuge as well. You'll likely hear the squabbling of American coots—often misidentified as ducks and famously belligerent when nesting. If you spot a hunched figure that looks like a little old man it's probably a black-crowned night-heron. The creature stalking through the shallows spearing fish or standing atop a rock surveying its feeding ground is a great blue heron. The lakes and wetlands are also home to other birds, such as northern harriers, redwing and yellow-headed blackbirds, and various songbirds.

In spring, usually peaking around late March, a beloved migrant tops off the refuge wildlife list—the sandhill crane. Thousands of these stately birds stop over at the refuge and vicinity on their way north each year, in turn attracting many human visitors. Although the cranes frequently feed in nearby fields, they can often be seen from the roads. To celebrate their arrival, the nearby town of **Othello** holds a festival, typically slated for the last weekend of March *(for information contact Othello Chamber of Commerce, 509-488-2683).*

Several walking trails wind through the refuge, including some interpretive paths. The 1-mile-long **Frog Lake Trail** starts at water level and works up through sagebrush grasslands to the tops of rimrock cliffs, passing through many different habitats. At water level you might spot a muskrat or beaver, but as you rise through the sage, look for coyotes, mule deer, snakes, and California quail. Up near the rim, look for species that like to nest up high. You may see colonies of mud nests that house cliff swallows. In the holes and on the ledges of the basalt walls, great-horned owls, American kestrels, and red-tailed hawks make their homes.

Canoeing is permitted on both **Hutchinson** and **Shiner Lakes,** where you can get close-up views of great-horned owls and canyon wrens along the cliffs. If you prefer to stay in your car, pick up an interpretive auto tour map at refuge headquarters in Othello. This 23-mile route takes about one-and-a-half hours and visits prime bird-watching habitat. ∎

Sandhills on Stage

With luck, visitors to the refuge in spring may witness the courtship ritual of the sandhill cranes. Svelte except for the fluffy bustle of their tail feathers, these elegant birds stand about three and a half feet tall, with a wingspan of more than 6 feet. Adults are usually gray with whitish faces and scarlet caps; juveniles blend gray with a rich cinnamon color. Imagine this bird jumping, bowing, bobbing its head, flinging grass, and racing about with wings extended. During all these gyrations sandhills let loose their distinctive call, a rattling trumpet heard for more than a mile.

Lake Roosevelt, Grand Coulee Dam

Grand Coulee

■ 50 miles long ■ Central Washington, from the dam southwest toward Lenore Lake ■ Camping, hiking, boating, swimming, fishing, dry falls ■ Contact Grand Coulee Dam Area Chamber of Commerce, P.O. Box 760, Grand Coulee, WA 99133; phone 509-633-3074 or 800-268-5332

FOR MOST PEOPLE, the name Grand Coulee brings to mind the mammoth dam that restrains the Columbia River in central Washington. But the dam got its name from the Grand Coulee, a geological feature that begins near the dam and runs southwest. A coulee is a deep gully, typically dry, that was created by water. The basalt foundations of the Grand Coulee were laid by ancient lava flows that covered much of the Pacific Northwest. Later, uplifting in the mountainous region to the north and a series of powerful ice age floods resulted in the deep ravines that now characterize this region. Although many coulees exist in the channeled scablands—the expanse of eastern Washington shredded by those prehistoric floods—this particular coulee earned the adjective "grand" because it is the largest of the scabland canyons. It is about 50 miles long, ranging from 1 to 6 miles wide, and is nearly 1,000 feet deep.

In the 1950s the Bureau of Reclamation filled a long stretch of the Grand Coulee with water for irrigation. The resulting narrow, 31-mile-long reservoir bears the name **Banks Lake** and is a favorite haunt of boaters, campers, and fishers. About 12 miles from the Grand Coulee Dam on Wash. 155, which runs along the eastern shore of Banks Lake, **Steamboat Rock** juts 670 feet into the nearly always sunny blue sky. This butte anchors **Steamboat Rock State Park** *(Electric City, 509-633-1304),* where visitors can enjoy 900 acres of camping, swimming (from a sandy beach, no less), picnicking, and boating. If you don't mind sweating a bit, you can hike up to the top of Steamboat Rock and drink in the views from the flat, 640-acre summit, which was an island during the ice age floods. East of the highway from the state park sprawls the 3,000-plus acres of **Northrup Canyon**, a maze of forested ravines that lace the coulee. To find out about hiking Northrup, you'll need to contact the rangers at Steamboat.

The **Lower Grand Coulee** starts from the southern end of Banks Lake. Wash. 17 will take you about 20 miles south along the shores of the natural lakes that stretch along the bottom of the canyon. At **Soap Lake** you can feel the natural chemical in the water that gives it a soapy texture. From **Lenore Lake** you can take a short spur road and a short trail up to some caves, once used by prehistoric hunters, that formed when the giant floods plucked out chunks of basalt from the stone wall.

The showstopper of the lower coulee and of the entire Grand Coulee is **Dry Falls.** You wouldn't think that a waterfall with no water would rate much attention, but Dry Falls conveys a visceral sense of the unimaginable scale of the ice age floods. Stop at the **Dry Falls Interpretive Center** *(509-632-5214)* and gaze out over this awesome basalt basin, where flood waters once poured over the 400-foot-high, 3-mile-wide cliffs, creating a waterfall almost three times the height of Niagara Falls. The visitor center provides good interpretive displays about the floods. If you're careful, you can hike down into the coulee on a couple of unmaintained trails. ▪

Damming the Salmon

Prior to western settlement, millions of salmon crowded up the Columbia and its tributaries each year to spawn. Most of them traveled beyond the site of the mile-wide, 550-foot-high Grand Coulee Dam. Even a lesser dam would have harmed the salmon runs, but a significant number of fish could have traversed the dams via fish ladders. However, 550 feet is too high for fish ladders, and the salmon stocks that had spawned above the dam for eons have vanished—a steep environmental price to pay.

Houseboat, Grand Coulee reservoir

Turnbull National Wildlife Refuge

■ 15,628 acres ■ Eastern Washington, 15 miles southwest of Spokane
■ Hiking, wildlife viewing, auto tour ■ Adm. fee charged March–Oct. ■ Contact the refuge, 26010 S. Smith Rd., Cheney, WA 99004; phone 509-235-4723

TURNBULL NATIONAL WILDLIFE REFUGE is located about 40 miles from the Idaho border in eastern Washington. This location puts it much farther east than the rest of the central plateau sites, and the difference shows. The lands here aren't as arid as those on the western side of the Columbia Basin. You'll still see some sagebrush, but these 15,628 acres offer a mosaic of habitats that includes native prairies, ponderosa pine forests, and aspen groves, as well as lakes, ponds, sloughs, and marshes.

Like Grand Coulee (see p. 161), Columbia National Wildlife Refuge (see p. 159), and the Palouse Falls State Park (see p. 158) to the west, Turnbull lies within the channeled scablands created by massive ice age floods. In some of the refuge's uplands you'll see the deep scars where water and debris ripped through the basalt. But the more luxuriant vegetation makes many of the old wounds less apparent than in the arid sites. Turnbull also differs from most of the other plateau sites and from almost all the country's other national wildlife refuges in what it doesn't have. Many wildlife refuges allow some combination of hunting, fishing, boating, grazing, mining, off-road vehicles, and oil and gas exploration, even though these intrusions often conflict with the goal of protecting wildlife. Turnbull provides a 2,200-acre public-use area for hiking, biking, and wildlife observation, but the rest of the refuge is off-limits to humans.

The mosaic of habitats enables Turnbull to support more than 250 species of birds, mammals, reptiles, amphibians, and fish. A variety of ducks, geese, and swans migrate through, including green-winged teal, buffleheads, handsome wood ducks, northern shovelers, elegant tundra swans, and many other waterfowl species, many of which also nest on the refuge. Nearly two dozen species of migrating shorebirds also use the wetlands, including crowd pleasers such as the American avocet and the long-billed dowitcher. In the aspen, alder, dogwood, and other trees that prosper in the riparian areas, you can spot warblers, black-chinned hummingbirds, song sparrows, willow flycatchers, and other neotropical migrants here from Central and South America for the northern summer. When the trees die, they become homes for cavity-nesting creatures, such as woodpeckers, nuthatches, chickadees, chipmunks, squirrels, and bats. Large mammals that roam the many refuge habitats include elk, mule deer, white-tailed deer, coyotes, porcupines, and badgers. River otters, beavers, and muskrats ply the refuge waters, along with such amphibians as the long-toed salamander and Pacific chorus and spotted frogs.

Turnbull is also known for its spring wildflowers, which usually peak in early May. From the headquarters you can take an auto tour route that loops through a variety of habitats. Several short hiking trails leave from stops along the route and the parking lot at the comfort station. ■

North Cascades

Canoeing at Ross Lake, North Cascades National Park

A QUICK LOOK at a map tells you a great deal about the
northern Cascades. Put your fingertip on the green
square of Mount Rainier National Park and drag it
north by northeast, up the spine of the Cascade Range to
Manning Provincial Park and Cathedral Provincial Park in
southern British Columbia. That's about 170 miles as the
crow flies—and there's no other way to make this crossing
because there isn't a single road running north-south
through this largely wild region. And your finger will

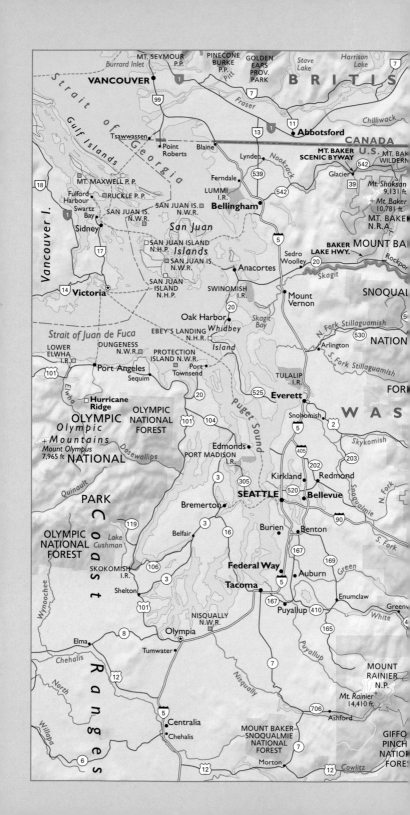

encounter only a few major east-west roads that cross the northern Cascades. What it will encounter again and again are the map lines that denote wilderness areas, national parks, provincial parks, and other outdoor havens.

When you leave the map and enter the real northern Cascades, what you will experience again and again is exquisite high country. The lack of roads and development stems from the region's mountainous character, starting with the southern anchor, Mount Rainier. At 14,410 feet, its summit is the highest place in the Northwest, and it falls just a few feet short of being the highest place in the lower 48 states. Another big volcano, Mount Baker, anchors the northern end of the region. Of course, the rest of the mountains fall short of such lofty heights, topping out in the 7,000- or 8,000-foot range, but they number in the hundreds and most are rough as a ripsaw.

By now you may be thinking you'd better hire a Sherpa to guide you through the northern Cascades. Indeed, the majority of the region does demand advanced backcountry skills of its visitors. But ample portions are accessible to moderately fit and experienced day-hikers and backpackers. And that handful of roads does make it possible for anyone to see some of the high country, including a few of the best spots.

Though defined by its high mountains, the northern Cascades offer visitors much more than peaks. You can see glaciers by the dozen, some within easy viewing distance of roads, some so close to trails that hikers can touch them. During the summer you can stroll through subalpine meadows brilliant with wildflowers—an immense canvas of warm Renoir colors. You can breathe deep the cool air rushing from the icy waters of a creek or a river or a thrumming waterfall. At lower elevations you can step quietly through old-growth forests, roofed by stately conifers, some of them more than 500 years old, more than 250 feet tall, and so thick that it takes four or five adults linking hands to encircle one.

A rich assortment of wildlife inhabits these wildlands. In the high country you're almost sure to see marmots and pikas, whose whistling and bustling about always entertains. Mountain goats and bighorn sheep also wander the steep slopes and high meadows, and can be seen fairly consistently in favored areas. In the fall, salmon are even more reliable, showing up in waterways at certain times to spawn. Most impressive, the region's checklist includes species that are rare or extinct in most of the nation, such as wolverine, lynx, and even those paragons of wildness, wolves and grizzlies.

Bear in mind that high country means cold and snow; a record-setting 95 feet fell on Mount Baker during the winter of 1998-99. At higher elevations, sunny skies and snow-free trails usually reign only in July, August, September, and parts of June and October. The short summers seem to be all the more lively, however, as birds, bees, flowers, shrubs, and trees appear to pack 12 months of energy into four months of activity. ■

Descending trail on Mount Rainier

Mount Rainier National Park

■ 235,612 acres ■ Western Washington, southeast of Seattle 60 miles
■ Best season summer; snow closes most roads and trails during other seasons.
Timing depends on elevation. Road between Nisqually entrance and Paradise
plowed year-round. Parking can be difficult at Paradise and Sunrise on pleasant
weekends; visit on weekdays, arrive early in the day, and carpool if possible
■ Camping, hiking, bird-watching, wildlife viewing, wildflower viewing ■ Adm.
fee ■ Contact the park, Tahoma Woods, Star Route, Ashford, WA 98304;
phone 360-569-2211. www.nps.gov/mora/

MOUNT RAINIER IS THE HIGHEST and most massive peak in the Pacific
Northwest. From Seattle, the 14,410-foot mountain is 60 miles away yet
looms large on the horizon. You can even see it from the Coast Ranges
summits more than 200 miles to the south, deep into Oregon. Throughout history native peoples, pioneers, climbers, painters, and sightseers
have been drawn to this towering volcano. How could Congress not
proclaim Mount Rainier and vicinity a national park? They did so in 1899.

But the real genesis of Mount Rainier took place much earlier, about
a half-million years ago. Molten rock erupting from a weak spot in the
earth's crust started the process. Over time sluggish lava flows and further
eruptions continued to build this composite volcano until about 6,000
years ago, when it is thought to have reached as high as 16,000 feet above
sea level. Geologic evidence indicates that a major landslide, now known
as the Osceola Mudflow, occurred at this time, depositing mountain-
borne rock in nearby river valleys, filling in former arms of Puget Sound,

Alpenglow on Mount Rainier

and reducing the mountain's summit. Another major eruption occurred 2,500 years ago, creating a second volcanic cone at the summit, and several minor eruptions shook the mountain sometime around 1840. Today Mount Rainier is still a work in progress, prone to the occasional mudflow or exhalation of steam and ash. Indeed, scientists are certain it will erupt again, although they are unable to predict when that might occur.

The mountain and the federally protected acres that surround it offer visitors much to do. Lower elevations in the park (as low as 1,880 feet above sea level) harbor vast expanses of old-growth forest. Along with the big trees you'll see a verdant understory, diverse wildlife, creeks, meadows, and waterfalls. A 240-mile trail network enables hikers of all abilities to venture off the road and into the wild. And wild it is, with 97 percent of the park designated as wilderness. During the summer months, the park service helps visitors enjoy and understand all these natural assets through a wide offering of interpretive talks, walks, and slide shows.

Lupine blooms in a meadow

What to See and Do

Longmire Area

Most visitors drive into Mount Rainier National Park through the southwest entrance on Wash. 706 and follow the Nisqually River 7 miles through lovely lowland forest to the Longmire area. This was the earliest part of the park to be developed; the first road to Longmire was completed in 1893, although James Longmire had cleared a trail to his homestead there by 1885. An easy 0.7-mile path called **Trail of the Shadows** recounts this early settlement. In Longmire you'll also find park headquarters, a small museum that describes the area's history, a wilderness information center *(summer only)*, and the National Park Inn *(360-569-2275)*.

A few other trails originate in Longmire, but they pale in comparison with those waiting farther along the road. Except, of course, for the aptly named **Wonderland Trail**. This route is a circle, so it doesn't exactly start at Longmire, but it is here that most visitors first cross its path. This 93-mile trail winds all the way around Mount Rainier, passing through deep forest, skirting along overgrown creeks and lakes, rising into alpine meadows, and edging so close to glaciers that you can feel their icy breath. Visitors who lack the time and the stamina for 93 miles can fashion shorter loops by combining the Wonderland with numerous access trails.

Continuing northeast, the road begins climbing out of the lowland forest and up the southern flank of the mountain. About 3.5 miles out of Longmire, you can pull over and take a short walk to view Van Trump Creek tumbling over **Christine Falls.** Another 1.5 miles brings motorists to **Glacier Bridge.** Park in one of the paved pullouts near the bridge and proceed along the walkway to get a look at the valley gouged by **Nisqually Glacier.** Glaciers are a prominent feature of the park's landscape. Aerial views reveal 25 glaciers radiating out from Mount Rainier's crest like the legs of a starfish. Some 3 miles past the bridge you'll come to the short but steep trail to **Narada Falls,** where the Paradise River takes a 168-foot dive off a rocky ledge.

Paradise

About a mile east of Narada Falls, visitors encounter the turnoff to Paradise. Who can resist? Go 2 miles up this winding road and you'll emerge from the trees into lustrous subalpine meadows backed by an awesome view of Mount Rainier. Paradise lives up to its name, being as close to heaven on earth as a place can get—or at least any place you can reach by paved road.

Begin by strolling into the **visitor center** *(open May– mid-Oct., weekends rest of year)*. The center doubles as a museum, which spirals up through several levels of exhibits on Mount Rainier's geology, ecology, and wildlife; it also covers the history of climbing the mountain. At the top, enormous windows afford expansive views of Mount Rainier and the surrounding landscape.

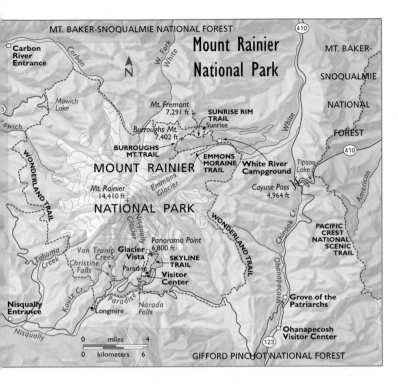

The heart of the famed sub-alpine meadows of Paradise sprawl up the mountainside north of the visitor center. John Muir once called these meadows "the most luxuriant and the most extravagantly beautiful of all the alpine gardens I have beheld." In July and August, with the snow finally melted, these slopes are ablaze with flowering plants. Larkspur, columbine, monkey flower, Indian and magenta paint-brush, avalanche lily, shooting star, and dozens of other species unfurl their technicolor blossoms in order to attract pollinators.

These enticements draw many admirers, but unlike the bugs, bats, and birds that pollinate the plants, humans do them no good. In fact, over the years humans have damaged the meadows. Sometimes the harm stemmed from plainly foolish acts, such as grazing cattle on the fragile meadows. Most often, however, the injury resulted simply from people loving them to death, tramping all over the plants in an effort to get close to those beautiful blooms.

The moral of the story: Stay on established trails. The **Skyline Trail** is a good example. You'll see plenty of blooms up close if you take this 5.5-mile loop. It starts at the **Paradise Inn** *(360-569-2275),* the grand old lodge just northeast of the visitor center, and, if you're going clockwise, heads almost straight up the mountain. Take it easy. Not only is the trail fairly steep, but you're at high altitude—the visitor center sits at 5,400 feet

Nisqually Glacier

Debris Flows

Exploding peaks and lava rivers aren't the only geologic hazards spawned by Mount Ranier. Of more immediate concern to visitors are debris flows called lahars, which occur several times a decade on some streams. Though the causes of debris flows are poorly understood, they may stem from three major phenomena: the sudden drainage of meltwater from glacier cavities; flooding following intense rainfall; or rock avalanches. Any one of these conditions could trigger a flow of rock, soil, and water down stream channels.

The mass of rock and soil moves at about 10-20 miles an hour, but the occasional large flow roars like a freight train, generates strong winds and dust clouds, carries huge boulders, shakes the ground, and wipes out trees, roads, bridges, and almost anything else in its path. Debris flows most often occur during hot, sunny weather. Very few people have ever been caught in a flow and no one in recorded history has been killed by one. But in the unlikely event you hear the rumble of a flow, or if you're by a stream that starts rising rapidly, move to ground 160 feet or more above stream level.

Visitors can see evidence of past flows at Tahoma Creek, Nisqually River, and Kautz Creek. In 1947, 50 million cubic yards of debris steamrollered more than 5 miles down Kautz Creek from the Kautz Glacier, burying the road under nearly 30 feet of mud and debris. To see giant boulders deposited by the flow, hike the Wonderland Trail to Kautz Creek.

and Skyline, the highest trail in Paradise, climbs to 7,200 feet. One minute of vigorous uphill striding in this thin air can leave unacclimated sea-level dwellers gasping.

First you'll pass through those luxuriant meadows; pause to smell the lupines or to examine the partridge foot (the divided leaves look like bird feet). Rivulets of icy snowmelt slither past, adding the sparkle of reflected sunlight to the meadows' palette. Hoary marmots scamper about, mouths often filled to overflowing with leaves, flowers, and other vegetation.

About a mile from the lodge, the trail passes a short side trail that leads to **Glacier Vista.** As the name suggests, the viewpoint gives hikers a great look at **Nisqually Glacier** from just a few hundred yards away. This glacier has the largest surface area (4.3 square miles) of any glacier in the 48 contiguous states. In its prime, back in 1970, the Nisqually Glacier was something of a speed demon. That May it moved as rapidly as 29 inches a day. When you've finished savoring the view of the glacier, raise your gaze and behold the big picture. You can see for miles, all the way to some of Mount Rainier's fellow Cascades volcanoes: Mount Adams, Mount St. Helens, and, far away in Oregon, Mount Hood.

Another half mile and 464 vertical feet up, the trail deposits visitors at **Panorama Point.** From this vantage you'll get big views, as well as an outstanding look at the Paradise meadows below. Just past Panorama Point, hikers come to an alternate route, the **High Skyline Trail.** This trail adds three-quarters of a mile to the loop but it also bypasses a part of the older Skyline Trail that often poses a hazardous crossing on a steep snowfield. Take the High Skyline Trail to avoid a possible fall. From the point at which the High Skyline Trail rejoins the main route, the Skyline Trail heads down through acres of meadows, ponds, creeks, and waterfalls, proof that the Paradise area more than deserves its name.

East Side

From Paradise, the road heads downhill, of course. Going east, travelers pass creeks, waterfalls, lakes, and several trails as they descend into the low-elevation forest in the southeast corner of the park. Here, near the entrance and visitor center at Ohanapecosh, the road intersects Wash. 123, which runs up the east side of the park. Just before reaching Wash. 123, stop and take the 1.2-mile loop hike through the **Grove of the Patriarchs.** People often describe old-growth forests as majestic, but if ever there were a time to use that adjective, this is it. This grove of western redcedars and Douglas-firs comes right out of J.R.R. Tolkien's novel, *The Hobbit.* Tall, massive, and gnarled, many are more than 500 years old; some are twice that age. Touching a living thing that was ancient when Europe was still mired in the Middle Ages can induce a deep sense of calm. The Grove of the Patriarchs is a good place for on-the-go types to ease off the accelerator.

Drive north on Wash. 123 for about 11 miles and you'll rise to Cayuse Pass (elevation 4,694 feet) where Wash. 123 dead-ends into

Wash. 410. If the idea of an easy mile-long hike around a lake framed by wildflowers is appealing, detour east on Wash. 410 a couple of miles to **Tipsoo Lake.** The main park route continues north on Wash. 410, arriving 3 miles later at the spur road to the **Sunrise** and **White River** areas. It's a slow, 9-mile haul to the end of the road at Sunrise, but it's worth the effort. Along the way, detour to the White River Campground and take the easy 3-mile (round-trip) **Emmons Moraine Trail** for close-up views of **Emmons Glacier** and Mount Rainier. Stand back from the moraine near the terminus of the glacier: Rocks fall frequently.

Back on the spur road, as you near the Sunrise area you will be above tree line; at 6,400 feet, Sunrise is the highest point in the park to which you can drive. From the parking lot, visitors enjoy fine views of the Emmons Glacier, the mountain, and, on clear days, distant Cascade volcanoes. Like Paradise, the Sunrise area boasts subalpine and alpine meadows alive with wildflowers. But because Sunrise lies in the mountain's rain shadow, it gets less precipitation than does Paradise. In these meadows, you'll find plants that have adapted to drier conditions, including beargrass, desert parsley, and species of cinquefoil, paintbrush, and buckwheat. This information and more is available at the Sunrise Visitor Center (*July–Labor Day*).

The Trails

More than a dozen trails beckon travelers away from the road and the Sunrise parking lot. At only 1.5 miles long, the easy Sourdough Ridge Nature Trail is a good introductory loop. It serves up wildflowers and views of the mountain to go with the interpretive information. Just as easy but twice as long as Sourdough is the Sunrise Rim Loop trail. It offers much the same benefits plus a view of Emmons Glacier. The path to Mount Fremont presents a stiffer challenge. This 5.6-mile trail (round-trip) gains 1,200 feet in elevation as it ascends to the old fire lookout atop the peak. Don't be surprised to share the path with a mountain goat; they often show up along this route.

To drink deeply of the alpine, take the **Burroughs Mountain Trail** from the Sunrise Visitor Center all the way to Second Burroughs and back, a distance of 7 miles with an elevation gain of 1,000 feet. You'll start amid those lush subalpine blooms and the scattered, stunted, high-elevation trees, but soon you'll leave the trees behind, and the plants will be shorter and hug the ground. This is true alpine, where the deep cold and furious winds of winter rule, where life hangs on rather than prospers. In this wide open high country you feel as if you're at the top of the world. Snow often stays on the ground up here well into July, so tread carefully, especially on steep slopes. And stay on the established trails—the plants here have enough trouble surviving without the additional stress of being trampled. Needless to say, without so much as a foot-high plant to block the view, the vistas from the Burroughs Mountain Trail are truly inspiring. ■

Lake Wenatchee Area

■ 381,490 acres ■ North-central Washington, north of Leavenworth 20 miles
■ Best season summer ■ Camping, hiking, boating, canoeing, snowmobiling,
cross-country skiing, snowshoeing, dog-sledding, bird-watching, wildlife viewing,
wildflower viewing, auto tour ■ Trailhead parking permits required in summer;
ski parking permits required in winter ■ Contact Lake Wenatchee Ranger
District, Wenatchee National Forest, 22976 State Hwy. 207, Leavenworth, WA
98826; phone 509-763-3103.

THE LAKE WENATCHEE AREA doesn't
offer any scene-stealing attractions,
yet the charms of the place add
up. Groves of massive cedars; a
scenic drive along a wild river;
ospreys diving into a lake; meadows
fragrant with wildflowers; river
otters approaching your canoe:
These and many other features
form an appealing mosaic.

Due to its relatively low
elevation and its location on
the Cascades' east side, the Lake
Wenatchee area has longer,
warmer summers than the high
Cascades or the western side of the
range. Lake Wenatchee and Fish
Lake form the area's hub, and the
riparian corridors of the Chiwawa
River, White River, and Little
Wenatchee River form the spokes.
At the center of things is the lake.

Brilliant fall colors along the Chiwawa River

What to See and Do

Five miles long and a mile wide,
ringed by forest and marsh, fed by
two rivers and numerous creeks;
Lake Wenatchee is a beauty. Such
a setting has drawn the attention
of many people over the years,
but **Lake Wenatchee State Park**
(*21588A Hwy. 207, Leavenworth.
509-763-3101*), on the southeast
tip of the lake, still offers a sem-
blance of wildness. So do two trails
leaving from the Glacier View

Campground at the end of Cedar
Brae Road. One half-mile hike
leads to **Hidden Lake** while another easy trail skirts part of the
lake's shore for 1.2 miles.

Smaller but wilder **Fish Lake**
is located about a mile northeast
of Lake Wenatchee State Park.
Informal trails and a rough road
provide access to some of the
shoreline, which is lined by
ponderosa pine, Douglas-fir,

western hemlock, vine maple, and alder. But the best vantage point from which to enjoy Fish Lake is in a small boat or canoe, which can be rented from Cove Resort (509-763-3130) on the south shore or at Cascade Hideaway (509-763-5104) on the north shore. Paddle to the 200-acre bog at the west end of the lake, which recently was declared a research natural area. Much of this area is a floating preserve that harbors several rare plant species, such as carnivorous sundews and some varieties of fern and sedge. Boaters likely will spot river otters, beavers, and mule deer, and on rare occasions a sandhill crane. The bog and lake also attract many birds. Look for the flamboyantly feathered wood ducks, loons, bald eagles, pileated woodpeckers, great blue herons, and ospreys.

Auto Tour

Beginning just south of Fish Lake the Chiwawa Valley auto tour heads north 24 miles up the **Chiwawa River.** Stop at the Wenatchee Ranger Station to pick up an interpretive guide. The road was cut in the early 1900s as a wagon route to provide access to upriver mining camps. Today the Chiwawa Valley Road (Forest Road 6200), most of which is unpaved, takes motorists to 15 campgrounds and 22 hiking trails, and provides a scenic drive for those who prefer to experience the area from their cars. From the **Chiwawa River Bridge** and various pullouts, you can scan the river for chinook salmon, cutthroat and steelhead trout, the widely imperiled bull trout, and other native species. The robust fish popula-

tions result from healthy habitat. Note the fallen trees and brush in the water, the shade produced by the bankside vegetation, the little rapids called riffles that mix oxygen into the water, and the occasional deep pools where fish feed and rest. These elements constitute a vibrant natural river, a rarity in this era of dams and development. Near Mile 17 you'll come to **Blue Pool,** where you'll see a natural flood plain, another component of a healthy river. Near the end of the main road a short spur winds up to the **Phelps Creek Trail,** an easy 5-mile path to **Spider Meadows**—and hundreds of acres of wildflowers.

Following the White River

Another river road beckons at the northwest tip of Lake Wenatchee. Though only about half as long as the Chiwawa route, the road follows a stretch of the **White River** that is equally wild and pretty and leads to campgrounds and hiking trails. Near the river's mouth, where it flows into the lake, wetlands yield views of many of the same animals that inhabit the marsh at Fish Lake. In the fall you can see sockeye salmon spawning in the river. Near the end of the road pull over and admire **White River Falls.** At the end, two fine trails lead into the **Glacier Peak Wilderness: White River Trail,** which runs along the east bank, and **Indian Creek Trail,** which parallels the White River's west bank 2 miles before branching west along Indian Creek. Glacier Peak's forested valley features some ancient western redcedars that measure 10 feet in diameter. ∎

Alpine Lakes Wilderness

■ 400,000 acres ■ Southeast Washington, east of Seattle 35 miles ■ Open year-round; best season summer ■ Camping, hiking, backpacking ■ Parking permit required at most trailheads ■ Contact Wenatchee National Forest, 215 Melody Lane, Wenatchee, WA 98801; phone 509-662-4335; or Mount Baker-Snoqualmie National Forest, 21905 64th Ave. W., Mountlake Terrace, WA 98043; phone 425-775-9702. www.fs.fed.us/r6/mbs/wilderness/alakes.htm

THINK OF THIS GRAND EXPANSE of the Cascades as an endangered species. Designated wilderness areas are in short supply in our overdeveloped world. The size of Alpine Lakes Wilderness—about 400,000 acres— makes it uncommon indeed. And the fact that Alpine Lakes is located a mere one hour's drive east of Seattle and the Puget Sound metropolitan area by interstate highway makes it downright rare; seldom does one find a vast wilderness so close to a heavily urbanized region. But that proximity also accounts for the endangered status of Alpine Lakes. Wilderness-starved visitors flock to the area, and among the crowds are those who carelessly trample fragile vegetation, cause erosion by cutting trails, and corrupt the solitude in popular sections. Like an endangered species, this special place needs care and protection, not only by its administrators but also by the general public. Forest Service managers have instituted a number of regulations that are doing much to lessen the damage, but visitors also must act responsibly—by following those rules and by generally taking it easy on this overloved land.

It's easy to understand the popularity of Alpine Lakes. For one thing, some 500 lakes dot this wilderness. A sprawling network of rivers and creeks round out the aquatic riches of the area. Those waterways course down from peaks that range as high as 9,415 feet and slither through alpine meadows brimming with wildflowers.

Alpine Lakes hosts a tremendous variety of plants and animals thanks to its wide elevation range and extensive west-east breadth. The wilderness runs from the west side of the Cascades across the crest to the east side of the range. Precipitation varies from 55 to 180 inches a year on the west side and around the crest to as low as 10 inches a year in the lowest areas of the east side. Western redcedar, western hemlock, mountain hemlock, and hulking Douglas-firs dominate west-side forests while smaller Douglas-firs and an array of pines—ponderosa, larch, lodgepole, and whitebark—are more common on the east side. Most animals range on both sides of the crest, and include black bear, elk, Columbia black-tailed deer, mountain lion, beaver, and, at higher elevations, mountain goat.

In order to tour Alpine Lakes properly you must leave your car behind. The basic method of transportation within the wilderness is your own two feet, although visitors do explore on horseback occasionally. More than 450 miles of trails provide both day hikes and backpacking opportunities, a few of which are mentioned below.

Backpackers on trail to Enchantment Lakes

What to See and Do

Many notable trails head south into the wilderness from US 2, on the north side of Alpine Lakes, or from spur roads that branch south from the highway. Located along Forest Road 6412, **Dorothy Lake Trail** climbs a fairly steep 1.5 miles through dense forest to the north end of picturesque Lake Dorothy. Day-hikers often never make it farther than the first stretch of lakeshore, but backpackers usually continue along the east side of the 2-mile-long lake, where primitive campsites are available. This trail can get crowded, especially on summer weekends.

Somewhat less crowded and less steep than the Dorothy Lake Trail is the **Tonga Ridge Trail**. To reach the trailhead, turn south off US 2 onto Foss River Road and go 4 miles. Take a left onto Tonga Ridge Road (Forest Road 6830), and continue for 6 miles, then take the Forest Road 310 spur 1 mile to its end and the trailhead. This route ascends gradually for 4.6 miles through second- and old-growth forests and across the broad back of **Tonga Ridge**, whose open meadows yield fine views and, in the early fall, juicy huckleberries.

On the south side of the Alpine Lakes wilderness, I-90 provides access to another complex of trails. The most popular is the 3.5-mile, moderately difficult hike to **Snow Lake**. It heads northwest from the ski area at Snoqualmie Pass and climbs along rocky slopes above the headwaters of the South Fork Snoqualmie River. Enjoy the surrounding peaks from a saddle graced by heather and huckleberry before descending to Snow Lake. Or pitch your tent on one of the primitive designated campsites.

Enchantment Lakes

On the east side of Alpine Lakes, the road along Icicle Creek reaches deep into the wilderness. Numerous trails heading north and south from the beautiful creek quickly lead into the wilds, though it takes long, hard hours to reach the area's most renowned destination: the Enchantment Lakes. But many people make the trek, drawn by the profusion of alpine lakes and lakelets and the views of granite spires and high mountains. These alpine lakes can be reached using the Snow Lake Trail (8.5 miles one way) or the Stuart Lake Trail via Colchuck Lake (5.5 miles one way). Both trails are located off Icicle Creek Road and are extremely steep. The trip is best done in two days, with an overnight stop at one of the other lakes along the way. The Enchantment Basin is a limited use area; for maps, reservations, and permits, inquire at the Lake Wenatchee Ranger District (22976 Hwy. 207, Leavenworth. 509-763-3103)

People who grouse about getting permits should recall the aim of the 1964 Wilderness Act: to preserve habitat for native animals and plants, to preserve landscapes, and to provide humans with a sanctuary. Recreation in wilderness areas comes second and must not degrade those primary purposes. So tread lightly, and smile when you get that permit. ■

North Cascades National Park

■ 700,000 acres ■ North-central Washington, off US 20 between Burlington and Twisp ■ Best seasons summer and fall ■ Camping, hiking, backpacking, mountain climbing, boating, fishing, mountain biking, horseback riding, wildlife viewing, wildflower viewing ■ Contact park, 502 Newhalem St., Rockport, WA 98283; phone 206-386-4495. www.nps.gov/noca/; or Lake Chelan Chamber of Commerce, P.O. Box 216, Chelan, WA 98816; phone 509-682-3503. www.lakechelan.com/

THIS IS ONE OF THE WILDEST places in the United States. Fortunate visitors may hear the howl of a wolf, the definitive call of the wild and a sound rarely heard south of Canada these days. If you're lucky you even may see one of the handful of grizzly bears that make their home here, another threatened species that typically roams only large, unspoiled landscapes. Of course, it's extremely unlikely that you'll encounter one of these creatures, but what you will see for sure is the land they call home.

Covering nearly 700,000 acres, the North Cascades National Park Service Complex includes North Cascades National Park, Ross Lake National Recreation Area, and Lake Chelan National Recreation Area. A sliver of the Okanogan National Forest is also considered part of the region. A full 94 percent of North Cascades is designated wilderness and all of it is rugged. Everywhere you look, stony mountaintops streaked with snow stab thousands of feet into the sky. More than 300 alpine glaciers cling to the flanks of these jagged peaks—that's more than half the glaciers in the contiguous United States. Just below the peaks, meadows bring life to the harsh high country. Lower still, heavily forested slopes angle down into valleys laced with lakes, rivers, and creeks. You may spot mountain goats, moose, harlequin ducks, snowshoe hares, lynx, spotted owls, hoary marmots, pikas, and many other species—the list is wonderfully long.

Hardy backcountry travelers are drawn to North Cascades like bees to honey. Long trails lead backpackers far into the wilderness, but parts of the complex don't even have trails. Trekkers must forge their own way, often with the aid of mountaineering gear. But North Cascades also offers several points of entry for those visitors who lack the skills of Daniel Boone. The North Cascades Highway (Wash. 20) cuts east to west through the complex, opening the heart of the area to view and providing access to trails that penetrate the wilds. The highway is open from approximately mid-April to mid-November (depending on snow depths). At Ross Lake, boat trips take visitors into the interior of the complex. And here and there back roads nibble at the edges of North Cascades.

What to See and Do

Most visitors get to know North Cascades via the **North Cascades Highway.** This paved road runs east-to-west along the **Skagit River** through the middle of the **Ross Lake National Recreation Area**

Spires of Pickett Range

and then dives down its eastern flank. In the tiny town of New-halem, near the point at which Wash. 20 enters the park complex from the west, you'll find the **North Cascades Visitor Center.** The center is open from mid-April to mid-November (depending on snow depths) and on weekends during the winter. In addition to the basics—information counter, bookstore—the center houses a fair number of museum-like exhibits. Several trails also fan out from the center or from nearby campgrounds. One educational path called the **"To Know a Tree" Nature Trail** (an easy third of a mile one way) zigzags through the forest from one type of tree to another, identifying and providing information about each species. In the fall, visitors to the center might see spawning salmon nearby in the Skagit or in **Goodell Creek.**

Three miles east along the highway brings motorists to **Gorge Creek Falls.** Park and walk out on the bridge to savor this 242-foot cascade and to stroll the new (1999) interpretive **Gorge Overlook loop trail** (half mile, easy, wheelchair accessible). On the other side of the highway is a decidedly less-natural sight: the 300-foot-high **Gorge Dam** plugging the Skagit River. This and the two larger Diablo and Ross Dams farther upriver were built by a regional utility many years before the establishment of the national park complex. Efforts are being made to mitigate the harmful effects of the dams, but their presence is a blot on the wild character of this strip of North Cascades.

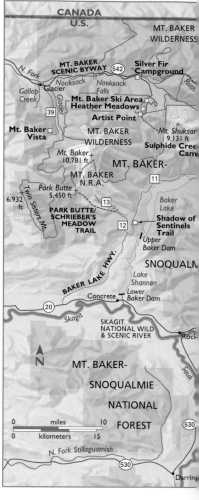

About 5 miles east of Gorge Dam, just past Diablo Lake, **Thunder Creek Trail** heads south from the Colonial Creek Camp-ground. The path wiggles 38 miles through the midst of the wilder-ness to the Stehekin Valley, via Park Creek Pass. However, most people bite off just the first mile. This flat segment runs through old-growth forest along **Thunder Creek** to a bridge over the creek. Take time to appreciate the massive

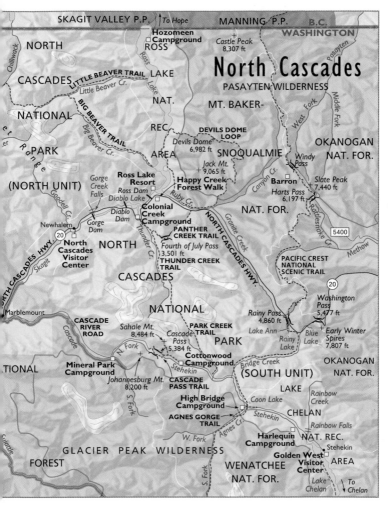

western redcedars and Douglas-firs, some of them a strapping 6 feet in diameter. Note, too, the light green color of the creek water. Glaciers high in Thunder Creek's watershed grind the rock beneath them into a fine dust —commonly called glacial flour— that gets washed into the creek. The flour becomes suspended in the water and refracts light in a way that humans see as green with a touch of turquoise.

A mile farther up the Thunder Creek Trail from the bridge, hikers reach the start of the **Fourth of July Pass Trail**. Three miles of steep walking up this route takes you to the 3,500-foot pass below Ruby Mountain, where you'll enjoy panoramic views of surrounding peaks. You can then either go back the way you came or take the **Panther Creek Trail** down to a point on the highway about 8 miles east of Colonial Creek Campground.

Cyclists on trail with view of Liberty Bell Mountain

On the road again, drive a little more than 4 miles northeast from the Colonial Creek Campground to **Happy Creek Forest Walk**. Suitable for wheelchairs, this one-third-mile boardwalk circles through a nice old-growth stand along **Happy Creek.** Interpretive signs reveal some of the secrets of the ancient forest.

Okanogan National Forest

The traveler heading east on Wash. 20 will leave Ross Lake National Recreation Area and enter the **Okanogan National Forest** *(1240 S. Second Avenue, Okanogan, WA 98840. 509-826-3275)*, a grand forest framed on both sides by mountains 7,000 to 8,000 feet high. For 20 miles you'll cruise through this living postcard, pacing Granite Creek, until you reach Rainy Pass, elevation 4,860 feet.

Several outstanding trails begin at the Rainy Pass rest area. The paved, flat, 1-mile path (one way) to **Rainy Lake Trail** is one of the most popular routes in the North Cascades. It slips through a forest of mountain hemlock and Pacific silver fir spiced with a few Englemann spruce. After crossing several spritely creeks the trail ends on a platform looking out at **Rainy Lake.** This pocket lake may be modest in size—perhaps a third of a mile long and half as wide—but any modesty about its looks would be false indeed. Its green-blue waters pool in a cirque, an amphitheater-shaped bowl at the head of a glacial valley. Rocky walls rise hundreds of feet above the still water, which is disturbed only by ripples sent out by the long waterfall splashing into the far end of

the lake, fed by a melting glacier high up the mountain.

Another trail originating at the rest area, is the **Maple Pass Loop**, which circles 7.5 miles through some high country so exquisite that the strain of the 1,800-foot elevation gain is quickly forgotten. The trail begins in tall timber interspersed with lush avalanche meadows. Hikers may discover that they're sharing this trail with porcupines, some of which get surprisingly big, perhaps 3 feet long and 35 pounds. But not to worry, porcupines don't really throw their quills; only people pushy enough to press close to one of these docile vegetarians will get a taste of those barbed ice picks.

About 1.5 miles up the trail, a spur path leads a half mile down to **Lake Ann**, a pretty little lake attended by ponds that rests at the

Lichens

You'll see lichens, a composite life-form that consists of an algae and a fungus, all over North Cascades forests; some dangle from tree limbs like green hair, some blanket rocks, and some that look like rubbery lettuce blow down from the canopy and litter the trails. Lichens provide nesting material for birds and they chemically alter nitrogen from the atmosphere to create a form plants and animals can use. During the winter, when food is scarce in most Northwest forests, lichens make up a key element in the diets of some deer and elk.

bottom of another classic cirque. The main trail continues up and soon emerges from the forest into the subalpine environment. Fairly steep switchbacks lead up one side of the cirque; the views down to Lake Ann get better with every step. You top out in alpine meadows at **Heather Pass**, where the vistas will compel you to sit a spell. When you're ready, turn south and follow the trail as it slowly ascends a ridge that affords views both east and west. Again, look about at the jagged pinnacles and numerous glaciers. Then look around your feet at the red-purple heather, the penstemon, saxifrage, and perhaps some glacier lilies growing there.

View from the Ridge

The ridge finally tops out at **Maple Pass**, 6,600 feet above sea level. From one point you can see both Lake Ann and Rainy Lake, not to mention all the mountains sawing the horizon. Note the alpine larches scattered about just south of the pass—these trees are found only near tree line in a few spots in the interior Northwest. Unlike other evergreens, this conifer's needles turn a brilliant gold and drop to the ground in late summer and fall. Somehow this deviant act of deciduousness befits the severe landscape of this high, exposed pass, where the sparse vegetation and scarcity of life—you'll be hard-pressed to spot so much as an ant—attest to scouring winds and biting winter temperatures.

From Maple Pass the trail descends steeply east toward Rainy Lake, following a ridgeline that tightropes just north of the lake. You'll see the meadows that blanket the bench above the waterfall at the head of the Rainy Lake cirque and enjoy aerial views of the upper falls. Occasionally mountain goats graze this green haven engulfed by steep, rocky slopes, veined with rivulets of icy glacial water, and graced by a sparkling pond. After a mile or so, the trail reenters the old-growth forest and switchbacks down to intersect the Rainy Lake Trail. Go north and you'll be back to the rest area in 10 or 15 minutes.

From Rainy Pass the highway descends briefly then climbs again even higher to Washington Pass (elevation 5,477 feet). You'll drive past hillsides that positively glow, their steep slopes draped in luminous meadows laced with curving streams and plumed by small waterfalls. Behind and above you, the sharp pinnacles of Early Winter Spires and Liberty Bell Mountain pierce the sky. Pause to appreciate the privilege of driving through the sort of wild and rough terrain that usually must be earned by hours or even days of tough hiking.

Near the top of Washington Pass you'll come to the start of the **Blue Lake Trail**, which climbs 2 miles through forest and subalpine meadows to **Blue Lake.** Along the way hikers enjoy views of Liberty Bell, Early Winter Spires, and other peaks. Mountain goats frequent the meadows and rocky slopes around the lake.

Less than a mile east, the highway crests at Washington Pass. From the picnic area a short loop trail leads up to a lookout with 360-degree views. If you're planning to continue driving east, linger on one of the benches and take a good, long look. The road

Gray wolf

Don't Build It and They Will Come

Wolves don't like people. More accurately, they don't like the development that so often comes with us. They aren't likely to move into a landscape littered with logging operations, ski resorts, vacation homes, mines, roads, and the other paraphernalia of industrial civilization. But wolves have moved into the North Cascades—a tribute to its wildness.

Actually, it's more correct to say that wolves moved back to the North Cascades. This area once supported plenty of wolves, but by the end of the 19th century they had been shot, poisoned, trapped, or driven away, as was the case throughout nearly the entire contiguous United States. During the following century, lone wolves occasionally passed through, but it wasn't until 1991 that a gray wolf began showing up regularly in the Hazomeen area of Ross Lake National Recreation Area, marking the return of wolves to the North Cascades. Since then other wolves have moved across the border from Canada into the North Cascades, and the numbers seem to be increasing. Now it remains to be seen whether these icons of the wilderness will establish a breeding population in the area.

Visitors probably won't see a wolf; the odds are up there with the likelihood of winning the lottery. The chances are better that you'll hear wolves howling or spot their tracks, but even such indirect encounters are rare. Many visitors, in their eagerness to have contact with wolves, often make wishful identifications. Rangers report that people sometimes mistake coyotes for wolves, and occasionally even take a raccoon for a wolf. (Perhaps it was dark and there was a lot of undergrowth obscuring the animal.) But you don't need to see wolves to appreciate their presence and the wildness of the home to which they are finally returning.

heading east leaves North Cascades; Washington Pass informally marks the area's eastern boundary.

North of the Highway

Many visitors to North Cascades never venture beyond the highway corridor, except perhaps to hike one or two of the shorter trails that branch out from the road. Though the corridor is undeniably marvelous, you'll miss out on the full North Cascades experience if you limit yourself to this narrow strip. For example, the section of the complex north of Wash. 20 is a vast wilderness that sprawls all the way up to Canada. No roads and few trails brave these 500 square miles of imposing mountains, glaciers, rivers, and forests. Expert backpackers and climbers will find many challenges and rewards in this section's backcountry.

Novices won't find many opportunities to explore the north, but there are a few, nearly all of which are tied to Ross Lake. (The lake is actually the reservoir created by the Ross Dam on the Skagit River.) This long, skinny body of water runs some 25 miles along the east side of the north section, from the North Cascades Highway to just beyond the Canadian border. If you happen to be in Hope, British Columbia, you can drive a 40-mile gravel road to the Hozomeen area on northern tip of the lake and boat or hike into the wilds. From the North Cascades Highway, you can only enter by foot, horseback, or boat.

The Ross Lake Resort (206-386-4437) runs a water taxi that will take hikers and campers to various camp sites and trailheads on the lakeshore. For instance, you might motor a few miles up-lake to the mouth of **Big Beaver Creek,** where a trail heads northwest for 17 miles into the heart of the north section and meets the **Little Beaver Trail,** which leads east, back to Ross Lake. This path tunnels through a barely touched forest that is home to black bear, lynx, and deer. The Big Beaver Creek riparian zone harbors numerous marshes and ponds. If you're quiet and patient, around dusk you may spot some of the beavers that created those ponds. In the same area during the day, look for river otters, ducks, and a variety of marsh birds, such as common yellowthroats, red-winged blackbirds, and tree swallows. About 3 miles from the lake, the trail enters one of the largest stands of old-growth western redcedar in the contiguous 48 states. Some of these trees are more than a thousand years old and a mind-boggling 15 feet in diameter. How far you choose to follow the trail depends on your legs and where you want to spend the night.

To the South

The south section of the complex is just as big and handsome as the north section, and it's a little more accessible. You can even drive a little way into it on the **Cascade River Road.** This 23-mile road, most of it unpaved, leaves the North Cascades Highway in Marblemount, just west of the national park complex. It snakes southeast along the **Cascade River** through an increasingly wild and scenic landscape until it reaches the Mineral Park Campground.

Paddling up Devil's Creek, a tributary of Ross Lake

Avalanche lily, Fisher Basin

Wildflower meadow

From there it arcs northeast and follows the North Fork Cascade. After crossing into the south section, the Cascade River Road continues several miles along the gorge of the North Fork then ascends into the high country.

Cascade Pass Trail

The drive itself is an attraction, but most people come here to hike the Cascade Pass Trail. The trail climbs about 1,800 feet in 3.7 miles to 5,384-foot **Cascade Pass,** then descends 2,600 feet in 5.5 miles into the Stehekin Valley to join with the trail system there. Many people make a day hike of going to the pass and back. This historic notch in the mountains, once used by Native Americans and early explorers, has become so popular that it actually can get crowded. All those people can

harm the fragile alpine vegetation, so please stay on the trails. Don't worry; you'll see more than enough spectacular scenery from the established paths.

As soon as you get out of your car, keep your ears open. While you go about preparing your gear and head up the first part of the trail, you may hear a sharp crack, like a rifle shot, echoing through the North Fork gorge and off the stone walls of the encircling mountains. Usually that crisp report is followed by a deep-throated rumbling, tumbling landsliding noise that reverberates in the canyon and may go on for a minute or more. You're listening to the sound of geology in action, as great chunks of ice split off the north face of 8,200-foot **Johannesburg Mountain,** a mile away across the gorge.

The trail proceeds via moderate switchbacks through the tall trees for a couple of miles, occasionally delivering views to the west and south. Then the forest begins thinning out and the trees are much shorter as the terrain grades into open parkland. Pikas scurry about the rock-jumbled slopes and plump marmots whistle if they're not snoozing in the sun. Meadows of grasses and wildflowers appear between the rock piles along with the occasional stunted subalpine tree. Look for glacier lilies, arnica, yarrow, bluebells, and monkshood.

By the time you reach the pass, nearly all the trees have melted away and you mount the crest amid that dizzying openness of the alpine. Mountains and glaciers lean close on the sides. Behind stretches the green of the meadows and forests you've just left and ahead and below spreads the head of the verdant Stehekin Valley.

If you yearn to ascend yet higher, near the pass the **Sahale Arm Trail** heads north up the steep slope toward Sahale Glacier and the top of **Sahale Mountain,** elevation 8,484 feet. As you're puffing slowly up the first part of the trail, you may hear a sound coming from the thick heather that surrounds the path, an odd sort of gurgling that seems like a cross between a puppy whining and the muted cry of a red-tailed hawk. This would be blue grouse muttering about whatever it is that grouse mutter about. You'll immediately grasp the origin of the term "grousing."

Perhaps half an hour of labor will earn you a broad, nearly flat ridge thronged with heather. The trail curves along this ridge for maybe a mile, giving you ample time to catch your breath and drink in the sweeping vistas, unobscured by trees. You're apt to see more pikas and marmots.

The final half mile of the trail climbs a steep slope covered with loose rock. Why should you bother? The answer lies just over the lip of the mountainside. You

Where the Action Is

Though the population of Stehekin could fit inside a moderately large restaurant, they provide visitors to the south end of North Cascades with a surprisingly extensive menu of activities. Local ranchers will set you up with a guided horseback trip to Coon Lake, or even a multi-day horse-packing adventure that allows customers to hike while horses haul the gear. You can rent a mountain bike and pedal the approximately 20 miles of the Stehekin Valley Road to Glory Mountain and to all points in between. Guides will take you down the lower 11 miles of the Stehekin River on a raft; the first half of the run offers some exciting but not intimidating white water, and the last half is a peaceful and scenic float. For a finale, you can take off in a floatplane from the dock at Stehekin for a flight-seeing tour over Lake Chelan and the surrounding peaks. For information on these and other activities, contact the Lake Chelan Chamber of Commerce (see p. 183).

Hikers, Cascade Pass Trail

top out on a starkly beautiful and blessedly flat area that's a jumble of boulders and bedrock outcrops. And right in front of you is the **Sahale Glacier.** As tempting as it is, don't climb onto the glacier: You should never do so without a guide or the appropriate safety equipment. But you can walk across the bedrock to the edge of the glacier, where it's about chest-high and there's no danger of falling rock. Before turning back, stand quietly and you can hear rivers being born as the ancient ice melts and whispers downslope through the rocks, seeking the sea.

Lake Chelan National Recreation Area

Improbably, the final major port of entry to North Cascades lies 50 miles southeast, in the small town of **Chelan,** on the edge of the eastern Washington desert. The town cozies up to one tip of the

almost 55-mile-long, 2-mile-wide **Lake Chelan.** The other tip of the lake extends a few miles into the national park complex's south section, and the **Lake Chelan Boat Company** *(P.O. Box 186, Chelan, WA 98816. 509-682-2224 or 509-682-4584)* takes advantage of this connection. Throughout the year the company runs one passenger boat up and down the lake, and during the warm months two other vessels are added to the fleet, including a high-speed catamaran. The slowest boat takes four hours to reach the dock in the south section; the catamaran zooms there in just over an hour. You can also get there in 30 minutes via a scenic floatplane flight *(Chelan Airways, 509-682-5065)* out of Chelan.

But faster isn't necessarily better for visitors who aren't short on time. Lake Chelan invites leisurely cruising. A natural lake raised 21 feet by a dam, it occupies a trough gouged out by glaciers. It is one of the country's deepest lakes, reaching down almost 1,500 feet, the last 400 below sea level.

Cruising Lake Chelan

The trip starts amid the high-desert hills around Chelan, many of them dotted with houses and orchards. The development soon is left behind as the boat enters national forest lands and the arid hills give way to low mountains and conifer forest. With each mile the mountains get higher and the forest thicker, and by the time you cross into North Cascades, 4 miles from the end of the lake, the peaks soar more than 8,000 feet and the forest is lush and deep. The only reason to rush up this lake is to spend more time in the area at the end of the line before your boat goes back to Chelan.

One way to have it all is to travel fast in one direction or to stay overnight at one of the lodges and campgrounds in **Stehekin** (see sidebar p.193), the village in which the dock is located. No roads go to this back-of-beyond municipality of some 100 residents, spread out over the lower 9 miles of the **Stehekin Valley.** An unpaved road runs about 20 miles up the valley, but the handful of vehicles that use it were barged in. Buses facilitate travel on this road, carrying sightseers and dropping off hikers, and you can rent mountain bikes near the dock. For information about recreation in the valley, stop in at the **Golden West Visitor Center,** on the hill above the dock.

Many visitors thoroughly enjoy themselves without ever leaving the road. They stroll along the lakeshore near the landing or take the shuttle to the more distant reaches of the valley. But people who want to venture farther afield will find many trails branching off the road. From the information center, you can take the three-quarter-mile **Imus Creek Nature Trail.** Just over 3 miles up the road, a 5-minute walk will lead you through the forest to a viewpoint near the base of 312-foot **Rainbow Falls.** In autumn, stop in at the **Harlequin Campground,** just up the road from the falls. In the **Stehekin River** and tributary creeks, hundreds, even thousands of salmon spawn in the clear, shallow water. The **Agnes Gorge Trail** intersects the road about 10 miles upvalley, near the High Bridge Campground and winds southwest 2.5 miles through a diverse forest to the narrow, 210-foot-deep gorge.

At the end of the road is Cottonwood Campground where you'll find the Cascade Pass Trail (see p. 192). In 1995 a flood washed out part of the road, so for the indefinite future the last 2.5 miles past Flat Creek are closed to vehicles. You can hike or ride a bike or a horse the last stretch to the campground. From Cottonwood, you head northwest on the Cascade Pass Trail along the upper reaches of the Stehekin River to where the 1.5-mile **Horseshoe Basin Trail** branches off and heads north up a moderately steep slope. The trail more or less follows a creek. Trees and brush eventually give way to open basin. It's a cirque bounded by rock walls hundreds of feet high. From the rim of this half-circle of cliffs, dozens of waterfalls dive to the rocks below. ■

Methow Valley

Pasayten Wilderness

■ 530,000 acres ■ North-central Washington, northeast of Seattle about 250 miles ■ Camping, hiking, boating, bird-watching, wildlife viewing, wildflower viewing ■ Best season summer; snow-free times of year vary from place to place due to differences in precipitation. Harts Pass typically open July–mid-Oct. ■ Contact Methow Valley Ranger District, Okanogan National Forest, 502 Glover, Twisp, WA 98856; phone 509-997-2131. www. fs.fed.us/r6/oka

TO PUT IT SIMPLY, the Pasayten is big and wild. This designated wilderness encompasses more than half a million acres. Straddling the Cascades divide and abutting the Canadian border, the Pasayten sprawls more than 50 miles west to east, which results in a tremendous breadth of climate and habitat. On the west side the annual precipitation averages more than 100 inches while on the east side the average is about 30 inches. Throughout the wilderness you'll encounter tall peaks; 58 summits surpass 7,500 feet. You'll also find a lot of water, including more than 100 lakes, scores of rivers and creeks, and water locked up in mountain glaciers. Wildlife thrives in this unspoiled place. Moose, black bear, mountain lion, wolf, grizzly, bighorn sheep, and wolverine can all be found here, as well as the largest population of lynx in the lower 48 states.

What to See and Do

For the experienced backcountry traveler, the options are dazzling. More than 600 miles of trails snake through the wilderness, the longest a leg-straining 73 miles. On the east side, you might try the 18-mile (one way) **Chewach Trail** to **Remmel Lake.** It shadows the banks of the **Chewach River,** passes **Chewach Falls,** continues through river-bottom forest and emerges into meadows colored by lupine and Indian paintbrush before reaching the lake. Another

18-miler, the **Devils Ridge Trail,** leaves **Ross Lake** on the east side and heads deep into the western Pasayten Wilderness, climbing through forest to Dry Creek Pass and ascending the 6,982-foot **Devils Dome** for a fine view of glacier-clad **Jack Mountain,** the Pasayten's highest point at 9,065 feet.

A handful of roads come near the Pasayten, giving less ambitious travelers a chance to peek into its confines or even take a day hike a few miles into its interior. One of the best is the road to Harts Pass (Mazama Road, which becomes Forest Road 5400). You can catch it in Mazama, just off Wash. 20. Of the 20 miles to Harts Pass, about 7 are paved; the remainder are dirt, with some narrow spots where the road clings to steep slopes. The road follows the **Methow River** and then **Rattlesnake Creek** through the drier forests typical of the east side, winding higher and higher until it reaches 6,197-foot **Harts Pass.** Near the pass, take the 3-mile spur road up to Slate Peak.

Along the Pacific Crest

About halfway up the spur, stop at the **Windy Pass Trail.** Part of the Pacific Crest Trail, which runs from Canada to Mexico, this 3.5-mile segment cuts along steep slopes and over rolling hills and ridges to **Windy Pass.** Most of the time the trail stays above tree line and the views are generous. In season, watch for wildflowers and migrating birds of prey. You'll pass above the old mining town of **Barron,** where thousands of optimists lived in the late 19th century. You can still see evidence of the town and the gold mines.

Back on the spur road, continue up to the parking lot just below **Slate Peak.** You'll have to hike up the steep last quarter mile of the road to the 7,440-foot summit. The summit used to be higher, but during the 1950s the military blasted it off to create a flat base on which it built a Cold War radar station. The MiGs never came and the radar station is long gone, but the spectacular 360-degree vistas remain. To the west and south lie the saw-blade pinnacles of the Cascades, including the **Pickett Range,** 44 miles in the distance. The volcanic cone of **Mount Baker,** 52 miles to the west, also is prominent. A mere 19 miles north is **Castle Peak,** a Pasayten landmark that hovers over the Canadian border. These and many other mountains are indicated by interpretive signs located around the rim of Slate Peak.

Sitting right on the edge of the Pasayten Wilderness, Slate Peak also provides close-up views of the wilderness that extends north and east from the peak's base. You can gaze down on the broad, glacial valley of the **West Fork Pasayten River.** You'll see the **West Fork Pasayten Trail** go across a bit of open terrain near Slate Peak and then descend into the dense green sea of timber that throngs the river valley bottom. You might venture a few miles along this path into the wild. If you don't want to go any farther than Slate Peak, scan the nearby landscape with your binoculars, and you might pick up a deer or a hawk. It's also just possible that you could see a grizzly or a wolf—very unlikely, but a possibility just the same. ■

Following pages: Fall storm approaches Harts Pass

Mount Baker

■ 1.7 million acres ■ Central Washington, just west of North Cascades National Park ■ Best season summer; major roads and Heather Meadows area can get crowded. Snow typically closes higher elevations mid-Oct.–July ■ Camping, hiking, boating, downhill skiing, wildflower viewing ■ Parking fee at Heather Meadows ■ Contact Mount Baker Ranger District, Mount Baker-Snoqualmie National Forest, 2105 State Route 20, Sedro Woolley, WA 98284; phone 360-856-5700

AT 10,781 FEET HIGH and mantled by snow and 14 glaciers, Mount Baker rises above nearby peaks like a colossus. You won't be surprised to learn that this commanding volcanic peak lends its name to the major elements of what is referred to as the Mount Baker area. These elements include the Mount Baker National Recreation Area (where the mountain itself resides), the Mount Baker Scenic Byway, and the Mount Baker-Snoqualmie National Forest. The only exception is Baker Lake—perhaps they just forgot the "Mount."

The Mount Baker area is rugged territory cut by rivers and forested by Douglas-fir, cedar, mountain hemlock, and other conifers, though much of the old-growth outside the wilderness has been logged. Located in extreme northwest Washington, touching the border with Canada and only 30 miles from the Strait of Georgia, the Mount Baker area receives prodigious amounts of precipitation. In the winter of 1998-99, a record 95 feet of snow fell. The snowpack may keep subalpine meadows covered until into July or August, but those flowers and grasses are unquestionably well watered.

What to See and Do

Mount Baker Scenic Byway

The Mount Baker Scenic Byway, which approaches the area from Bellingham to the west, consists of the last 24 miles of Wash. 542 (during winter the first 21 miles of the byway are plowed to provide access to the Mount Baker Ski Area). Start at the **Glacier Public Service Center** (360-599-2714. mid-May–mid-Oct.), located in the little town of Glacier. It's a joint operation of the National Park Service and the Forest Service and its staff will give you lots of information about the Mount Baker area. Shortly after you drive east from the center, you'll see **Glacier Creek Road** (Forest Road 039) branching south. Take this spur 9 miles to its end and you'll come to **Mount Baker Vista,** which provides superb views of the **Coleman Glacier** and **Mount Baker,** just a mile or so away. From the junction with Forest Road 039, the byway leads through a blend of old-growth forest and big second-growth forest along the **North Fork Nooksack River.** This wild river starts life in the snow and glaciers of Mount Shuksan, northeast of Mount Baker, and cuts deep into the land on its way to the sea, in places carving a gorge several hundred feet deep.

Hikers near Artist Point

Snowboarder, Mount Baker Ski Area

About 2 miles from Glacier, adjacent to the Douglas-fir Campground, you'll see the start of the **Horseshoe Bend Trail.** It's the first of nearly 20 trails that branch off the byway or its spur roads. The 1.5-mile Horseshoe Bend Trail follows the bank above the North Fork Nooksack then loops back to the trailhead. During the fall watch the shallows for spawning chinook salmon (also known as king salmon). This, the largest of all salmon species, was recently placed on the federal endangered species list, but its condition seems to be improving. To see a lot of salmon, visit during the big pink salmon runs, which take place during odd-numbered years in **Gallup Creek,** right in the town of Glacier, or in **Thompson Creek,** a mile south of the highway on Glacier Creek Road. All year, but especially in fall and winter, more salmon run through the creeks in northwest Washington than in any of the lower 48 states.

Another 5 miles along the byway takes motorists to **Nooksack Falls,** where the river plunges more than 100 feet over rocky outcrops. Past the falls the road slips through some fine old-growth western hemlock, Douglas-fir, and western redcedar. Some specimens of these trees are preserved in the **North Fork Nooksack Research Natural Area,** which gives scientists baseline information and offers passersby glimpses of some of the plant world's giants. About 14 miles from Glacier lies the **Silver Fir Campground,** so named because, at about 2,000 feet elevation, the campground marks the transition zone where silver fir mixes with lower-elevation tree species. Near Silver Fir, **Anderson Creek Road** (Forest Road 3071) heads southwest 4 miles to some extensive beaver ponds.

Heather Meadows

Now comes the good part. Sure, those first 14 miles of roaring river and towering trees are great, but the last 10 miles of the byway are one of the most dramatically beautiful drives in the Northwest. Just past the Silver Fir Campground, the road turns south, leaves the North Fork Nooksack, and starts climbing. Soon you emerge from the forest into open, sparsely treed subalpine terrain. Switchbacking several miles up mountainsides steep enough to induce vertigo, you'll cross into the storied **Heather Meadows area.** Here the trees have shrunk to cowering knots of stunted evergreens and the slopes belong to sweeping blankets of heather, huckleberries, blueberries, and wildflowers. Tarns—little alpine lakes—wink in the sunlight and slender creeks wriggle down the mountainsides, sometimes leaping down small waterfalls.

A couple of miles into Heather Meadows you should stop and stroll around **Picture Lake.** The lake itself certainly warrants a photo, but that's not how it got its name. Stand on the northwest rim of the lake and look southeast and you'll get the picture. The reflection of **Mount Shuksan** in

Where the Glaciers Are

Glaciers still move ponderously down the mountain slopes, sculpting the land, adding minerals to the food web, and pouring meltwater into creeks. You can hike to a glacier on one of several trails. On Mount Baker's south side, the Park Butte Trail leads up to Park Butte, which commands grand views of Easton Glacier. The Railroad Grade Trail branches off the Park Butte Trail and takes you right to the glacier. On Mount Baker's northwest side, the Heliotrope Ridge Trail provides up-close views of the Coleman Glacier; a branch, the Hogsback Route, ascends to the glacier. From the Heather Meadows area, the Picture Lake Trail yields views of several of Mount Shuksan's glaciers; the Artist Ridge Trail does likewise for Mount Baker's glaciers.

the still water, with the 9,127-foot peak itself in the background—it's about 3 miles away—is reputed to be one of the most photographed mountain scenes on the continent.

As you continue you'll pass several trails that will take you into this ethereal realm. A 1.5-mile (one way) path ventures to **Bagley Lake** and meets up with the **Chain Lakes Trail,** which traverses Table Mountain and enters the **Mount Baker Wilderness** as it drops down to the **Chain Lakes.** The **Fire and Ice Trail** is a half-mile interpretive loop that starts at the Heather Meadows Visitor Center *(July– early Oct.).* The trail explains how volcanic action and glaciers sculpted this landscape with an artistry to which Rodin could only aspire.

The road ends at **Artist Point** with a scenery crescendo. You're standing atop a high divide— 5,140 feet—with Mount Shuksan appearing a few miles to the east, Mount Baker looming even higher a few miles to the southwest, and the high country of the north Cascades sprawling before you in every direction. The easy, 1-mile (one way) **Artist Ridge Trail** takes you toward Mount Shuksan until you get the feeling it's going to wash over you.

One end of the aforementioned Chain Lakes Trail leaves from Artist Point. If you and your party are up to maneuvering along a narrow path with some steep drop-offs, the **Table Mountain Trail** will take you 1.5 miles into the alpine world atop **Table Mountain.** (No dogs are allowed, and you should think twice about taking children.) From the flat top

savor the views of Mounts Baker and Shuksan.

From the South

It's tough to compete with the Mount Baker Scenic Byway, but some of the other parts of the Mount Baker area rise to the challenge, especially in the wilderness. Even a few of the places accessible by road or day hiking rank pretty high on the wow index. On the south side of Mount Baker, visitors can enter the area via the Baker Lake Highway, off Wash. 20. Near the southwest shore of **Baker Lake,** the **Shadow of the Sentinels Trail** loops half a mile through a grand stand of old growth. Some of the trees are almost 700 years old and 7 feet or more in diameter. The flat path is a combination of pavement and boardwalk, and it has notably informative interpretive signs that offer insight into the forest community. One sign bears a haiku that includes the phrase "quieting the mind": What better place for that pursuit? Another flat and easy route—but unpaved and unsigned—starts at the northern tip of Baker Lake. For 3 miles the **Baker River Trail** heads upstream along the eponymous river, passing beaver ponds and old growth, including some enormous western redcedars. After a mile the trail enters a remote corner of **North Cascades National Park** (see p. 183) and proceeds 2 more miles amid the gathering mountains to Sulphide Creek Camp.

Another rewarding trail can be reached by leaving the Baker Lake Highway just inside the national forest boundary. Head northwest on Forest Road 012 for 3.5 miles and go north and then west 6 miles on Forest Road 013 to its end, in the **Mount Baker National Recreation Area.** The first mile or so of the **Park Butte/Schrieber's Meadow Trail** is fairly easy and gets you to **Schrieber's Meadow**. Then the trail starts climbing, but not too steeply, passing through forest and eventually rising to a heather-drenched saddle above tree line. A short but strenuous ascent of a ridge with dizzying drop-offs to either side brings you to the old fire lookout atop **Park Butte,** 5,450 feet above sea level. From here you can savor a panorama that take in Easton Glacier, the Twin Sisters Range, the Black Buttes, and Mount Baker, its summit a mere 4 miles away—and looming a mile higher. ■

Mount Shuksan and Picture Lake

Manning Provincial Park

■ 19,383 acres ■ Southwest British Columbia, 100 miles east of Vancouver ■ Season mid-May–mid-Oct.; snow covers the park rest of year. Blackwall Road typically closed Thanksgiving–mid-May ■ Camping, hiking, backpacking, boating, canoeing, mountain biking, horseback riding, downhill skiing, cross-country skiing, wildlife viewing, wildflower viewing ■ Contact the park, Box 3, Manning Park, BC V0X 1R0; phone 250-840-8836. www.env.gov.bc.ca/bcparks

THE TREES TELL THE TALE. In the heart of Manning Provincial Park grow Engelmann spruce, lodgepole pine, alpine larch, and alpine fir, typical Cascades species. But as you head northeast out of the park, you'll see black cottonwood along the waterways and ponderosa pine on the slopes—trees that prefer drier climates and lower elevations. As the trees indicate, the landscape is changing.

This British Columbia provincial park lies at the northern end of the Cascades, the range that defines the Northwest. Appropriately, the Pacific Crest Trail ends its 2,650-mile run in Manning Provincial Park, perhaps unwilling to come down from the mountaintops to the flatlands of the Kamloops Plateau, which lies just beyond the park. Happily, the high country goes out with a bang, not a whimper.

View of Cascades from atop Blackwall Peak

Located across the border from Washington's Pasayten Wilderness (see p. 196), Manning Provincial Park exhibits the same enticing blend of 7,000-foot peaks, wild rivers, forested glacial valleys, and thriving wildlife. Visitors will see a wide variety of flora and fauna due to the park's considerable east-west reach, ranging from coastal species in the west to sagebrush-country species in the east. The park is especially well known for its subalpine wildflower displays, probably the finest to be found in British Columbia.

What to See and Do

The westernmost part of Manning Provincial Park consists of a long, narrow finger along the Sumallo and Skagit Rivers. Near the confluence of these rivers is **Sumallo Grove,** where a vaulting stand of western redcedar and Douglas-fir can be explored via a half-mile interpretive loop trail. The presence of western redcedar, which prefer cool, moist climates, indicates that this river valley is an outpost of coastal habitat. Another favorite route is the 8-mile **Skagit River Trail,** which starts in Sumallo Grove, crosses into adjacent **Skagit Valley Provincial Park** *(contact Cultis Lake Provincial Park Office, P.O. Box 3010, Cultis Lake, BC V2R 5H6. 604-824-2300),* and continues alongside the Skagit in the verdant valley bottom. Coastal

Cyclists, Lightning Lake

flora also prevail in neighboring **Rhododendron Flats,** just east of Sumallo Grove. Stroll the loop trail just under half a mile through the flats in early to mid-June and drink in the beauty and fragrance of the blooming red rhododendrons.

The vast majority of Manning's trails and other recreational opportunities lie in the southern portion of the park. Ground zero is the visitor center and nearby **Manning Park Resort** *(250-840-8822),* both right off Crowsnest Highway. The visitor center *(mid-May–mid-Oct.)* has a few displays depicting the area's natural and human history and plenty of information about recreation opportunities in the park.

Across the highway from the Manning Park Resort, a paved road winds 6 miles up a steep grade to **Cascade Lookout.** The views spread south across the park and well across the American border into Washington. Note the mix of tall, jagged peaks and somewhat shorter, rounded peaks; the mas-

sive glaciers of the last ice age were so thick that they steamrollered everything but the highest pinnacles. As you stand there admiring the view, Cascade golden-mantled ground squirrels and yellow-pine chipmunks will accost you, begging for handouts. Enjoy watching them, but please don't feed them.

Blackwall Peak

From the lookout the road becomes gravel and continues 4.5 miles up into the subalpine to **Blackwall Peak,** which yields even better vistas than does the lookout. Park your car and walk to a nearby high point and you'll have unobstructed views in all directions. However, most people don't come to Blackwall Peak to look somewhere else. They come to look at the subalpine meadows that begin around Blackwall and extend north along the broad, rolling landscape for about 15 miles. During the summer a diverse display of wildflowers illuminates these meadows. The first wave of color erupts right on the heels of the snowmelt, about mid-June to mid-July, as yellow avalanche lilies, white spring beauties, and creamy western anemones burst from the soil into the sun, sometimes blossoming even before the leaves on the plants begin to grow. The second and bigger wave rolls into the meadows in mid-summer, with a ten-day peak usually in late July or early August. Particularly prevalent are red Indian paintbrush, blue lupine, and yellow arnica, but many other species join in the rush to reproduce before the snows and harsh weather return.

Park naturalists often lead wildflower walks in this area. One of their favored routes is a 1-mile loop along **Paintbrush Nature Trail,** which starts at the **Naturalist Hut** near the parking lot. Here visitors make the acquaintance of many of the flowering plants and learn a bit about the community in which they live. You'll see white Indian paintbrush, a less common cousin of the abundant red paintbrush. Western anemone graces parts of the trail; it's as well known for its stringy seedheads (moptops) as for

> **Whistle Pigs**
>
> Whistle Pig is an old-time name for a marmot, a large, furry rodent. The yellow-bellied marmot is found mainly along the road cuts and at lower elevations. The hoary marmot is the classic herald of the high country, sounding its high-pitched whistle whenever an intruder enters the alpine community.

its large white blooms. On hot, rocky sites lance-leaved stonecrop grows, putting out small yellow blooms. Look closely and you'll see that those lance-shaped leaves are leathery and succulent, evolved to retain moisture. Many plants in the open and nearly treeless environment on the ridge tops have adaptations designed to make the most of the water that comes their way. That seems odd in habitat that lies beneath the snow most of the time, but exposure to high, moisture-stripping winds and the intense high-elevation sun parch these meadows. That is why wooly pussytoes have fuzz that diffuses UV rays and lupines are shaped to collect water at their base.

If the wildflowers at Blackwall Peak aren't enough, hike a few miles north on the moderately difficult 13-mile (one way) **Heather Trail**. This route passes through tens of thousands of acres of subalpine meadows.

Plants occupy center stage at Blackwall Peak, but take a moment to appreciate the animals, too. Hoary marmots and pikas inhabit the rocky slopes and gather food

Sunlight on a pond

plants from the meadows. Another common mammal, but one that's rarely seen, is the pocket gopher. The work of these subterranean dwellers is readily visible, however; the long stripes of turned-over soil veining the meadows result from the gophers' digging. Their plowing is critical to the health of all those flowering plants. If a noisy Clark's nutcracker (see p. 211), a member of the jay family, flies up to you while you're surveying the scene, it's looking for food. About 80 to 90 percent of this bird's diet consists of the seeds of whitebark pines, a tree species that grows in harsh, high-elevation terrain, such as Blackwall Peak. To withstand brutal cold and wind, the whitebark pine has evolved small limbs that are nearly as flexible as rope so they won't snap during winter

gales. But the species needs Clark's nutcrackers to spread its seed. It's a symbiotic relationship, because the nutcrackers, too, must survive the rigors of winter, and in order to do so each bird buries some 10,000 whitebark pine seeds in scattered sites. The birds dig up their caches as needed during the winter, but they never need or find them all, so the leftovers sprout into nicely spaced whitebark pine seedlings.

When you wind back down the road from Blackwall Peak, explore the area south and west of the highway. The **Gibson Pass Road**, which runs west toward the ski area from the Manning Park Resort, brims with fine trails and appealing sights. Less than a mile from the resort, the road crosses the Similkameen River. Here the 1.2-mile **Canyon Nature Trail**

Gray jay, also known as a whiskey jack

loops up the west bank and back down the east bank, with 17 marked stations where you should consult your interpretive booklet. You'll learn about dwarf mistletoe, the sex life of cottonwoods, and the signals that tell conifers when to let loose their winged seeds. Across the road, before the bridge, is the horse corral, where visitors can sign on for guided rides along the park's many equestrian trails. A few hundred yards farther down the road brings you to another interpretive loop, the one-third-mile **Rein Orchid Trail.** Board-walks circle through a bog, where rein orchids bloom in early summer and beavers can be seen at dawn and at dusk.

Lightning Lake Trails

About a mile west of the Rein Orchid Trail, **Lightning Lake** meets Gibson Pass Road. You can rent canoes at Manning Park Lodge *(250-840-8822)* and paddle this slender, 1.5-mile-long lake or walk around it on the flat and easy, 5.6-mile **Lightning Lake Loop** trail. Diving ducks and loons frequent the lake and numerous chipmunks scamper about on terra firma. Around **Rainbow Bridge** at dusk you may glimpse beavers at work. Now and then visitors encounter black bears on this trail, too; stay alert and keep your distance if you spot one. At the far end of **Lightning Lake** you can join the **Lightning Lakes Chain** trail, which continues southwest several miles, linking Lightning Lake to Flash Lake, Strike Lake, and Thunder Lake. Several long, more demanding trails originate at Lightning Lake.

Bird Brains

Experiments have shown that a Clark's nutcracker, often found near timberline, has a remarkable capacity to remember mental maps. When pine nuts are in season for a brief time in the fall, Clark's nutcrackers gather and cache thousands of them over wide territories. When winter comes and there's little to eat, the nutcrackers consult their mental maps and return with startling accuracy to their stores. One study discovered that the birds find their caches about 90 percent of the time.

One of the most popular and most strenuous day hikes climbs to the top of **Frosty Mountain;** at 7,900 feet it's the highest point in Manning. Two routes reach the peak, one a 14-mile round-trip from the Lightning Lake day-use area, the other a slightly longer loop that also can be started from the day-use area. Both trails inflict an elevation gain of nearly 4,000 feet on hikers' knees. But Frosty's sub-alpine meadows burst with flowers and the view from the top can make you forget your aching legs. During the fall you can relish a half-mile stretch of alpine larches, those uncommon deciduous conifers whose needles turn golden and drop in fall.

Skyline I Trail

Also originating at Lightning Lake is the wonderful **Skyline I Trail** (yes, there also is a Skyline II

Trail), which takes hikers through deep forest, fine meadows, and along a high ridgeline that yields outstanding views. The loop, which includes short portions of two other trails, is about 13 miles long and involves an elevation gain of about 2,500 feet, so be prepared and be fit. If you reverse the direction described below, you'll have a longer but gentler ascent and a steeper descent—pick your poison.

Park at Spruce Bay, next to Lightning Lake Campground, and head south on the **Lightning Lake Trail.** In about half a mile you'll arrive at the start of the Skyline I Trail. Take it northwest up the heavily forested slope amid trees bearded by lichen and coated with moss. The path is well maintained and not too steep. Tread softly and you may hear the rising echo of loons calling from Lightning Lake below. Their vocalizations, which

Rosy spirea

sound like yodeling, announce that they have claimed a bit of lake for breeding territory.

After a couple of miles the grade steepens. Soon you pass into a recent burn, scorched by fire in 1994. A few trees still stand, to the delight of the hairy woodpeckers that chip away at the bark searching for tasty bugs. Wildflowers, shrubs, and tree seedlings thrive in the open space created by the fire. Often mule deer come to feed on the tender new undergrowth.

As you labor up the steep trail, the openings created by the fire reveal that you're ascending a sharp ridge, with views to either side, including a fine look down on Lightning Creek and the chain of Lightning Lakes. The views get better and better until you top out on the knob that marks the start of the broad skyline ridge. You've pretty much left the trees behind, except for a few misshapen whitebark pines, and from the knob you can see a vast expanse of the northern Cascades. Sit a while and pick out the glaciers, avalanche chutes, lakes, cirques, rivers, and other details that give depth to this masterpiece of a landscape.

From the knob, the trail runs across the broad, gently rolling ridge through subalpine meadows thick with blossoms during the summer. The purple-blue of lupines dominates the color scheme, but the red of Indian paintbrush, the yellow of lance-leaved stonecrop, and a rainbow of other hues blend with the lupine. Occasionally you'll come across a small patch of tiger lilies, their showy, speckled orange flowers swaying atop 3-foot stems.

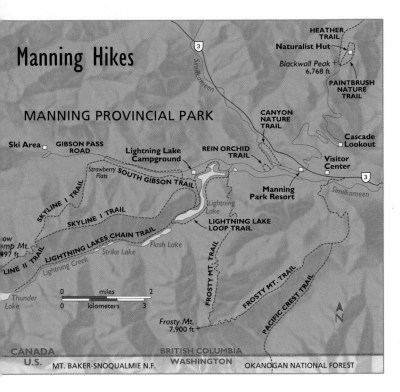

Sometimes tracking right down the middle of the ridge, sometimes clinging to the south slope, the trail goes from knob to knob for a couple of miles, serving up a steady diet of grand views and beaming wildflowers. You might see a northern goshawk glide past at eye level or a mule deer browsing on a distant mountainside.

From the last of the several knobs the trail starts a gradual descent from the ridge. For a mile or so it passes through patches of trees and sprawling meadows. Less exposed and better watered than the meadows on the ridge, these produce much taller plants, such as the head-high cow parsnip and the waist-high hellebore—lovely with its deeply grooved, spiraling leaves but a deadly poison. Black bears favor these meadows, so keep an eye out and make noise so you don't surprise a napping bear.

After about 6.5 miles, you'll meet up with the Skyline II Trail. Make sure you stick with number one, which makes a sharp turn to the north. You'll steadily descend through forest for several miles to **Strawberry Flats,** a rich botanical area that includes a strange brew of alpine, interior, and coastal plants. You'll see skyrockets, bluebells, tiger lilies, mountain forget-me-nots and, of course, strawberries—in all, more than 150 species, which is some 25 percent of all the floral species found in Manning. From Strawberry Flats walk a couple of miles east on the easy **South Gibson Trail** back to the Spruce Bay parking lot. ■

Hiking near Ladyslipper Lake

Cathedral Provincial Park

■ 82,667 acres ■ South-central British Columbia, on the Washington border ■ Best season May–mid-Oct., but snowstorms can occur any time. Hikers should be prepared for extreme weather year-round ■ Camping, hiking, backpacking, boating, horseback riding, wildlife viewing ■ You cannot drive into the park in your own vehicle ■ Contact BC Parks, District Manager, Box 399, Summerland, BC, V0H 1Z0; phone 250-494-6500. www.elp.gov.bc.ca/bcparks/explore/parkpgs/cathedra.htm

CATHEDRAL PROVINCIAL PARK'S 82,667 acres harbor the beautiful peaks, forests, meadows, and lakes familiar to admirers of the northern Cascades. But Cathedral also includes flora, fauna, and terrain typical of the drier transition landforms between the Cascades of Washington state and the interior plateaus of British Columbia.

The park consists almost entirely of wilderness; only a small rustic lodge, a ranger station, a teeth-rattling dirt road that grinds up to the lodge and ranger station, a few small campgrounds, and several trails reveal the presence of humans. The lodge, ranger station, and campgrounds lie in the Cathedral Lakes area, the heart of the park and the destination of most visitors. Note that you cannot drive into the park on your own; vehicles must be left in a parking lot at the entrance, from which you can hike into the park or pay the operators of the Cathedral Lakes Lodge *(888-255-4453)* for a ride. It's a hard, all-day hike up to the lodge/lakes area, so most people opt for the lodge's four-wheel-drive vehicle ride. Make reservations well in advance for the ride, and even further in advance if you'd like to stay at the popular lodge.

What to See and Do

Wide-ranging backpackers can find many compelling places, but visitors can experience the essence of the park by exploring the Cathedral Lakes area. **Quiniscoe Lake** serves as the area's hub and is the location of Cathedral Lakes Lodge *(888-255-4453 reservations; 250-492-1606, summer only)*, the ranger station, and one of the campgrounds. The lake rests in a bowl at an elevation of 6,800 feet, almost encircled by a wall of mountains that looms 1,000 to 1,500 feet higher. Many visitors enjoy evening walks along the easy 1-mile trail that rings the lake. Look for rein orchids, globeflowers, and marsh marigolds in the wetlands that edge Quiniscoe.

Several moderate trails fan out from the lake. A nearly flat path leads a mile to **Lake of the Woods.** Another easy walk curves 2 miles through the forest to **Glacier Lake.** More ambitious hikers may prefer the 3-mile, moderate, somewhat up-and-down **Diamond Trail,** which circles **Scout Mountain** and passes through gorgeous subalpine meadows perfumed by thick expanses of blue lupines.

All of the above trails are lovely trails, but to experience the park more fully you must hike up into the alpine. The **Rim Trail** is the park's showcase route, running along the edge of the wall of mountains that cups **Cathedral Lakes.** Three trails switchback up to the Rim Trail, which in turn allows hikers to fashion a variety of loops, including a grand tour of the entire rim. Note that the rim tour takes a full day to complete.

For the grand tour, start out on the Diamond Trail and turn southeast toward **Red Mountain**. (Yes, it's red.) You'll get to experience some of those fragrant subalpine meadows before the trail rises into the world above the trees. Sit beside one of the sloping rock piles for a spell—the 1,000-foot elevation gain and thin air will encourage you to take a breather—and you'll likely see pikas. (Yanks say PIE-ka and Canadians say PEE-ka, a pronunciation that seems better suited to these charming little critters.) Part of the same family as rabbits and hares, pikas look as if they are related to guinea pigs. You'll hear them squeak as they scamper about the rocks collecting vegetation for the winter. They gather flowers, grasses, and sedges into piles that occasionally measure as much as 2 feet high and 3 feet across. After their haystack dries—sometimes they

Pyramid Lake

turn over their piles to promote drying—the pikas tuck their food under the rocks. Some naturalists assert that they can predict the harshness of the coming winter by the size of the pikas' food caches. You'll probably also see hoary marmots sunning and playing on those rocky slopes. Rangers say that the park's marmots are exceptionally hefty, weighing 25 and even 30 pounds.

When the trail crests on Red Mountain, it levels out and heads south, roughly following the rim above Cathedral Lakes. This is harsh, exposed alpine country, where plants hunker low to the ground and trees and shrubs refuse to grow. Mostly the terrain seems to grow rocks. But visitors typically don't notice either the ground-hugging plants or the rocks right away: The views command attention. As you walk the next couple of miles, at times you can see far to the west (Mount Baker, 100 miles away in Washington); at times you can gaze down at the Cathedral Lakes to the east, and sometimes you can see dozens of miles in every direction. And everything you behold is wild.

Closer at hand, you may spy a white, black-horned, goateed, 150-pound mammal shambling along the rim—a mountain goat. These animals inhabit the plateaus during the summer, males usually going their solitary way and females and their kids clustering in groups of ten or so. If you watch for a while, you may witness their legendary agility as they negotiate slopes so steep that most humans wouldn't want to tackle them without a rope. During mid-to-late-August you may also spot bighorn sheep.

The Cascades at sunset, from Cathedral Provincial Park

Near the southern end of the loop, you'll encounter the **Devil's Woodpile.** This formation of columnar-jointed basalt inspired the authors of the park's brochure to describe the woodpile as "a tangled heap of rocks that might serve as the ingredients for Satan's blast furnace." A little farther on the trail passes through another striking rock formation known as **Stone City,** which consists of massive boulders of quartz monzonite eroded into odd shapes. From here you can see far south into the American Cascades; the border is less than 5 miles away. At Stone City the loop cuts east on the **Ladyslipper Trail** and winds back down to Quiniscoe Lake. However, hikers can continue south on informal routes about a mile to the **Giant Cleft,** a deep split in the granite face of a mountain. ■

Altitude Sickness
Altitude sickness can cause headaches, fatigue, drowsiness, and nausea. More extreme altitude disorders can result in disorientation, fluid in the lungs, swelling of the brain, and unconsciousness. Such symptoms typically occur well above 8,000 feet and accompany exertion—climbing a mountain, for instance—but even casual hikers to the high country should be alert to signs of altitude sickness. The usual advice is to rest, drink plenty of fluids, and descend to 5,000 feet or lower. The best prevention is acclimatization: spend a couple of days at middle elevations before going higher.

North Coast

Sunset at Wickaninnish Beach, Pacific Rim National Reserve

WHAT IS "THE COAST"? Is it the intertidal area, the land that's exposed at low tide and submerged at high tide? Is it all the land between the crest of a coastal mountain range and the ocean? Are you on the coast as long as you can hear the music of breaking waves or catch a whiff of the fresh, briny smell of the sea? As these ideas suggest, there is no precise definition of coast. A coast is a zone of influence with no exact boundaries. It includes such places as an estuary, in which seawater may push

many miles up a river, profoundly altering the river's ecology; a coastal forest whose dominant tree species rely on ocean fog for moisture; or islands tucked into coastal nooks and crannies, sheltered from the storms that hammer open-ocean islands. The north coast features all these variations on the coastal theme, and more.

Running from southwest Washington up to southwest British Columbia, the north coast of the Pacific Northwest exhibits great diversity. You'll find plenty of classic coastline, such as the rocky, wave-blasted shores and sandy beaches of Pacific Rim National Park Reserve. You'll also find not-so-classic sites, such as Nisqually National Wildlife Refuge, ensconced at the southern tip of Puget Sound some 100 miles by water from the open Pacific, yet fundamentally shaped by the rising and falling of the tide. Most anomalous of all are the mountains in Olympic National Park and in Garibaldi Provincial Park. As you wander through beflowered alpine meadows and watch mountain goats perched on rocky crags, the coast seems far away. Yet salt water flows just a few miles from both these places and the maritime climate reaches out to help shape these mountain fastnesses.

In addition to its diversity, the north coast is noted for its wildness, especially along its classic coastal strips. Olympic National Park and Pacific Rim National Park Reserve harbor long stretches of essentially untouched beaches, tide pools, and shoreline forests. You may see rocks plastered with hundreds of colorful sea stars, black bears foraging on the beach, stands of 200-foot-tall and 500-year-old trees, and bald eagles snagging fish at the mouths of creeks. And if you're willing to hike a few miles, you may see such wonders without another human being in sight, even in the middle of the summer months. Along the north shore of Olympic National Park, for example, you can sit in solitude beneath a giant spruce near the water's edge and gaze out at gleaming tide pools, surf-splashed towers of stone, and slowly heaving kelp beds where sea otters play. Sometimes the wildness seems so complete that you get the feeling that no human before you has left footprints in the sand.

When planning a trip to the north coast, bear in mind the first word in the term "rain forest." Surprisingly little rain falls during the summer and early fall, but winter is another story. Storms marked by waves higher than a two-story house and torrential downpours beset the coast, quickly adding inches to annual precipitation figures that can be measured in feet. Other hazards are present throughout the year. If you're planning to hike along the beach, know the local tides so that you don't get trapped between two headlands. That grand forest right on the edge of the sea—one of the north coast's finest attractions—also presents some dangers: Dead logs tumbling about in the surf can knock you off your feet, so stay clear of these potential bonecrushers. Finally, keep an eye out for rare sneaker waves. They're not tidal waves and they're not very common, but these unpredictable large breakers can sucker punch unwary tide-poolers or wading children. ■

Spearhead Range, Garibaldi Provincial Park

Bird-watching at Grays Harbor NWR

Grays Harbor National Wildlife Refuge

■ 1,800 acres ■ North coast of Washington, 8 miles west of Aberdeen ■ Best months late April–early May for viewing migrating shorebirds; to avoid crowds go early in the morning ■ Boat trips, bird-watching ■ Donations ■ Contact Nisqually National Wildlife Refuge Complex, 100 Brown Farm Rd., Olympia, WA 98516; phone 360-753-9467. For recorded information about Bowerman Basin, phone 360-532-6237

BOWERMAN BASIN MAY NOT LOOK like much to human eyes, but to vast numbers of shorebirds it means the difference between life and death. These few hundred acres of tidal mudflat and wetland in Grays Harbor provide food and shelter to hundreds of thousands of migrating shorebirds. It is one of only five key staging areas in North America, and the only one on the West Coast outside Alaska.

Shorebirds migrate between their nesting grounds in the Arctic and their wintering grounds in Central and South America. Traveling such long distances, sometimes flying hundreds of miles without stopping, drains these birds of energy. In order to complete their migration, they must find superabundant food resources and rapidly replenish their energy reserves so they can move on. However, development has eliminated or degraded many of their stopover sites, magnifying the importance of the few that remain, such as Bowerman Basin. Fortunately, when development threatened the basin in the 1980s, Grays Harbor National Wildlife Refuge was established to protect this shorebird sanctuary.

Those hundreds of thousands of northbound shorebirds pack the basin during a short period each spring, usually peaking from the end of

April through the beginning of May—check with the refuge for the best times to visit. The time of day also is critical. Plan to be there sometime during the period from an hour or two before high tide to an hour or two after; that's when the birds concentrate on the feeding grounds. During peak times the U.S. Fish and Wildlife Service asks people to call the refuge in advance for parking and shuttle bus information (the shuttle bus leaves from Hoquiam High School). If you happen to visit when the shuttle bus is not running, ask the Nisqually staff, who oversee Grays Harbor, for directions to the basin. Boat trips leave from nearby Westport to observe offshore seabirds *(360-733-8255. Fare)*.

The shorebirds have become a big draw in recent years. And why not? So many birds in such a small place present quite a spectacle. The most common species is the western sandpiper. Short-billed and long-billed dowitchers, semipalmated plover, and dunlins also show up in enormous numbers, and about a dozen other shorebird species round out the scene. Follow the new 1-mile (one way) boardwalk on the **Sandpiper Trail**—it will keep you from wading through several inches of water and mud as you head for the tip of the Bowerman peninsula. When you first arrive, you'll most likely just gape for a while at the sheer volume of avian activity. Once you're able to focus, pick out a bit of mudflat, train your binoculars on individual birds, and watch carefully. You may discern order in what at first appears to be chaos.

One pattern involves the connection between the feeding habits of shorebirds and the nature of their bodies. Western sandpipers, for instance, use their inch-long bills to pick invertebrates from the surface of the mudflats. Their short legs won't take them out in the water where black-bellied plover prowl for snails, shrimp, and even some small fish. Nor can the sandpiper, with its stubby bill, probe deep into the burrows of crustaceans and marine worms, as the long-billed dowitcher can. Other anatomical differences compel other shorebirds to seek different foods in different places. Biologists call this resource partitioning (see sidebar p. 241). It limits competition among species and allows a wide range of birds to get the food they need at the same site, using the available resources as fully as possible.

Shorebirds aren't the only feathered visitors to the refuge. Like lions following the migrating wildebeest on the Serengeti, peregrine falcons migrate with the shorebirds and prey on them. Given that these powerful falcons are the fastest animals in the world and can reach speeds of more than 150 miles an hour, you'd think they could snatch one of the thousands of shorebirds in the basin as easily as we take a chicken leg from a plate. But it's not so easy. When a peregrine bullets toward a flock of sandpipers, they flurry into the air en masse. Peregrines prefer to zero in on a single target, so this swirling swarm of madly flapping birds sometimes confuses the falcon, causing it to lose track of its intended meal. On the other hand, many peregrine assaults end with an explosion of feathers and a shorebird lunch. But as long as places like Bowerman Basin remain intact, plenty of other shorebirds will survive. ■

Mallards, Nisqually NWR

Nisqually National Wildlife Refuge

■ 3,000 acres ■ Northwest Washington, 8 miles east of Olympia, off I-5 ■ Best months May-Oct., but open year-round ■ Hiking, bird-watching, wildlife viewing ■ Adm. fee ■ Contact the refuge, 100 Brown Farm Rd., Olympia, WA 98516; phone 360-753-9467. www.r1.fws.gov/nisqually/

NISQUALLY NATIONAL WILDLIFE REFUGE is only 2.7 miles wide and 3.1 miles long, but plenty of wildlife seeks refuge in the **Nisqually River Delta.** One of the few undeveloped estuaries left in Puget Sound area, the delta is highly productive and serves as the home for some 300 species of animals and as a migratory stop for some 130 species of birds. The salt marshes and tide-enriched mudflats teem with invertebrates that feed hungry herons, killdeer, sandpipers, gulls, and ducks.

One-third of the refuge's 3,000 acres are enclosed by the **Brown Farm Dike,** which keeps salt water out and creates the freshwater habitat favored by the 20,000 waterfowl that rest or overwinter here. Cattail-framed freshwater marshes shelter bitterns, frogs, marsh wrens, and salamanders. Rodents throng the adjacent grasslands, attracting coyotes, hawks, and owls. Scan the bluffs above the refuge and you may spot bald eagles, ospreys, and a great blue heron colony. Sometimes you'll even glimpse salmon and steelhead migrating upriver.

Several trails meander through the refuge. The 1-mile **Twin Barns Loop Trail** is a fully accessible, interpretive boardwalk (with two spurs, benches, and an observation platform) located near the visitor center. To get a thorough look at all the different habitats, take the 5.5-mile **Brown Farm Dike Trail.** Photo blinds, a river overlook, and an observation tower enhance your viewing opportunities. The refuge also features a visitor center that is open Wednesday through Sunday. ■

Olympic National Park

■ 922,000 acres ■ Northwest Washington on the Olympic Peninsula, south of Port Angeles off US 101 ■ Best season summer. West side of the park gets immense amounts of rain during the rest of the year, and snow inhibits travel in the high country in winter ■ Camping, hiking, backpacking, bird-watching, wildlife viewing, wildflower viewing, tide-pooling ■ Adm. fee ■ Contact the park, 600 E. Park Ave., Port Angeles, WA 98362; phone 360-452-0330. www.nps.gov/olym/home.htm

SCENE I: ATOP YOUR HIGH-COUNTRY perch you turn slowly in a circle. To the south a jumble of snowcapped peaks, glaciers clinging to their flanks, etch a jagged skyline. Below them, thickly forested slopes curve down to thickly forested valleys where icy rivers run unseen amid the trees. Dropping your gaze to the lower, flatter mountaintop on which you're standing, your eyes feast on an opulent subalpine meadow in the full blush of spring—which comes in July at this elevation and latitude. Wildflowers paint the landscape almost every color on the artist's palette. Roly-poly marmots scoot through the foot-high vegetation, occasionally emitting high-pitched squeaks and whistles. On a nearby slope, a black bear roots for tasty bulbs.

Scene II: Standing in the midst of a low-elevation forest, you can't see more than couple of hundred feet in any direction. Green embraces you, from the moss-draped spruce and hemlock trees that hover far above to the sorrel and sword ferns that live on the larger branches of the trees and also blanket the ground. If you're lucky you may see a herd of the uncommonly large elk that roam this temperate jungle.

Scene III: You stroll along one of the most remote coasts in the contiguous 48 states. With the mist-veiled forest at your back, you look out to sea. Just offshore, 100-foot sea stacks—rock pillars—thrust out of the water, their bases home to barnacles and sea lions, their tops a refuge for squawking seabirds. At the edge of the shore, the waves rear and break, thumping the rocks and sand, sending diamonds of spray into the salty air. Up the beach, tide pools serve as outposts of the sea, harboring marine animals and plants until the tide returns.

Sol Duc Falls

What to See and Do

Start at the **Olympic National Park Visitor Center,** in Port Angeles, near the northeast border of park. After you're loaded down with ideas and literature, check out the numerous exhibits. More information can be found at the centers at the Hoh Rain Forest, on the park's west side, and at Hurricane Ridge, thousands of feet above Port Angeles.

High Country

Many visitors are surprised to learn that the highest peak in the park measures only 7,965 feet; it looks so much taller, more like those famous 14,000-footers in the Colorado Rockies. In a way, the high Olympics are the equal of the Rockies. Bear in mind that the Rockies start from a high plateau of 5,000 or 6,000 feet, whereas Mount Olympus and its brethren rise essentially from sea level; that

means the Olympics' elevation above the surrounding country-side is comparable to that of the 14,000-footers. The Olympics are at least as rugged, too, due to eons of carving by ice age glaciers and erosional forces that are still at work. Today 60 mountain glaciers crown the tallest peaks and valleys of the park's high country, although most glaciers are not actively sculpturing the area now.

From the main visitor center, you can reach the park's most accessible slice of high country by driving 17 miles south from Port Angeles to Hurricane Ridge. The paved road ascends through forest and foothills and ends in the mountains at 5,242 feet. Even from the parking lot, you'll find that the views command attention. Sawtooth summits greet you from the east, west, and, especially, the south, where the bulk of the park

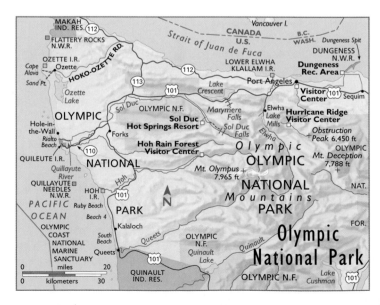

Roosevelt elk, Hoh River Trail

spreads before you. Once you've taken a deep drink of the vistas, tour the **visitor center,** which has good interpretive displays on the surrounding country.

Just outside the visitor center, the **Meadow Loop Trail** winds through the lovely subalpine meadows that grace the south slope of **Hurricane Ridge.** The easy trail actually consists of several intersecting paths of half a mile or less that circle amid the purple lupine, magenta paint-brush, and other wildflowers. Often you'll spot black-tailed deer—please don't feed them.

You're also likely to see Olympic marmots. These social, playful rodents are real crowd pleasers. As they scurry about in their colonies, they greet and groom each other and let loose piercing whistles. And they eat. Due to the high country's severe winter weather, these marmots hibernate for eight or nine months a year, so during the salad days of summer they gorge themselves to put on fat for the winter. By fall some of these pudgy critters weigh 10 or 15 pounds.

Olympic marmots are endemic to the Olympic Peninsula, meaning that this species lives nowhere else. In fact, the peninsula abounds with endemic species, including the Olympic chipmunk and the snow mole and Flett's violet and Piper's bellflower. Because massive

Following pages: Wildflowers flourishing on the Hurricane Hill Trail

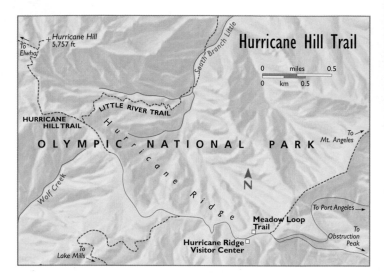

glaciers essentially surrounded the peninsula during the ice age, the plants and animals there were isolated. Over hundreds of thousands of years, they adapted to glacial conditions; some of the peninsula's inhabitants evolved into distinct species and subspecies.

Hurricane Hill Trail

The park's most famous—and definitely one of the most crowded —hike begins at the visitor center. Try it during off-season or off times. The 1.5-mile Hurricane Hill Trail climbs, sometimes steeply, to the 5,757-foot summit of **Hurricane Hill**, where an exotic alpine world and world-class views await.

The partly paved path begins at a little above 5,000 feet and ascends about 700 feet up Hurricane Ridge to the summit. The first part ascends through a subalpine meadow—the riot of wildflowers makes resting a pleasure. The trees, mostly wind-stunted subalpine firs, get even sparser, shorter, and more contorted as you gain

elevation. By the time you reach the saddle about halfway up, few trees obstruct the generous views. Scan the hillsides and you'll sometimes see deer or black bear. After dipping momentarily at the saddle, the trail rises fairly steeply through more superb meadows to the expansive, flat-top summit, which is laced with informal trails—please don't make any new ones in this fragile habitat.

Bunchberry

Hanging moss

Wildflowers and marmots compete for your attention, but you'll probably lose yourself in the views of the high country to the south, the islands in the Strait of Juan de Fuca, the Cascade Range, and Vancouver Island in Canada.

Alpine Zone

To see more of the high country, there's a terrible but wonderful side road you may want to take. As you head back toward Port Angeles on the main park road, almost immediately after leaving the Hurricane Ridge Visitor Center parking lot, turn southeast on the twisting, rutted dirt road that edges 8.4 miles along Hurricane Ridge to **Obstruction Peak.** (The road is generally open from midsummer to early fall.) You'll get grand views of the high country, including Mount Olympus, along the way. At the summit of Obstruction Peak, elevation 6,450 feet, a couple of trails lead into the alpine zone, the world above tree line. Without trees to protect them, alpine plants hug the ground and animals live in burrows to survive the blasting winds that rake the tundra.

These trails into the alpine continue for miles, eventually meeting up with other trails, which in turn intersect yet more trails. Altogether, more than 600 miles of hiking trails thread through the park, most of them in the mountains. This extensive trail network allows you to explore many great high-country spots, but before setting out be sure to contact the park staff for the necessary information and make sure you've got the equipment, skill, and stamina you'll need.

Low-elevation Forests

The park's low-elevation forests are among the richest and most biologically productive places on earth, especially on the wet west side. Generally defined as the lands between sea level and 2,000 feet, these seas of green crest hundreds of feet overhead, forming a canopy of western hemlock, western red-cedar, Douglas-fir, and, in the temperate rain forests, Sitka spruce. These four conifer species grow taller than 200 feet on the Olympic Peninsula. Except in the drier areas, on the east side, a luxuriant understory of vine maple, salmon-berry, dogwood, and ferns crowds beneath the canopy. Many cool rivers and creeks pass through on their way from the high country to the sea, and wildlife abounds, from stately elk to the cult favorite banana slug (see sidebar p. 57).

Many visitors first encounter unspoiled low-elevation forest at **Lake Crescent,** about 15 miles west of Port Angeles on US 101. (Most of the Olympic Peninsula's low-elevation forestlands are either privately held or part of the **Olympic National Forest,** and have been heavily logged for many years.) You can see some of the forest just by driving the 8 miles of US 101 that curve right along the shore of this deep glacial lake. To walk through a representative section of forest, take the **Marymere Falls Trail,** a 1-mile one-way route that leads from the lake's south

Deer in Olympic National Park

shore to a 90-foot waterfall. Note that the first three-quarters of a mile is an easy hike, but the final quarter mile is very steep.

Just a couple of miles west of Lake Crescent, a road branches off 12 miles southeast from US 101 up the **Sol Duc River** through another splendid expanse of low-elevation forest. Near the end of the road you'll find the Sol Duc Hot Springs Resort *(360-327-3583)*, where some swimming pools filled with spring water serve as the focus for a lodge and spa. At the end of the road, about 1.5 miles past the resort, you'll find the start of the **Sol Duc Falls Trail.** The grade is almost flat, the hemlock-fir forest is lovely, and you'll reach **Sol Duc Falls** after about a mile. Stand on the bridge or viewing platforms and see the river crashing into the narrow chasm.

Continue counter-clockwise around the park to reach the rain forest, a realm so striking that it's sometimes considered to be separate from the rest of the low-elevation forest. Most people associate rain forest with the tropics, but a rare relative of those steaming jungles can be found in New Zealand and southern Chile, and on the Pacific Northwest coast. This is temperate rain forest. Although it rarely freezes, it may be cooler than the tropics. It receives impressive amounts of rain: about 120 to 170 inches a year, more than anyplace else in the lower 48 states. The park's prime rain forests are located in the low western valleys. Cool ocean currents and prevailing westerly winds bring clouds packed with moisture onto the

Return of the Sea Otter
The kelp beds off the Pacific Northwest coast once teemed with sea otters, but fur hunters wiped them out. In the late 1960s, U.S. military teams about to conduct nuclear bomb tests on the remote Alaskan island of Amchitka relocated some of the sea otters that lived there. Two groups released on the west coast of the Olympic Peninsula took hold, and now over 600 hundred sea otters populate the nearshore waters off the coastal strip of Olympic National Park.

peninsula. When these east-bound clouds pile up against the Olympic Mountains, they release their load of water on the valleys below. Marvelous rain forests blanket the lower sections of the Quinault and Queets River Valleys, but the most accessible and most popular rain forest in the park lies in the **Hoh River Valley,** on the park's west side.

At the center of the Hoh sits the **Hoh Rain Forest Visitor Center,** which offers interpretive displays and a variety of activities, notably guided hikes. For an introduction, head out from the visitor center on the paved mini-trail to the three-quarter-mile **Hall of Mosses Trail.** Look up at the bigleaf maples along the loop and you'll see how this trail got its name: Dense curtains of club moss hang down several feet from the branches of the maples. That moss provides some of the green in this astoundingly lush ecosystem, where nearly

Ruby Beach, Olympic National Park

every square inch of earth is covered by vegetation. Even the rocks appear green. Sorrel, lichens, mushrooms, trillium, and vanilla leaf throng the spongy forest floor. Ferns seem to be everywhere, on the ground and up in the trees: Licorice, deer, bracken, lady, oak, wood, and maidenhair are just some of the species you may see.

Sitka spruce, western hemlock, and other conifers, some of them more than 1,000 years old, form the roof of the rain forest. And when these giants fall, they help build the floor, too. In this climate it takes hundreds of years for a big tree to decompose, so you'll see massive logs strewn all over the place. Fallen trees play a vital role in giving seedlings a start in life. Because the ground cover is so thick, it's difficult for tree seeds to sprout and grow on the forest floor, so they often take root on top of those downed trees, creating so-called nurse logs.

Spruce Nature Trail

You can see more examples of nurse logs along the Spruce Nature Trail, a 1.25-mile route that circles from the mini-trail out beside the Hoh River and back. Park guides and interpretive signs add depth to this trail. For example, you can learn about the root race that occurs as seedlings compete to send their roots around or through a nurse log in order to be the first to reach the nutrients in the soil. In the end only one seedling in a thousand will grow to maturity. And you'll be informed that the fog that often shrouds the rain forest on summer mornings enables some of the vegetation,

notably Sitka spruce, to survive. Very little rainfall occurs during summer, but the fog provides 20 to 30 inches of precipitation. While gawking up at fantastic, tree-house gardens of moss, lichens, and ferns, you'll learn that the park is home to more than 130 species of epiphytes, air plants that grow on plants but are not parasites.

The rich plant life of the rain forest supports a food chain that nourishes abundant wildlife, though animals often are hard to spot amid the dense vegetation. If you glance at the trail now and then you'll probably see a yellow banana slug oozing along. Douglas squirrels usually make an appearance. If you're lucky you may sight a green tree frog, a snowshoe hare, or a coho salmon. The most prized sight is of a Roosevelt elk, the Pacific Northwest native that »is cousin to the more common Rocky Mountain elk. Roosevelt elk are more social than Rocky Mountain elk and bigger; a bull may top 800 pounds. The park is home to the largest remaining herd. In fact, protecting Roosevelt elk was one of the main reasons for the establishment of Olympic National Park; it was nearly called Elk National Park.

The Coast

Sixty-three miles of wilderness coastline form the western border of the park. No oceanfront condos, no souvenir shops, no seafood restaurants with fish nets hanging from the ceiling. Just sandy beaches, tide pools chockablock with life, sculpture gardens of wave-carved rocks, a brooding forest cloaked in fog, and shorebirds prancing at the water's edge. The park's coastal strip is the longest undeveloped shoreline in the contiguous 48 states.

The southernmost 10 miles, between South Beach and Ruby Beach, seem less wild because US 101 runs just behind the shore, but that also means this is the park's most accessible stretch of coast. Eight named beaches invite motorists to pull off and take short trails down to the sea. At **Kalaloch,** especially near the mouth of Kalaloch Creek, you'll find vast piles of driftwood to explore; just bear in mind that even 100-foot logs, if they're stacked loosely, sometimes will roll when you climb on them, and be aware that high surf can move the logs, even toss them like matchsticks. **Beach 4** offers excellent tide-pooling in the rocks near the north end of this otherwise sandy beach. Rangers conduct guided tide-pool walks here. Did you know that barnacle larvae attach to rocks with glue from their heads? And look for streaks on algae-encrusted rocks. That's where limpets—cows of the intertidal— have been grazing.

Northern Shoreline

At **Ruby Beach,** the end of the park's accessible southern shoreline, US 101 turns inland. The northern 50-plus miles of coast constitute a remote wilderness. People can hike this whole stretch, but they must deal with numerous hardships and dangers, especially treacherous overland trails across headlands and the trap of the incoming tide. Don't attempt this hike, or any section of it, without first talking to park staff and getting their brochure called the "Olympic Coastal Strip."

A couple of spur roads and relatively short hiking trails allow visitors to sample this wilderness coast. Wash. 110 leads to **Rialto Beach,** near the mouth of the **Quillayute River.** Look for bald eagles in the estuary. A 1.5-mile walk north on a beach takes you to **Hole-in-the-Wall,** a striking rock formation and tide-pooling area.

Anyone willing and able to walk 9 flat miles can get a strong dose of wild coast by hiking the triangular route created by the **Ozette Lake–Cape Alava–Sand Point Trail.** From the ranger station at the north end of **Ozette Lake,** off Hoko-Ozette Road, take the 3-mile trail that angles southwest to **Sand Point.** You'll pass through brushy woods, cross bogs and marshes via boardwalks, and slip through towering coastal forest until you reach the Pacific at Sand Point. After soaking up the view, hike north along the beach for 3 miles. This is a relatively easy and safe stretch, but there are a couple of minor headlands and the beach is narrow, so use caution.

While strolling this ruggedly handsome shore, watch for black oystercatchers munching on mussels, bald eagles wheeling overhead, and tufted puffins and rhinoceros auklets bobbing on the swell. Occasionally you'll even spot black bears rummaging through the tide pools. When you reach **Cape Alava,** you're at the westernmost point of the contiguous 48 states; the rocky cape has excellent tide pools. To return back, take the 3.3-mile trail back to Ozette Lake. ■

Mountain goat

Mountain Goats

Mountain goats have charisma to spare. Those comically somber faces made long by drooping beards. That thick, long-haired coat of pure white. Their acrobatic moves on treacherous mountain slopes. Visitors to Olympic National Park love watching these critters. As one local wag put it, mountain goats are high on the warm-white-and-woolly index.

But they don't belong in the park. Though mountain goats are native to other parts of Washington, they didn't penetrate the isolation of the Olympic Peninsula until ecologically naive people introduced them back in the 1920s—before the park was established—so that they could be hunted. As a result, the high-country ecosystem didn't evolve with goats as part of the mix, and some of the plant species are suffering from the unaccustomed grazing, trampling, and wallowing.

As the problems associated with non-native species became better known during the last couple of decades, the Park Service began a removal program, transplanting most mountain goats to the Cascades and some to the Rockies. By the late 1980s, they had cut the goat population from more than 1,000 to a few hundred, but they also had angered some animal lovers. Protests and complaints to politicians mounted and eventually, in 1989, the Park Service had to stop removing the mountain goats. Since then the park has tried other approaches, such as sterilizing goats, but with little success. While discussions and studies continue, between 300 and 500 of these non-native animals still roam the park's high country, damaging some of the continent's rarest natural communities.

Dungeness Spit, jutting into the Strait of Juan de Fuca

Dungeness National Wildlife Refuge

■ 631 acres ■ Northwest Washington, northeast of Port Angeles ■ Best seasons spring and fall ■ Horseback riding, bird-watching, wildlife viewing, beachcombing ■ Adm. fee ■ Contact the refuge, 33 S. Barr Rd., Port Angeles, WA 98362; phone 360-457-8451. www.dungeness.com/refuge/

DUNGENESS SPIT is one of the longest natural sand spits in the world. So what, you ask? How can a skinny, 5-mile crescent of mounded sediment piled up by waves and tidal currents form the foundation of a wildlife refuge?

The answer lies not in the spit itself but in the protection it affords from the wind and the sometimes rough seas of the Strait of Juan de Fuca. Behind that long barrier of sand, animals and plants find shelter in quiet bays, beaches, eelgrass beds, ponds, and tidal mudflats.

Your visit to Dungeness will begin at the parking lot at the extreme southwest end of the refuge, immediately north of adjacent Dungeness Recreation Area *(Clallam County Parks 360-683-5847)*. A trail runs 5.5 miles from the parking lot to the lighthouse near the tip of the spit. The first half mile winds through the mainland forest to the rim of the ocean bluff, where there's an interpretive overlook. From this point you can see the spit and the strait beyond. There is also a platform deck equipped with a telescope for getting a detailed view of the refuge. Check out the bluffside trees for roosting bald eagles.

From the overlook the trail descends to the spit and heads out along this narrow strip of land, bounded by the strait on one side and **Dungeness Harbor** on the southeastern side. As you walk the trail, scan the harbor (which is more of a natural bay than a working harbor) for the black brant. Dark and stocky, the brant is a small, sea goose that drinks salt water and feeds on saltwater plants. About 1,500 winter in the refuge and up to 8,000 migrate through in the spring, peaking in late April.

The Dungeness refuge is one of the best places in Washington to see harlequin ducks, a species of concern in the state. These diving ducks get their names from the male's beautiful patchwork plumage of gray, white, russet, and black. Harlequins breed in high mountain streams during the summer, but they come down to the shore to pass the fall and winter. You may spot them loafing on gravel beaches, feeding in shallow water —primarily on small crabs—or engaging in courting rituals. In the protected waters and tidal flats, your binoculars also may pick up plover, common murres, buffleheads, and dunlins. You may also see tufted puffins, some of which nest on nearby **Protection Island NWR** *(closed to the public to protect nesting seabirds and seals).*

Harbor seals frequent not only the harbor but much of Dungeness; as many as 600 have been counted in the refuge. The tip of Dungeness Spit is a major beaching and pupping site for harbor seals. Such sites are critical to the well-being of the seals, serving as a place to rest, mate, give birth, and nurse pups. Unfortunately, harbor seals are sensitive to human intrusion. They have abandoned another traditional haul-out site within the refuge—a spot on Graveyard Spit—most likely due to disturbance from people. For this reason, the tip of Dungeness Spit is closed to visitors. In fact, several other refuge species suffer when disturbed, so the managers have instituted a number of other closures for certain places at certain times of year. ■

A Place at the Table

To understand how different species of shorebirds manage to peacefully coexist, train your binoculars on the mudflats in the Dungeness NWR at low tide and note the relation between each species' bill and legs and the feeding niche it occupies. Look in the algae-flocked mud up near the tide line and you may spot a least sandpiper scooting around on its stocky legs, snatching up worms and snails with its short bill. You may see a marbled godwit nearby, probing deep burrows with its two-toned, upturned, 6-inch bill in search of juicy invertebrates that the sandpiper could never reach. Farther out, in the shallow water of the receding tide, foraging dowitchers stalk about on their long legs, their feathered bodies safely above water that would swamp a stumpy sanderling. Different bills and different legs lead to different uses of resources, which allows dozens of different shorebird species to share the bounty of the mudflats.

Following pages: Beachcombers on Dungeness Spit

Exploring a tide pool at Rosario Beach

Deception Pass State Park

■ 4,128 acres ■ Northwest Washington, 60 miles north of Seattle on Whidbey and Fidalgo Islands ■ Best months May-Sept., but the park gets very crowded ■ Camping, hiking, swimming, bird-watching, wildlife viewing, beachcombing ■ Adm. fee ■ Contact the park, 5175 N. State Hwy. 20, Oak Harbor, WA 98277; phone 360-675-2417. www.parks.wa.gov/deceptn.htm

SANDY BEACHES, dramatic ocean views from seaside cliffs, old-growth forest, freshwater lakes and marshes, tide pools, wildlife: Deception Pass State Park is a place of great natural abundance. It's not surprising that the park gets almost six million visits every year, making it Washington's most popular state park. Unfortunately, both the sheer number of visitors and the development that caters to them have diminished the park's natural bounty. If concession stands, radios playing music, thronged picnic grounds, and crowded beaches decrease your pleasure in a park, don't despair. You can still savor the wild side of Deception Pass State Park if you visit during the off-season—the summer months are typically the most crowded—or explore the area early in the morning or later in the evening.

The 4,128 acres of the park straddle two islands: **Whidbey Island** to the south and **Fidalgo Island** to the north. (Several ferries and a bridge service these islands.) You may enjoy starting in the middle, by walking out onto **Deception Pass Bridge,** the longer of the two spans that constitute the 1,487-foot link between the islands. You'll get a grand view of the rocky, forested islands and the blue-green sea 182 feet below. When the tide is running, the water squeezing through the narrow channel seems more river than ocean.

Just off the highway in the Whidbey unit of the park, you can get information and advice at the park office. Ask for the interpretive handout for the nearby **Caretakers of the Forest Trail.** As you walk the short trail, you can learn how to tell a true fir from an imposter (such as Douglas-fir), how burls form, and how birds aid red huckleberry plants (their seeds can't germinate until their outer coatings are removed by passing through the digestive system of a bird). Across **Cranberry Lake** from the Caretakers of the Forest Trail is the **Sand Dune Trail,** an 0.8-mile stroll along the lake's marsh and along the ocean beach. For an overview of the Whidbey Island unit and views of the surrounding area, take one of the two short trails (each a third of a mile) to **Goose Rock Summit.**

The most popular trails lie to the north, across the bridge on Fidalgo Island. Two of these—the **Lighthouse Point** and **Canoe Pass Vista Trails**—can be combined into a nice, 2-mile route that passes through a forest of western redcedar and Douglas-fir, along the beach, and beside a marsh. Look for wildflowers in the spring and allow time to soak up great views of **Canoe Pass,** the narrower of the two passages that separate Fidalgo from Whidbey.

Stirring coastline views can be had even more easily by taking the quarter-mile **Rosario Head Trail.** From the 100-foot bluffs, you can see a sizable expanse of the Strait of Juan de Fuca. At low tides during the spring and summer, fine tide pools emerge at the base of the bluffs. ∎

Butterflies of the Sea

When you're ogling tide-pool life at Rosario Beach, don't forget to look for nudibranchs (pronounced NEW-duh-branks)—sea slugs. These aren't your garden-variety slugs. The 1- to 2-inch-long *Phidiana crassicornis,* one of the more common sea slugs in the region, looks like a translucent, illuminated vacuum cleaner made of liquid opal topped with a swaying garden of gold-orange poppies. You also may sight a *Hopkinsia rosacea,* which looks like a hot-pink feather duster, or an *Aeolidia papillosa,* which calls to mind a Salvador Dalí rendition of a Lhasa apso. Some Northwest nudibranchs reach nearly a foot in length, but the majority range from 1 to 3 inches. You'll need a magnifying loupe to see why some marine biologists refer to sea slugs as the butterflies of the sea.

In the San Juans

San Juan and Gulf Islands

■ 786 islands ■ Northwest Washington, in the straits between Washington and Vancouver Island ■ Best months May-Sept. ■ Camping, hiking, boating, boat tours, kayaking, biking, bird-watching, wildlife viewing, wildflower viewing, tide-pooling, whale-watching ■ Contact San Juan Islands Visitor Information Service, P.O. Box 65, Lopez Island, WA 98261; phone 360-468-3663 or 888-468-3701. www.guidetosanjuans.com; or Tourism Association of Vancouver Island, 335 Wesley St., Nanaimo, BC V9R 2T5; phone 250-754-3500

OCEANIC ISLANDS hold a special allure for many travelers. Their mountains, forests, and shorelines seem somehow more exotic than their mainland counterparts. Indeed, an island by definition is a place apart, not easily reached. Instead of merely firing up the Buick, travelers often must journey by boat to reach an island, which adds to the sense of mystery for those of us who are more accustomed to the rhythms of the freeway than the rhythms of the sea.

The San Juan Islands and the Gulf Islands are among those that can only be reached by boat—or small plane—yet they are more easily reached than most islands because an extensive ferry network serves them (see sidebar opposite). This ferry service has led to a compromise between isolation and accessibility; the islands regularly visited by the ferries have been developed to varying degrees, while the bypassed islands are largely if not entirely unpeopled (of course, some are private islands and a few are provincial parks). However, even the most developed islands are lightly settled and blessed with natural beauty and pockets of wildness. Friday Harbor, by far the most populous town in the San Juans, has a population of only 1,730. And the entire 74 square miles of Saltspring, by far the most populous Gulf Island, is home to only about 10,000 people. It should be noted that remoteness alone doesn't account for the lack of development; conscientious land-use planning also has helped preserve the natural surroundings.

This archipelago of 786 islands—some more than 15 miles long, some mere rocks that submerge at high tide—straddles the border between the United States and Canada. Those islands south and east of the sharp-angled international boundary fly the stars and stripes and those to the north and west wave flags bearing the bright red maple leaf, but in bio-geographical terms these islands belong together. They lie in the Strait of Georgia, bounded by the Washington mainland and Vancouver Island. (When he explored the region in 1792, Capt. George Vancouver is said to have mistaken the strait for a gulf—hence the misnomer Gulf Islands.) Shielded from Pacific storms by Vancouver Island and the Olympic Mountains, the San Juan and Gulf Islands bask in some of the region's driest and sunniest weather (about 18 to 30 inches of rain a year, almost all in the winter).

Most visitors who don't have their own boats stick to the dozen or so major islands, which are served by public ferries. These few islands also have nearly all of the archipelago's roads and tourist facilities. Travelers who want to venture to the other islands can charter a boat or catch a water taxi, or view them in passing from a ferry or a whale-watching cruise.

What to See and Do

San Juan Islands

As its name indicates, **San Juan Island** anchors the San Juan Islands. Being the most developed of the group, its charms are more pastoral than natural, but it does possess some worthwhile sites for the outdoor traveler. **American Camp,** a unit of **San Juan Island National Historical Park** *(Cattle Point Rd. 350-378-2240)*, offers several trails that lead through woods and along an unspoiled stretch of southeastern shoreline. In the forest look for deer, foxes, and the glorious pileated woodpecker. Now that the ivory-billed woodpecker is thought to be extinct in North America due to loss of habitat, the

Planning Ahead

The ferries get very crowded during the summer and on fair-weather weekends; waits of several hours aren't uncommon at peak times. Try to go early or late in the day or at a less popular time of year. Likewise, island lodging for the summer can get booked up well in advance, so reserve early. For information on ferry reservations to the San Juan Islands, contact Washington State Ferries, 206-464-6400; to the Gulf Islands contact BC Ferries, 250-386-3431.

Great blue heron at South Pender Island

pileated woodpecker is by far the largest woodpecker in North America, measuring some 16 to 17 inches from the tip of its tail feathers to its scarlet crown. The coastal trail skirts a lagoon where you may see kingfishers, great blue herons, and bald eagles. Bald eagles also have been known to nest in a tree right outside the visitor center.

Drive east from American Camp and in a few minutes you'll come to **Cattle Point,** land's end for southern San Juan Island. Walk to the nearby high point and enjoy views of the San Juans, the Olympic Mountains, and Mount Baker and Mount Rainier, more than 75 miles in the distance.

On the Trail of Killer Whales

As you motor along the scenic, lightly developed western shore of

Look Who's Talking

Killer whales make a lot of noise. For one thing, they emit a rapid series of clicks to echolocate, sometimes transmitting as many as several hundred of these high-energy clicks per second. But the sounds they use to talk to one another are much more elaborate, as befits these very social animals. According to the book *Killer Whales*, scientists divide these vocalizations into three categories: whistles, variable calls, and discrete calls. When members of a pod of killer whales gather close together for an intimate chat, they seem to use the whistles and variable calls, which sound different from one time to the next. But the discrete calls sound exactly the same each time they're used.

Scientists who study killer whales are particularly interested in discrete calls, which may serve to keep foraging pods together. Each pod has its own dialect consisting of anywhere from 5 to 15 discrete calls. Some pods share a few calls, but the repertoire of one pod never overlaps completely with that of another pod. Those pods that share some common calls are said to belong to the same clan. Scientists can use these linguistic markers to identify killer whales. Researchers even have been able to figure out which whales held in captivity in aquariums belong to which pods by identifying their unique dialects.

San Juan Island, you'll come to **Lime Kiln Point State Park** *(360-378-2044 or 800-233-0321)*. On a typical summer day dozens of people will be standing on the stony bluffs and small beach of this modest little park, staring out to sea. Join the sentinels and, if you're lucky, you may discover the reason for their baffling behavior.

With binoculars at the ready, scan the surface of **Haro Strait.** If you see a plume of steam puff into the air, train your binoculars on that spot. Soon a pointed black fin will cut through the water's surface like a knife tip slicing through dark blue fabric. Finally, a body will appear as the creature comes up for air, and you'll get a glimpse of a killer whale, the species that everyone has been hoping to see.

Residents of the San Juans dote on killer whales, also known as orcas. Killer whale wind socks flutter from the decks of many houses, and the shops of Friday Harbor teem with killer whale photos, mugs, and T-shirts. Orcas occupy center stage at the **Whale Museum** *(62 1st St. N., Friday Harbor. 360-378-4710 or 800-946-7227)*. An excellent facility overlooking the harbor, the museum will teach you all sorts of things about all sorts of whales—including the fact that killer whales aren't whales; they're the largest members of the dolphin family. And in case you wondered, they're called killer whales because they are fierce hunters, feeding on salmon, seals, and other dolphins—but not on humans.

If you see one killer whale, you'll almost surely see more. Highly social animals, orcas

Sunlight streaming through morning fog, China Beach (see p. 255)

usually swim about in groups called pods. Scientists have labeled as residents the three pods that regularly forage in the waters around the San Juans in the summer and fall. J-pod has 28 members and K-pod includes 17 orcas; L-pod numbers a whopping 46.

The odds that a killer whale pod will pass by anytime soon are exceedingly small. But if you spend an hour or two at Lime Kiln Point during the summer, you at least have a better chance. The resident killer whales, particularly J-pod, spend much of May, June, and July preying on migrating salmon in Haro Strait, often near the shore.

However, if your heart is set on spotting orcas, you must venture out on a boat that is specifically seeking killer whales. These are often manned by someone who is in contact with the spotters who spend their days tracking the local orcas. And once a boat finds killer whales, it can stay with a pod for an hour or two, providing ample time to see a variety of behaviors and social interactions.

Whale Excursions

A half dozen outfits in the San Juans offer killer whale excursions, most of them are based in Friday Harbor. During the height of the killer whale season, from mid-May to mid-July, your odds of finding orcas are about 90 percent. Some tour operators are so confident of their ability to locate orcas that they offer a rain check to all passengers aboard a boat that fails to find killer whales. A word of caution: Sometimes ignorant boaters inadvertently stress the orcas by approaching too close or by get-

ting between a baby killer whale and the rest of its pod. To make sure you don't contribute to this harassment, go with a company that is a member of the Whale Watching Operators Association of the Northwest *(P.O. Box 2404, Friday Harbor, WA 98250; or contact Whale Museum 360-378-4710)*.

If you do catch up with a pod of killer whales, you'll soon understand what all the fuss is about. For one thing, they're beautiful animals, with their gleaming, smooth skin and those intricate black-and-white markings. They're big and powerful, too; females measure about 25 feet long and weigh about 7 tons and males run about 30 feet and 10 tons. Yet they maneuver quickly and gracefully, like the dolphins they are, as they pursue salmon or other prey. Sometimes orcas jump out of the water and reenter with a splash— a cannonball dive that puts all human attempts to shame. Fairly often they spyhop, rising maybe 6 feet out of the water, as if to have a look around. Orcas also slap the water with their long pectoral fins, swim along the surface upside down, do barrel rolls, and hammer the surface with their tails. These vocal animals have quite a vocabulary, but apparently they don't know the meaning of the word boring.

Other San Juan Islands

As if seeing orcas weren't enough, these excursions provide passengers with sightings of other wildlife and a chance to see some of the hundreds of small isles that throng the archipelago. You'll likely cruise past some of the islands and reefs that constitute

Living Dall's

As you ply the waters around the San Juan and Gulf Islands in a tour boat or ferry, often you'll see a group of what appears to be small killer whales. These winsome creatures are Dall's porpoises. Like killer whales, they sport pretty black-and-white markings, but, unlike killer whales, they belong to the porpoise family. (Killer whales are in the dolphin family.) Dall's porpoises also are much smaller than killer whales, measuring about 6 feet and weighing about 300 pounds. Strong and agile swimmers, Dall's porpoises can reach speeds of 35 mph. Each time they surface to take a breath they cast off a rooster tail of spray. Frequently, a pod of Dall's porpoises—anywhere from 5 to 30 individuals—will seek out a ferry or some other power boat and ride its bow wave. With evident glee, they weave in and out of the wave and dart over and under the bow, sometimes staying with the ship for hours.

the **San Juan Islands National Wildlife Refuge** *(360-457-8451)*.

The larger islands are topped with Pacific madrone and Douglas-fir, some of which contain bald eagle nests. Eagle pairs typically return to the same nest year after year, sometimes for decades, building them up into enormous castles of sticks and vegetation that weigh as much as a ton. Many of the rocks and reefs serve as nesting sites for seabirds, including puffins, cormorants, and auklets, and harbor seals often bask in the sun here. As you scan for killer whales, you may spot minke whales, pilot whales, harbor porpoises, and Dall's porpoises (see sidebar above), often mistaken for baby orcas due to their black-and-white markings.

Of the three other San Juan Islands served by the ferry—Lopez, Orcas, and Shaw—**Orcas Island** has the most to offer the outdoor traveler. Its rugged and scenic topography is crowned by **Mount Constitution,** the high point of 5,000-acre **Moran State Park** *(360-376-2326)*. You can hike or drive to the 2,409-foot summit and then ascend the old stone lookout tower for an even higher vantage point. Signs atop the tower indicate some of the sights this 360-degree view reveals, such as the Canadian Coast Mountains, Vancouver Island, the Gulf Islands, and Mount Rainier. Other trails and roads in the park lead through evergreen forests to lakes and waterfalls.

Moran State Park is the only large natural preserve on Orcas, but the island harbors many small pockets of undeveloped coastline and forest that visitors come across as they drive and cycle the bucolic byways. One such place lies a few hundred yards from the village of Eastsound. Head south on Prune Alley along the eastern shore of East Sound and park at the end of the road. Continue along the shoreline on foot and you'll soon enter **Madrona Point,** a hideaway that gets its name from the groves of Pacific madrones, easily identified by the bright orange-brown-yellow trunks and branches and peeling bark. Informal trails branch off in many directions. Hike down to a few of the secluded little beaches on the sound. At some beaches nearly every footfall stimulates buried clams to spout, sometimes as high as eye level. At others, the cold, clear water shelters intertidal riches, including barnacles, anemones, and, in places, an exceptional diversity and number of crabs.

Gulf Islands

Just across the Canadian border from the San Juans lies Pender Island, the southernmost of the major Gulf Islands. Actually, there are two islands, **North Pender** and **South Pender,** close together and connected by a short wooden bridge. Seven parks and more than 20 beach access points provide ample opportunities to enjoy the forest and seashore, especially on South Pender. Only about 300 people live there versus North Pender's population of 2,000. If you're up for a steep but rewarding 45-minute hike, take one of two trails to the 800-foot summit of **Mount Norman,** located a couple of miles south of the bridge, in **Mount Norman Regional Park** (250-478-3344). The closest trail head is about a quarter-mile down Ainslie Point Road from the bridge and the other is just off Canal Road about 1.5 miles from the bridge. You'll ascend through woodlands of maple, fir, and cedar speckled with wildflowers, including robust purple-blossomed foxglove, some of it so tall you have to look up at it. A wooden platform at the summit yields fine views of the islands and beyond.

Even better views await on several mountaintops on **Salt Spring Island** (Saltspring Island Visitor Center 250-537-5252), the largest of the Gulf Islands. The most accessible summit—you can drive there—is 1,980-foot **Baynes Peak,** located in **Mount Maxwell Provincial Park** (250-391-2300). However, the best hiking can be found at sea level, in **Ruckle Provincial Park** (250-391-2300. Adm. fee). Its 1,200 acres include interior second-growth forest and a long, dramatic stretch of Saltspring's southeast coast. Walk the shoreline trail, which curves along just above the water and the massive seaside rocks. In the intertidal area, look for narrow channels and crevices loaded with seaweed, sea stars, and other marine life.

Several Saltspring outfits offer visitors an unorthodox alternative to tide-pooling on foot: tide-pooling from a kayak, with or without a guide. Particularly on calm, sunny days, you can glide along atop the shallow, lucid water close to the rocks and in little coves, witness to the daily lives of the inter-tidal and subtidal communities. You'll likely see a headless rock sea cucumber, a big, flashy sunflower star on the prowl, and huge purple sea urchins. You'll see larger wildlife, too, such as bald eagles and harbor seals, as you stroke past the lovely shoreline of cobble beaches, stony bluffs, and conifer forest sprinkled with madrones. (Canadians call them arbutus trees.) On longer kayak trips, you might venture farther out and explore some of the islands near Saltspring, perhaps picnicking on your very own deserted island. ■

Claquot Sound and Meares Island

Juan de Fuca Marine Trail

■ 30 miles long ■ Southwest British Columbia, along the western shore of southern Vancouver Island off Hwy. 14 ■ Best season is summer ■ Camping, hiking, backpacking, wildlife viewing, tide-pooling ■ Camping fee ■ Contact BC Parks, South Vancouver Island District, 2930 Trans-Canada Hwy., Victoria, BC V9E 1K3; phone 250-391-2300. www.bcparks.gov.bc.ca

AMAZING HOW A FEW MILES can make quite a difference. On the southeast tip of Vancouver Island sits Victoria, the refined capital city of British Columbia, where tourists take high tea in the elegant Empress Hotel. On the western shoreline of the island, 40 miles distant, is the start of the Juan de Fuca Marine Trail, where black bears roam second-growth forests and human footprints are a relative rarity on remote beaches.

Beginning just west of the tiny town of Jordan River, at China Beach, the marine trail runs 30 miles northwest along the shore of the Strait of Juan de Fuca; it ends at Botanical Beach, just south of the small town of Port Renfrew. The shoreline is a wilderness—no hot dog stands, motels, or even a ranger station. Just beaches, tide pools, forests, wildlife, and solitude. The only significant development is the paved road, which is set back between 0.5 and 3 miles from the coast and goes all the way to Port Renfrew. One other artifact of modern civilization is all too evident, however: clear-cuts. The narrow band of forest that shelters the shore-hugging trail contains a fair bit of older second-growth, but most of the landscape surrounding the road has been heavily and fairly recently logged.

If you're a hardy, experienced backpacker and have several days, you may want to trek the entire length of the Juan de Fuca Marine Trail. The rewards would be great, but be prepared to deal with tides, bears, creek crossings, unpredictable weather, and some rugged sections of trail. Travelers with less time or experience can sample this wild coastline by stopping at any of four trailheads along the main road where spur roads and short trails lead down to the marine trail. If you want to take a long day hike over a section of the main trail, such as the 12 moderately difficult miles from Sombrio Beach to Botanical Beach, you can arrange for a van shuttle back to your car *(West Coast Trail Express 250-477-8700. May-Sept.)*.

Many travelers never go beyond **China Beach,** located at the start of the marine trail. From the parking lot off the highway, you walk down a broad trail through a deep-and-dark Sitka-spruce forest anchored by trees 8 feet in diameter. After a mere 15 minutes, you'll reach the fine sands of China Beach. You can wander along the shore at length to the southeast or a few hundred yards to the northwest end of the beach, where a waterfall dives into the sea.

At the far end of the marine trail, a few miles south of Port Renfrew via a good gravel road, you'll find the trailheads for **Botanical Beach** and **Botany Bay.** Don't miss this spectacular area. You can make a loop by hiking down to Botany Bay, then going southeast along the beach to Botanical Beach, and then returning to the parking lot on the **Botanical Beach Trail**—or by walking this triangle in reverse. You could cover this easy loop in an hour, but you'll likely want to allow several hours for exploring and lingering.

Botany Bay is small but striking. Lush forest presses against the beach. Massive slabs of ridged stone jut from the sand and the nearshore waters. If the tide is below 4 feet and you're sure of foot, you can walk out along these natural rock piers and look at the marine life and the crashing surf. Just offshore, burly sea stacks topped with trees stand guard at the entrance to the bay.

More dramatic scenery awaits at Botanical Beach in the form of craggy bluffs, dense forest, monumental rock formations, and the view across the mouth of the **Strait of Juan de Fuca** to the tip of the **Olympic Peninsula** and beyond to the open Pacific. But you'll probably spend most of your time looking at your feet. Well, not at your feet, literally, but at the marvelous tide pools underfoot, on the rock shelf that is exposed at low tide, especially tides of 4 feet or lower.

The unusual tide pools are themselves as compelling as the life within them. Instead of mere depressions in the intertidal rocks, they are finely sculpted aquariums, some oval, some nearly perfect circles, some but a foot across, some 20 feet from rim to rim. Many are as deep as they are wide. The biological riches in that limpid water include gooseneck barnacles, black leather chitons, sea stars, shore crabs, and vast colonies of purple sea urchins. You may also see forest dwellers grocery shopping in the tide pools, from raccoons and river otters to deer and black bears. ■

Following pages: Along the Juan de Fuca Marine Trail

Pacific Rim National Park Reserve and Vicinity

■ 123,000 acres ■ Southwest British Columbia, along the southwest coast of Vancouver Island, 60 miles west of Port Alberni ■ Best months June-Aug. ■ Camping, hiking, boat tours, kayaking, wildlife viewing, tide-pooling, natural hot springs ■ Adm. fee ■ Reservations required to hike the West Coast Trail ■ Contact the park, 2185 Ocean Terrace Rd., Ucluelet, BC V0R 3A0; phone 250-726-7721. www.harbour.com/parkscan/pacrim/

THE WEST COAST of Vancouver Island exists beyond the bounds of the urban world of malls and traffic jams, even beyond the rural realm of farms and pastures. Scarcely a handful of fishing villages and logging camps interrupt the wildness of hundreds of miles of storm-lashed beaches and dense rain forest. The only paved-road access to this raw coastline, the sole significant link to civilization, is Highway 4 to Pacific Rim National Park Reserve and vicinity.

Via road, hiking trail, floatplane, tour boat, or kayak, you can explore this otherwise inaccessible coastline. You can walk along a broad, sandy beach where the only eyes watching you belong to a bald eagle perched in one of the fringing spruce trees. You can kayak through a maze of small islands and land on one that strikes your fancy, claiming it—temporarily—as your own. You can crouch quietly at the lip of a tide pool and watch the maneuvers of crabs, sculpin, and sea stars. You can tread quietly through the green of the rain forest, gazing up at the canopy of moss-festooned cedars and hemlocks or down at the forest floor alive with ferns, fungi, nurse logs, and banana slugs. You'll be privy to a world that constantly changes yet remains essentially the same today as it was yesterday, the same as it was 1,000 years ago.

What to See and Do
Arriving at the Park
What's it to be? Highway 4, which slips through forested mountains and along the shores of Sproat and Kennedy Lakes for about 60 miles, or a packet freighter that travels about the same distance but follows a different and even more scenic route?

You'll be faced with this choice in Port Alberni, where the two packet freighters are docked; it is situated at the head of Alberni Inlet about 115 miles northwest of Victoria. The ships are set up for passengers as well as cargo, but they don't carry cars. So if you opt for a freighter (*contact Lady Rose Marine Services, P.O. Box 188, Port Alberni, BC V9Y 7M7. 250-723-8313 or 800-663-7192*), either someone in your party will have to drive to the park or you'll have to make do without your own vehicle. (Shuttle vans do operate in the park.)

Once the small coastal freighters, the M.V. *Lady Rose* and the M.V. *Frances Barkley,* depart from the Port Alberni docks, you'll cruise southwest for about the next two hours through the Alberni Inlet, a long, narrow channel framed by beefy mountains and fed by tumbling creeks and icy rivers. You'll likely see deer, Canada geese, and cormorants, plus the occasional black bear and trumpeter swan. The freighter will skirt a multitude of little bays and coves, sometimes stopping at one of these remote embayments to unload supplies for a settlement or a logging camp.

As the ship rounds Chup Point

Safe tide-pooling
Poking around in tide pools and on rocks exposed by low tides is one of the great pleasures of exploring the Northwest coast, but you must do it in a manner that is safe for both you and the rocky intertidal area's inhabitants. For your sake, always face the ocean and watch out for sneaker waves. Wear shoes with good traction and watch your step; wet or algae-covered rocks can be slippery. Know the tides; explore while the tide is ebbing and leave as it starts coming back in. For the sake of the resident flora and fauna, try not to step on living things, which can be quite difficult on thronged intertidal rocks. Never pry a tide-pool animal off a rock; they're literally hanging on for dear life. If you pick up a hermit crab, nudibranch, or some other unattached animal, always return it to the spot where you found it. In general, move slowly, watch carefully, and be gentle.

Sizing up a 700-year-old western redcedar

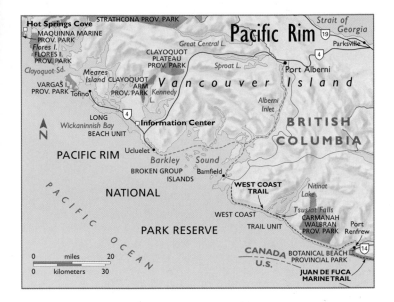

you'll enter **Barkley Sound.** At this point the freighter will head south to Bamfield or west to Ucluelet, depending on which sailing you've chosen. Either way, for the next two or three hours you'll slalom through hundreds of islands, some hardly large enough for a seagull to land on, some hundreds of acres in size. You'll see bald eagles atop some of those trees; a large population lives year-round in Barkley Sound. Other birds frequently sighted include common loons and surf scoters. Some of the islands serve as beaching spots for Steller's sea lions and harbor seals, and you'll sometimes see porpoises and gray whales in the channels.

West Coast Trail

If you go to the small fishing village of **Bamfield**, you'll be at the doorstep of the West Coast Trail, the southernmost of the three geographical units that constitute the national park. This internationally renowned route snakes 45 miles down the coast to Port Renfrew. Do not attempt the West Coast Trail unless you are physically fit, experienced, well equipped, and possessing a permit. This arduous trail passes through absolute wilderness; that is, both the beauty of it and the difficulty of it. Hikers who are willing and able will enjoy the privilege of abundant wildlife, pristine beaches piled with driftwood from savage winter storms, and virgin cedar and hemlock rain forest. Some veterans of the trail assert that cooling off in the shoreside pools below 60-foot **Tsusiat Falls** makes the entire trek worthwhile. From Bamfield you can day hike to the falls and back.

Broken Group Islands

If you select the packet freighter sailing that goes to Ucluelet, you'll pass through the Broken Group Islands, the middle unit of the national park. The Broken Group consists of about 100 islands and rocks scattered over 50 square miles in the middle of Barkley Sound. You also can visit the Broken Group aboard tour boats. But to thoroughly explore these islands, paddle among them in sea kayaks. Several islands have primitive campgrounds to accommodate multiday voyages. However, novice kayakers shouldn't set out on their own; the west coast of Vancouver Island is known as the Graveyard of the Pacific due to severe winter storms, summer fog, and strong tides. A number of commercial outfitters organize and lead journeys into the Broken Group; contact one of them for a worry-free expedition. *(information available from the park).*

Kayakers get a leisurely and intimate look at this enticing ecosystem. Suspended atop the clear water, you can watch barnacles filtering the water for food and hermit crabs search for more commodious shells. You can stop in the canopy of a kelp forest and look for the well-camouflaged kelp crabs. You'll paddle over oyster beds and past rocks thick with mussels. You'll raise your binoculars to watch a passing group of Dall's porpoises (see p. 252) or a basking harbor seal. And when it's time to rest, you can put ashore and picnic on a deserted beach or stroll along grassy bluffs.

Long Beach Unit

When you get off the packet freighter in Ucluelet *(visitor information 250-726-4611),* you'll step onto a paved road that in 5 miles connects to the highway back to Port Alberni. But instead of heading northeast to Port Alberni, take the highway northwest and in a couple of minutes you'll enter the **Long Beach Unit,** the park's most popular and accessible section. If you have no car, pick up The Link shuttle van *(250-726-7779)* to the Long Beach Unit and Tofina at the ferry dock.

The highway runs through the park for about 15 miles, providing access to forest and seashore. Though you'll find a restaurant, the visitor center *(250-726-4212. Mid-March–mid-Oct.),* and a few other trappings of civilization in the Long Beach Unit, the vast majority of the landscape remains wild, an unsullied slice of the primeval west coast of Vancouver Island.

Many visitors rush to the park's famous beaches, but you shouldn't overlook the inland attractions. (Not that they're very far inland; everything in the park is within a mile or so of the coast.) You might start with the **Rain Forest Trail.** Actually, this trail consists of two half-mile loops with interpretive signs that start at the same trailhead, right off the highway. A combination of dirt paths, boardwalks, and wooden stairs, the loops swing through an old-growth forest of hulking western redcedar, Pacific silver fir or amabilis fir, and western hemlock. About 120 inches of rain falls on the Long Beach Unit each year; robust vegetation bursts not only from the ground but from tree trunks, fallen trees, rock crevices, the branches of standing trees, and anywhere else a plant can grab hold.

Not far from the Rain Forest Trail, the high rainfall has produced a startlingly different

Grasses at Wickaninnish Beach

community. The **Bog Trail,** also a half-mile interpretive loop, winds through a poorly drained area in which much of the precipitation pools. (To prevent visitors from sinking, most of the path is a boardwalk.) The high water table and acidic conditions promote the growth of sphagnum moss, which blankets the bog's surface. In some places you can lightly press the "ground" and it will shake like jello. (Be gentle; the sphagnum community is fragile.)

The few trees that grow in the bog are stunted by the lack of nutrition; a 300-year-old shore-pine may be little taller than a basketball hoop. Though the bog lacks majestic, 250-foot trees, it boasts some awesome flora at the other end of the spectrum. Kneel on the boardwalk and scan the mat of moss for a carnivorous plant called a sundew. You'll recognize it by the sparkling droplets that dot the reddish fringes of its one-inch leaves. These are not raindrops but sticky traps set for small insects. When ants or flies become stuck to the leaf, it slowly curls around the victim and digests it with an enzyme. This meat diet provides the sundew with nitrogen, which is scarce in the nutrient-poor bog.

Wickaninnish Beach

Now back to those famous beaches. To make the acquaintance of the beach that gave this park unit its name, take the first available side road that leads to the coast. This 2-mile spur leads down to Wickaninnish Beach and Wickaninnish Centre. From a viewing deck beside the visitor center, you can look northwest and take in the whole 7-mile sweep of Long Beach, of which Wickaninnish Beach is a part. This broad, sandy beach gently curves along Wickaninnish Bay. Old-growth Sitka-spruce forest towers just behind the beach. Half-buried driftwood logs, creeks feeding into the Pacific, and rocky points at either end punctuate the fine sand expanse. About half a mile off-shore from the midpoint of Long Beach, sea lions bark and grumble from some small islands inevitably named **Sea Lion Rocks.** Long Beach begs you to take lazy, barefoot walks—you can stroll all 7 miles if you feel like it. (Crossing **Sandhill Creek,** a couple of miles down the beach from Wickaninnish, results in wet legs when the creek is running unusually high.) To see other parts of the beach with less effort, two other spur roads farther along the highway also provide access.

Long Beach is not the only beach worth visiting. Check out the rocky headlands that start just south of Wickaninnish Centre. You can reach them by taking the half-mile **South Beach Trail,** which curves along the edge of the shoreline Sitka-spruce forest. At several points you can walk down to coves interspersed among the headlands. Some of them harbor excellent rocky intertidal areas, rich with finger limpets, black chitons, gooseneck barnacles, purple shore crabs, and more than the usual sightings of sunflower stars—the largest and fastest of all sea stars. Don't overlook some of the large, shallow channels through the sand, where flounders ripple sideways over the sandy bottoms and Dungeness crabs come to molt, shedding their old shells by backing out through a slit in the abdomen. Sometimes the outgoing tide strands small fish in shallow pools and bald eagles and ravens swoop down to feed on them.

Storm-watching

Storms generate hulking 20- and 30-foot waves, whose size depends on the storm's area, wind speed, and duration. The storm can be just offshore or 1,000 miles away. In 1999, four huge storms battered the Northwest with waves whose "significant height" (the average of the highest one-third of the waves) measured more than 33 feet in deep waters. One storm in March packed a significant wave height of more than 45 feet, which means the biggest waves topped 80 feet. To see big waves, seek out a steep coastline—gradually sloping beaches make the waves break far offshore—and behold the force of nature from a safe vantage point.

South Beach

If you continue along the trail, you'll soon arrive at South Beach, which differs dramatically from the open, soft-sand expanse of Long Beach. The beach itself is small and consists of smooth pebbles that "sing" as the surf knocks them about. All around stand massive rocks, including a double sea arch. At the north-west end of the beach, waves snarl through huge surge chan-nels, creating a fury of spray and foam. South Beach is great for winter storm-watching (see sidebar this page), though you must exercise caution: The monster breakers occasionally rush up all the way to the edge of the forest.

Outside the Park

After passing through the park, Highway 4 continues for several miles until its reaches the little fishing and tourist town of Tofino (visitor information 250-725-3414). This is literally the end of the road. Past Tofino lies mile upon mile of wilderness, starting just outside of town with Clayoquot Sound. You may have heard of Clayoquot. For years local citizens and environmentalists have been fighting efforts to log the dense rain forests that cover the islands and mountains of this sublime sound. (Vancouver Island as a whole has been heavily logged.) Most of the sound's core area remains uncut, and efforts are being made to create a biosphere reserve here, ensuring that logging would be conducted in a sustainable manner.

One site of controversy in the late 1980s was Meares Island, a 20,000-acre island that lies just north of Tofino. You can take a water taxi over to Meares and hike the two-hour Big Trees Trail and see what it is the locals wanted to save and the timber companies wanted to cut. Meares shelters the world's largest known western redcedars, which measure as much as 15 feet in diameter, and some of Canada's largest hemlock and spruce.

The excursion to Meares Island is but one of dozens of outings for which Tofino serves as base camp. You can take four-hour or four-day kayak trips through Clayoquot Sound. A glass-bottom boat affords views of undersea life from a warm and dry cabin. Numerous tour boats conduct whale-watching trips, especially from about mid-March to mid-April, when migrating grays are passing close to shore.

One of the most popular destinations is **Hot Springs Cove,** part of **Maquinna Marine Provincial Park** *(250-954-4600),* located about 25 miles north of Tofino and accessible by boat or floatplane. From the park's dock, visitors hike about a mile on a boardwalk trail through the forest to a cluster of natural hot springs. The half-dozen rock pools vary in temperature from about 80°F to 120°F.

You can reach Hot Springs Cove quickly by air, but if you have time, take one of the small tour boats that operate out of Tofino. The best part of the trip is the four or five hours you'll spend exploring the sound on your way to and from Hot Springs Cove. You may see young bald eagles peering out from their treetop nest. Even when it's not peak gray whale migration, you'll often spot grays or perhaps a minke whale. Your captain may back into a 40-foot wide island channel overgrown by huge cedars and spruce, where a waterfall swan dives from the steep hillside above and bright ocher sea stars cling to the rocks in the clear water below. On rare occasions, fortunate visitors will spot a 40-foot shark off **Flores Island,** but don't worry, this is not a creature from *Jaws.* It's a harmless basking shark calmly feeding on plankton. Always, as you meander among the mountainous, heavily forested islands and the west-reaching fingers of mainland Vancouver Island, you will experience the fantastic wildness of Vancouver Island's west coast. ■

Sunshine Coast

■ 80 miles long ■ Southwest British Columbia, from Gibsons north to Lund ■ Best months late May–Sept. ■ Camping, boating, boat tours, kayaking, canoeing, wildlife viewing, scuba diving ■ Contact Upper Sunshine Coast, Powell River Visitors Bureau, 4690 Marine Ave., Powell River, BC V8A 2L1, phone 604-485-4701; or Lower Sunshine Coast, Gibson & District Chamber of Commerce, 668 Sunnycrest Rd., Gibsons, BC V0N 1V0, phone 604-886-2325. www.thesunshinecoast.org/

THOUGH IT BEARS the kind of name that tourism boosters would concoct, the Sunshine Coast comes by its label honestly. This 80-mile stretch of southern British Columbia coast, only 25 miles from downtown Vancouver, curves along the Strait of Georgia in the lee of Vancouver Island. Shielded from ocean storms, it gets a mere 35 to 40 inches of precipitation a year. But sunshine is hardly the only attraction. This ragged coastline brims with beaches, deep inlets, islands, isolated coves, lakes, rivers, waterfalls, and forests, all backed by the steep mountains of the coast range. Its topography makes the Sunshine Coast a boater's paradise. If you are boatless, you can weigh anchor aboard tour boats, charters, and guided kayak and canoe trips.

The Sunshine Coast at sunset

What to See and Do

Travelers also can drive the Sunshine Coast via Highway 101, aided mid-drive by a short hop on a car ferry. You can start by taking a ferry from Horseshoe Bay in the Vancouver area to Gibsons, which anchors the southern end of the Sunshine Coast. Or you can ferry over from Comox, on Vancouver Island, to Powell River, which is located about 15 miles south of Lund, on the northern end of the Sunshine Coast. The ferries get crowded during the summer and on weekends, so either arrive early or keep your schedule flexible.

Lund sits at the end of Highway 101, an extension of which begins in southern California and follows the coast north. As befits such a location, Lund is a tiny, edge-of-civilization place where you can sit and watch bald eagles fish in the harbor. Lund also serves as the gateway to sumptuous **Desolation Sound Marine Provincial Park** (*BC Provincial Parks 604-898-3678*), the province's largest marine park and one of the most scenic. From Lund you also can take a 15-minute hop on a water taxi to the enticing sandy beaches of **Savary Island.**

Just 15 miles south of Lund, Highway 101 takes you through a much larger town, Powell River, that serves as a staging area for many outdoor ventures. The **Powell Forest Canoe Route** loops through the mountains just east of Powell River, stringing together eight forest-fringed lakes with four other optional connections. The town also is a scuba-diving mecca. People who envision scuba diving as a tropical activity will be surprised by the dozens of fine dive sites and the rich underwater world populated by red coral, wolf eels, radiant sunflower stars, and 6-foot lingcod.

Regional and provincial parks crop up throughout the Sunshine Coast. The most unusual bears a fittingly unusual name: **Skookumchuck Narrows Provincial Park** (*BC Provincial Parks 604-898-3678*). Skookumchuck means "strong water" in the local Chinook language, which makes it an ideal name for this bottleneck in **Sechelt Inlet,** on the inland side of the **Sechelt Peninsula** near the town of Egmont. A 2.5-mile trail through a second-growth forest leads to two vantage points on the hillside right above the narrows.

Mac's Gift

Prospector James F. "Mac" Macdonald first visited Princess Louisa Inlet in 1919, and when he hit paydirt in 1926, he bought the property around Chatterbox Falls. "This beautiful, peaceful haven should never belong to one individual," he said. "I have felt that I was only the custodian of the property for Nature." True to his word, Mac gave the land to the public in 1953; during the summers he moored his houseboat there until 1972, his 83rd year.

Observing Tides

Get a tide table from a local store and arrive at the vantage points just before the tide shifts from outgoing to incoming or vice versa. Pick a time when there will be a large change in the height of the tide; from a low tide of 3 feet to a high of 13, for example. Outgoing tides are best viewed from **North Point** and incoming tides from **Roland Point** (another ten minutes down the trail). When the tide shifts, you'll witness the phenomenon of 200 billion gallons of water squeezing through the shallow, 200-yard-wide channel.

The still water of the inlet becomes an angry river, churning and swirling, reaching speeds of 15, even 20 miles an hour. Whitewater rapids appear where there are no rocks. Monstrous eddies send water in the opposite direction of the flow. Whirlpools pock the inlet's surface, some 50 feet wide and 6 feet deep. Logs sucked into this chaos can drift and spin for an hour without making any progress through the narrows. The difference in water level from one side of the narrows to the other can be more than 6 feet.

Princess Louisa Inlet

Princess Louisa Inlet, 30 miles north of Skookumchuck, is arguably the standout site on the Sunshine Coast. Contrary to what you might think, this inlet actually lies deep in the mountains. Several companies based around the Sechelt Peninsula offer boat tours that take 10 to 20 passengers on all-day, 100-mile round-trip voyages to this shoreline Shangri-la.

Some trips begin in **Pender**

Desolation Sound

Harbor, a natural bay on the peninsula's west side that is strewn with islands and coves. Resorts and waterfront homes dot the shore, but as you leave the harbor and turn north up **Agamemnon Channel** you quickly leave behind most signs of civilization. After half an hour the boat enters **Jervis Inlet,** which snakes 35 miles northeast through the Coast Mountains. Even in those first few miles, 5,000-foot snowcapped peaks rise up out of the depths of the ocean. About 10 miles up Jervis Inlet, you pass under the shadow of the area's highest peak, 6,480-foot **Mount Churchill,** a Matterhorn-shaped mountain.

Lower your gaze and you'll see slopes forested with yellow-orange madrones and conifers, shoreline rocks plastered with oysters and sea stars, bald eagles circling overhead, and, on rare occasions, mountain goats. And you'll see lots of waterfalls. If the snow is melting in the high country or if rain has fallen recently, many, many waterfalls may appear, some sliding hundreds of feet down those steep mountain slopes, some cascading thousands of feet. Often the falls take shape as thin white stripes ribboning down dark rock faces.

After about three hours you'll finally turn into Princess Louisa Inlet, a narrow, 5-mile long fjord framed by more 6,000-foot mountains, their massive granite faces streaked by dozens of waterfalls. At the end of the inlet lies **Chatterbox Falls,** which tumbles nearly a mile, tier by tier, until it finishes with a 120-foot plunge into the water. ∎

Garibaldi Provincial Park

■ 480,000 acres ■ Southwest British Columbia, 60 miles north of Vancouver
■ Best months July-Sept. ■ Camping, hiking, backpacking, skiing, back-country skiing, wildlife viewing, mountaineering ■ Camping fee ■ Contact BC Parks, Box 220, Brackendale, BC V0N 1H0; phone 604-898-3678

IMAGINE YOURSELF AN EAGLE flying over the middle of Garibaldi Provincial Park from east to west. Your shadow folds over jagged, 8,000-foot peaks, their upper elevations frosted in snow even in summer. Massive glaciers cling to the flanks of some of the mountains, the ice slashed with aqua-tinted crevasses. In the higher valleys, the green of alpine meadows mingles with the blue-green of glacial lakes, while the lower valleys and slopes bristle with a thick forest of Douglas-fir, western redcedar, and western hemlock. As you gaze down on this mountain redoubt, you probably never imagine this beautiful landscape is part of the British Columbia coast. But it is part of the coast. For as you exit Garibaldi at its southwest boundary, the salt water is a few miles ahead.

The relation of the park to the coast was evident right from the park's inception. Mount Garibaldi, the inspiration for the formation of the eponymous park, was discovered by a naval captain who was standing aboard a survey ship in Howe Sound, an arm of the Strait of Georgia. But even though this half-million-acre chunk of British Columbia's coast range is part of the coastal ecosystem, it differs radically from the Sunshine Coast beaches a few miles to the west.

Volcanic eruptions and a massive uplifting of granite provided the raw material for the park, but glaciers accounted for most of the dramatic surface landscape that you see today. During the last glacial period of the ice ages, which peaked about 15,000 years ago, mammoth flows of ice—up to a couple of miles long and a thousand feet thick—carved the cirques, U-shaped valleys, and many other park features.

Visitors without exceptional stamina and outdoor skills must gain access to Garibaldi from the west; to the east is raw wilderness. An hour's drive from the city of Vancouver on Highway 99 takes you to the southwest corner of the park, and from there the road continues along the western border. In five places spur roads take visitors east to the park boundary, each leading to one of the five access areas within Garibaldi. However, the park has opted for minimal development, with no elaborate visitor centers or bathrooms with hot showers, but merely established trails and the occasional pit toilet and patrolling ranger.

What to See and Do

Diamond Head Area

Visitors heading north from Vancouver on Highway 99 come to Mamquam Road, the first of the roads to Garibaldi, about 2 miles north of the town of Squamish. Take this logging road east about 10 miles to the section of the park

Atop Whistler Mountain

known as the Diamond Head area. When you leave the highway, you'll wind along the Mamquam River and Ring Creek and then cross into the park and climb northwest into the high country. You'll enjoy some fine views along the way, especially as you near the parking lot at the end of the road, which lies above 3,000 feet.

To get more than a glimpse of the Diamond Head area, you must forsake your car and take the trail that meanders generally northeast from the parking lot. Three miles of gradual ascent brings hikers to **Red Heather Meadows,** an expanse covered in summer with wildflowers and, of course, red heather. Four miles and many vistas farther up **Paul Ridge,** the trail hits **Elfin Lakes.** Here visitors can shuck their backpacks, loll by the small, icy lakes, and gaze at Columnar Peak, Mamquam Icefield, Opal Cone, and the Gargoyles, some dramatically eroded rock formations. Visitors equipped for overnight stays can camp near Elfin Lakes and take trails deeper into the park (public shelter is also available). Diamond Head is also a popular wilderness winter recreation area.

Black Tusk/Garibaldi Lake Area

Drive about 20 miles north from Mamquam Road on Highway 99 and you'll arrive at the second of the spur roads to Garibaldi. This 1.5-mile drive takes visitors up to the Rubble Creek parking lot, from which a trail leads into the heart of the park: The Black Tusk/Garibaldi Lake area.

The trail to Garibaldi Lake, nearly 6 miles one way with an elevation gain of about 2,500 feet, makes a long and tiring but worthwhile day hike. It switchbacks relentlessly uphill for the first 4 miles, but the grade isn't too steep and the trail generally is excellent. The scenery along this first stretch is gloriously monotonous and outstanding: acre after acre of gargantuan, old-growth western redcedar and Douglas-fir. After this 4-mile climb, you pass the **Barrier,** a wall of volcanic rock. From here the trail levels out as it leads from little **Barrier Lake** to slightly larger **Lesser Garibaldi Lake** to really large Garibaldi Lake.

Garibaldi Lake is the focal point of this diverse area. The west bank of the lake houses park rangers and a sizeable campground. (A smaller campground is located at Taylor Meadows, about a mile away.) The lake itself is stunning: almost 1,000 feet deep, several miles long, surrounded by sawtooth peaks and glaciers. No doubt some visitors pitch a tent by the lake and spend days there, savoring their surroundings.

But when you're ready to explore further, you have several dazzling options. An easy mile's walk northwest from the Garibaldi Lake campground, **Taylor Meadows** spreads its many-hued carpet across the relatively flat terrain between Taylor and Parnasus Creeks. The trail wanders amid the purple-blue of sweet-smelling arctic lupine; the magenta, tube-like blooms of Lewis's monkey flower; the delicate little pink blossoms of mountain heather; the radiant yellow of the glacier lily, which pushes up through the snow in its eagerness to begin reproducing; and a multitude of other wildflow-

Land Above the Trees

Some 40 percent of the tundra in North America is alpine tundra, where altitude more than latitude accounts for the defining conditions. By definition, alpine tundra exists above timberline and below the line of perpetual snow. The plants and animals that inhabit this harsh world have evolved some notable adaptations in order to survive the extreme cold, the scouring winds, and exposure to the sunlight of high elevations. Marmots, for example, lower their body temperatures to just above freezing and hibernate for as long as eight months. One species of alpine buttercup spreads its flowering process over four years as a way of dealing with the tundra's truncated growing season. Study this demanding realm, and you'll learn to appreciate the resilience of life.

ers. Taylor Meadows is particularly lush in July and August.

A fairly tough hike will take you north from Garibaldi Lake to the base of the isolated volcanic tower that is **The Black Tusk,** but you'll probably find the scenery along the way makes part of the 3-mile, 1,800-foot-elevation-gain push worth doing. The first half of the hike is pretty gentle and yet offers considerable rewards. Within half an hour of leaving the lake, you'll be strolling through subalpine meadows strewn with summer wildflowers and dotted with little lakes of dark blue water. At times the trail threads through steeply tilted meadows on the mountain flanks. As you look down the slope, flowers seem to be cascading to the earth below, and as you look up it seems as if a tidal wave of blossoms is about to crash on your head. Much of this hillside trail also yields fine views of Garibaldi Lake and the surrounding mountains, including The Black Tusk. You can continue along the trail, with care and caution, and right up to the summit of this 7,600-foot peak, though the last

few hundred yards require technical climbing.

People lacking ropes and expertise but seeking comparable views can branch off to the east about halfway up The Black Tusk trail and head about a mile and a half to the crest of **Panorama Ridge.** Stride for stride, this may be the most gorgeous hike in the park. You rise above the bonsai conifers near tree line and wind through a landscape of ground-hugging alpine plants. The trail curves past **Mimulus,** The Black Tusk, and **Helm Lakes,** the views improving with every step. As you approach the **Helm Glacier,** the trail turns south and starts climbing Panorama Ridge. Below to the west and north you can see the meadows, Helm Creek, and The Black Tusk.

The final half mile requires a reasonable level of fitness and agility. The trail gets steep and you must scramble over loose rocks and sometimes snow, even in summer. So you'll be out of breath when you reach the summit, but the views would take away your breath anyway. Standing atop the pinnacle—a fairly flat knob about

Following pages: Mountain biker heading into Singing Pass

the size of a large living room—
you get unobstructed views for
miles in all directions.

Directly below the ridge to
the south sprawls Garibaldi
Lake, its light blue-green glacial
water oddly reminiscent of tropical seas. To the north you can
gaze along the alpine meadows
bordering Helm Creek to the
forests around the **Cheakamus
River.** The Black Tusk looms
near, and not too much higher
than your 7,000-foot perch.
Also near eye level are **Gentian
Peak, Helm Peak, Mount Price,**
and a horizon full of other sharp-
shouldered mountains, many
draped with glistening glaciers.
Pull out your trail mix and sit
here a spell.

Northern Approaches

The third spur road angles off
Highway 99 about 7 miles north
of The Black Tusk/Garibaldi Lake
turnoff. From the logging road
turn left toward the park, where
the road dead-ends at a parking
lot, the jump-off point for the
Cheakamus Lake area. An easy
trail passes through old-growth
forest along the Cheakamus River.
Note the clear creeks feeding into
the Cheakamus, their crystalline
waters soon lost in the milky green
glacial river. The canopy of beefy
western redcedar, Douglas-fir, and
western hemlock creates a cool
forest floor, thick with moss,
robust skunk cabbage, and devil's
club reaching higher than your
head. After about 2 miles, the trail

comes to the west end of the lake, where there's a camping area. Mountains rise some 2,000 feet above, providing a scenic frame for this 4-mile-long lake. The trail continues along the northeast shore for another couple of miles, ending at a second camping area.

Less than 2 miles north of the road to Cheakamus, the highway enters the posh ski resort of Whistler Village. The fourth spur road used to lead from Whistler to the trailhead for the **Singing Pass area,** but collapses due to unstable soils have closed the road for the foreseeable future. Now this beautiful alpine area is accessible only to backpackers or to those who are willing and able to make the 15-mile round-trip trek. The rewards are a profusion of wildflowers and fine views of the Spearhead Mountains and Cheakamus Glacier.

Another option is to take the chair lift *(fee)* to the top of Whistler Mountain, then hike into Garibaldi over the **Musical Bumps** and over the Singing Pass before joining the closed road.

The last spur road takes off from Highway 99 about 8 miles north of Whistler. The 2-mile road leads to the 4-mile trail that climbs into the **Wedgemount Lake area.** This is one tough trail, ascending about 4,000 feet and, near the end, crossing a tricky, boulder-strewn slope. But the rewards include a slender 1,000-foot waterfall, a chance at sighting mountain goats, and terrific high-country views. ■

Backpackers on the Garibaldi Lake Trail

Other Sites

The following is a select list of other sites of interest located in the Pacific Northwest.

South Coast

Aufderheide Scenic Byway

This 60-mile scenic drive leads through a pretty section of the western Cascades in western Oregon. It follows three rivers and serves up some soaring old-growth forest. Snow closes the route in winter. The byway runs from just east of Blue River to Oreg. 58, through the town of West Fir. Contact the Middle Fork Ranger District, Willamette National Forest, P.O. Box 1410, Oakridge, OR 97463; phone 541-782-2283.

Bullards Beach State Park

A 3-mile drive through coastal forest and along a bird-rich estuary brings you to several uncrowded miles of sandy beach. Where the beach meets the mouth of the Coquille River stands a historic lighthouse. Bullards Beach lies just north of Bandon on the southern Oregon coast. Contact the Oregon Parks and Recreation Department; phone 800-551-6949.

Oregon Coast Aquarium

An outstanding aquarium devoted to regional marine life. The many acres of indoor and outdoor exhibits feature sea otters, wolf eels, sharks, moon jellies, puffins, and hundreds of other species. Docents, videos, and a learning lab make a visit informative as well as fascinating. Bring your curiosity to Newport, on the central Oregon coast. Contact the aquarium, 2820 SE Ferry Slip Rd., Newport, OR 97395; phone 541-867-3474. Adm. fee.

Rogue River Gorge

Surrounded by lush forest, walk along a paved interpretive trail that winds above this 40-foot deep, 25-foot wide chasm gouged from volcanic bedrock and collapsed lava tubes. The gorge is located about 12 miles north of Prospect. Contact Prospect Ranger District, Rogue River National Forest, 47201 Hwy. 62, Prospect, OR 97536; phone 541-560-3400.

South Cascades

Cove Palisades State Park

Beneath the striking basalt cliffs shimmers the Lake Billy Chinook, the mainstay of this 4,130-acre park in central Oregon. Cove Palisades is located about 10 miles southwest of Madras. Contact the Oregon Parks and Recreation Department; phone 800-551-6949.

Fort Rock State Natural Area

The area's centerpiece is a 325-foot volcanic tower that rises dramatically above the sagebrush flats of the high desert. Pronghorn, large herds of mule deer, and a variety of raptors inhabit the area. You'll find Fort Rock about 70 miles southeast of Bend, just off Oreg. 31. Contact the Oregon Parks and Recreation Department; phone 800-551-6949.

High Desert Museum

This excellent museum is devoted to the natural and cultural history of the high desert. Inside, you can take in displays on snakes, fish, lizards, burrowing owls, and other denizens of the desert. Outside, you can view porcupines, river otters, and birds of prey in their natural habitats. The museum is about 3 miles south of Bend on US 97, in central Oregon. Contact the museum, 59800 S. Hwy. 97, Bend, OR 97702; phone 541-382-4754. Adm. fee.

Julia Butler Hansen National Wildlife Refuge for the Columbian White-tailed Deer

Nearly 5,500 acres of Columbia River floodplain harbor river otters, bald eagles, Canada geese, beavers, elk, and endangered Columbian white-tailed deer. A dike road makes wildlife viewing easy. The refuge is located on the Columbia about 25 miles west of Kelso, in southwest Washington. Contact the refuge at P.O. Box 566, Cathlamet, WA 98612; phone 360-795-3915.

High Desert

Diamond Craters Outstanding Natural Area

Dirt roads lead motorists on a self-guided tour of high-desert lands characterized by craters, spatter cones, domes, lava tubes, and other volcanic features. Diamond Craters lies just east of the midsection of Malheur National Wildlife Refuge, in southeast Oregon. Contact Burns District BLM, HC 74, 12533 Hwy. 20 West, Hines, OR 97738; phone 541-573-4400.

Wallowa Lake State Park

A small (200-acre) park in a big setting, it sits at the southern end of this classic glacial lake beneath the high peaks of the Eagle Cap Wilderness. You can hike, picnic, swim, fish, or take the gondola 3,200 vertical feet up to the 8,200-foot summit of Mount Howard. Located in northeast Oregon a few miles from Joseph. Contact the Oregon Parks and Recreation Department; phone 800-551-6949.

Central Plateau

Mount Spokane State Park

A ski area in winter, 5,878-foot Mount Spokane serves as a superb lookout point during the summer. From Vista House, an old lookout, you can gaze into Idaho, Oregon, Montana, and Canada. This park is located 30 miles northeast of Spokane, in eastern Washington. Contact Washington State Parks; phone 509-238-6845 or 800-233-0321.

McNary National Wildlife Refuge

A self-guided trail lets you sample a few of this refuge's 3,629 acres of wetlands and grasslands. Up to 100,000 ducks, geese, and swans congregate here during spring and fall migrations. This wildlife spectacle occurs a few miles southeast of Pasco, in south-central Washington. Contact Mid-Columbia River National Wildlife Refuge Complex, P.O. Box 2527, Pasco, WA 99302; phone 509-545-8588.

William L. Finley National Wildlife Refuge

A remnant of the pre-agriculture Willamette Valley, these 5,325 acres include wetlands, bottomland ash forest, oak savanna, and other now-rare habitats. Famed for its waterfowl, the William L. Finley refuge also harbors deer, frogs, hawks, and a herd of elk. It is located 12 miles south of Corvallis in northwest Oregon. Contact the refuge at 26208 Finley Refuge Rd., Corvallis, OR 97333; phone 541-757-7236.

Little Pend Oreille National Wildlife Refuge

This diverse 40,000-acre refuge encompasses six forest zones, from the ponderosa pine and Douglas-fir below 2,000 feet up to the sub-alpine fir above 4,500 feet. The wildlife is likewise diverse and includes black bears, mink, golden and bald eagles, and the refuge's specialty—white-tailed deer. The refuge entrance is located 11 miles southeast of Colville, in northeast Washington. Contact the refuge at 1310 Bear Creek Rd., Colville, WA 99114; phone 509-684-8384.

North Cascades

Northwest Trek Wildlife Park

Northwest Trek falls somewhere between a zoo and wilderness. Visitors take a tram through the 435 acres of forest, wetlands, and meadows to view free-roaming bison, elk, bighorn sheep, and other native northwest animals. It is located in western Washington, 17 miles south of Puyallup on Wash. 161. Contact the park, 11610 Trek Dr. East, Eatonville, WA 98328; phone 360-832-6117. Daily, April-Oct., Fri.-Sun. Nov.-March, Adm. fee.

Skagit River Bald Eagle Natural Area

Each winter, peaking on about January 1, several hundred bald eagles come to this stretch of the Skagit to feast on spawned-out salmon. You can watch the eagles by joining volunteers armed with spotting scopes at designated viewpoints or by taking guided raft trips down the river. Look for the Bald Eagle Festival the first weekend in February. The eagles concentrate on the Skagit just east of Rockport, in northwest Washington. Contact the Upper Skagit Bald Eagle Festival, P.O. Box 571, Concrete, WA 98237; phone 360-853-7009.

North Coast

George C. Reifel Migratory Bird Sanctuary

The Fraser River delta and estuary are rich with bird-watching hotspots, and the George C. Reifel Refuge is perhaps the hottest of all. With a bird list that includes 268 species, it is best known for the 20,000 snow geese that flock here during the fall and early winter. The refuge is located about 45 minutes from Vancouver, at the mouth of the Fraser River in southwest British Columbia. Contact the refuge at 5191 Robertson Rd., Delta, B.C., V4K 3N2, Canada; phone 604-946-6980. Adm. fee.

Resources

The following is a select list of resources. Contact state and local associations for additional outfitter and lodging options. For chain hotels and motels operating in the Pacific Northwest, see p. 281.

OREGON

Federal and State Agencies

Forest Service Fall Color Hotline
800-354-4595 (only in fall)

Nature of the Northwest
800 N.E. Oregon St.,
Suite 177
Portland, OR 97232
503-872-2750

www.naturenw.org
The Forest Service's information center. Maps and books; information on campgrounds, cabin rentals, national forests, and Bureau of Land Management lands.

Oregon Department of Fish and Wildlife
P.O. Box 59
Portland, OR 97207
503-872-5268
www.dfw.state.or.us
Fishing and hunting information and licenses

Oregon Parks and Recreation Department
1115 Commercial St., NE
Salem, OR 97310
800-551-6949 for information
800-452-5687 reservations
www.prd.state.or.us

Oregon Tourism Commission
775 Summer St. NE
Salem, OR 97310
800-547-7842
www.traveloregon.com
Information on camping, lodging, outdoor activities, sites, events, and more.

Portland Oregon Bicycle Program
1120 S.W. 5th St, Rm. 730
Portland, OR 97204
503-823-CYCL
State bike trails information, maps

Outfitters and Activities

Hellgate Jetboat Excusions
966 SW 6th Street
Grants Pass, OR 97526
541-479-7204 or
800-648-4874

www.hellgate.com
Jet-boat tours to Hellgate
Canyon; white-water trips
through canyon.

High Country Outfitters
P.O. Box 26
Joseph, OR 97846
541-432-9171
Combo float and horse-
packing trips through
Hells Canyon.

**Hurricane Creek Llama
Treks, Inc.**
63366 Pine Tree Rd.
Enterprise, OR 97828
541-432-4455 or
800-528-9609
www.hcltrek.com
Week-long treks in Hells
Canyon and the Wallowa
Mountains. June-Aug.

**Oregon Guides and Packers
Association**
P.O. Box 673
Springfield, OR 97477
541-937-3192 or
800-747-9552
www.ogpa.org
Directory of Oregon out-
fitters; information on
packages and tours

Lodgings

**Oregon Bed and
Breakfast Guild**
P.O. Box 3187
Ashland, OR 97520
800-944-6196
www.obbg.com
For information on B&Bs
throughout the state.

**Crater Lake NP
and vicinity**
Southwestern Oregon Visi-
tors Association
88 E. Stewart Ave.
Medford, OR 97501
541-779-4691
Information on lodgings in
southwestern Oregon

Lodging is also available in
the distant gateway towns
of Klamath Falls (80 miles)
541-884-5193, and Medford
(60 miles) 541-779-4847.

Crater Lake Lodge; Mazama
Village Motor Inn
P.O. Box 2704
White City, OR 97503
541-830-8700 (winter),
541-594-2511 (summer)
Both located inside the
park. Both seasonal; length

of season varies for each.

Diamond Lake Resort
Diamond Lake, OR 97731
541-793-3333
Rooms and cabins.
Located a few miles out-
side Crater Lake NP.

Rocky Point Resort
28121 Rocky Point Rd.
Klamath Falls, OR 97601
541-356-2287
Rooms, cabins, camping;
boat and canoe rentals.

Mount Hood vicinity

Mount Hood Information
Center
65000 E. Hwy. 26,
Welches, OR 97067
503-622-4822 or
888-622-4822.
www.mthood.com
Information on lodging,
dining, winter recreation,
and more.

Timberline Lodge
Timberline Lodge, OR
97028
503-622-7979 or
800-547-1406 (reserva-
tions) www.timber-
linelodge.com
1937 stone-and-timber
lodge; luxury amenities.

Hells Canyon NRA

Gateway towns offer a wide
range of accommodations.
Contact the Chambers of
Commerce in Joseph, OR.
(541-432-1015), and Lewiston, ID (208-743-3531).

Copper Creek Lodge
P.O. Box 1243
Lewiston, ID 83501
208-743-4800 or
800-522-6966
22 cabins overlooking
river. Closed Jan.-Feb.
Accessible by river and
trail only.

Camping

Crater Lake NP

The national park offers
two campgrounds (Lost
Creek and Mazama); no
reservations. Tent sites only
at Lost Creek.

The Forest Service oper-
ates campgrounds in the
surrounding national
forests. Contact the Rogue

River (541-858-2200.
www.fs.fed.us/r6/rogue),
Siskiyou (541-471-6500.
www.fs.fed.us/r6/siskiyou),
Deschutes (541-388-2715.
www.fs.fed.us/r6/deschutes),
and Umpqua National
Forests (541-672-6601.
www.fs.fed.us/r6/umpqua)
for more information. Some
campgrounds may be
reserved (877-444-6777.
www.reserveusa.com). Ad-
ditional information on the
Great Outdoor Recreation
Pages (www.gorp.com).

Hells Canyon NRA

The Forest Service oper-
ates campgrounds in the
surrounding Wallowa-
Whitman (541-523-1405.
www.fs.fed.us/r6/w-w),
Payette (208-634-0700), and
Nez Perce (208-983-1950)
national forests. Additional
information on the Great
Outdoor Recreation Pages
(www.gorp.com).

WASHINGTON

State and Federal
Agencies

Washington Department
of Fish and Wildlife
600 Capitol Way N.
Olympia, WA 98501
360-902-2200
www.wa.gov/wdfw
Variety of information,
including regulations and
licensing for fishing and
hunting. Call the Recre-
ational Fishery Regulation
Hotline (360-796-3215)

Washington State Parks &
Recreation Commission
Information Center
P.O. Box 42662
Olympia, WA 98504
800-233-0321
www.parks.wa.gov
Information on services,
amenities, campgrounds,
and activities, including
winter recreation.

Washington State Dept.
of Transportation Bicycle
Hotline
360-705-7277
www.wsdot.wa.gov/Bicy-
cle-pages/List-Bike-
Maps.htm
Website provides a listing

of state bike trail maps available.

Washington State Ferries
2911 Second Avenue
Seattle, WA 98121
206-464-6400 or
888-808-7977 (or
800-843-3779, automated information only)
www.wsdot.wa.gov/ferries
Offers schedules, fares, and route information for state ferries in Puget Sound.

Washington State Tourism Division
P.O. Box 42500
Olympia, WA 98504
800-890-5493
www.tourism.wa.gov
Variety of travel and recreational information, including lodging, camping, whale-watching, and events.

Outfitters and Activities

Columbia River Journeys
P.O. Box 26
303-D Casey Ave.
Richland, WA 98352
509-943-0231
Offers boat tours of the Hanford Reach section of the Columbia River.
May–mid-Oct.

Gig Harbor Kayak Center
8809 Harborview Dr. N.
Gig Harbor, WA 98335
253-851-7987 or
888-42YAKIT
Offers instructional classes and kayak tours of South Puget Sound.

Information on skiing in Washington
800-278-7669
www.skiwashington.com
www.skinorthwest.com
Resort and other information pertaining to the ski industry in Washington.

Lake Chelan Boat Company
509-682-2224
Offers boat tours and ferry service to Stehekin, at south end of North Cascades National Park

Rainier Mountaineering Inc.
535 Dock St., Suite 209
Tacoma, WA 98402
360-569-2227 (May-Sept.),

253-627-6242 (Oct.-April)
www.rmiguides.com
Offers guided ascents of Mount Rainier.

Washington Trails Association
1305 4th Avenue, Suite 512
Seattle, WA 98101
206-625-1367
www.wta.org
Maintains hiking trails statewide.

Outdoor Education

North Cascades Institute
2105 State Route 20
Sedro-Woolley, WA 98294
360-856-5700 x209
www.ncascades.org/nci
Field-based educational programs and an Environmental Learning Center.

Olympic Park Institute
111 Barnes Point Rd.
Port Angeles, WA 98363
360-928-3720 or
800-775-3720
www.yni.org/opi
Field seminars on Olympic Peninsula natural history.

Washington State Audubon Office
P.O. Box 462
Olympia, WA 98507
360-786-8020
wa.audubon.org
Chapters throughout the state conduct tours for bird-watching, kayaking, etc. Call the Olympia office for local chapter information.

Lodgings

Mount Rainier NP

Alexander's Country Inn
37515 Hwy. 706 E.
Ashford, WA 98304
360-569-2300 or
800-654-7615
Located near the Nisqually entrance to the NP.

Mount Rainier Guest Services
P.O. Box 108
Ashford, WA 98304
360-569-2275
Operates two inns: The 25-room National Park Inn at Longmire; and the 126-room Paradise Inn (open June-early Oct.), located at 5,400 ft. elevation.

North Cascades NP

The town of Chelan offers a variety of accommodations. Contact the Chamber of Commerce (509-682-3503).

Cascade Mountain Inn
3840 Pioneer Lane
Birdsview
Concrete, WA 98237
360-826-4333
A small inn on 5 acres, located west of North Cascades NP.

North Cascades Stehekin Lodge
P.O. Box 457
Chelan, WA 98816
509-682-4494
Rustic lodge and cabins; myriad activities. Within Lake Chelan NRA. Access by boat, seaplane, or trail.

Ross Lake Resort
Rockport, WA 98283
206-386-4437
www.rosslakeresort.com
12 cabins and 3 bunk-houses built on log floats; on west side of the lake. Access by trail or boat only. Mid-June–Oct.

Olympic NP

Port Angeles, the main gateway town to Olympic NP, offers a variety of accommodations. Contact the Chamber of Commerce (360-452-2363) for more information.

Kalaloch Lodge
157151 Hwy. 101
Forks, WA 98331
360-962-2271
Lodge and 40 cabins on coastal strip of Olympic NP.

Lake Crescent Lodge
HC 62, Box 11
Port Angeles, WA 98362
360-982-3211
Within park on Lake Crescent, offers cottages and rooms in the 1916 lodge.
May-Oct.

Lake Quinault Lodge
P.O. Box 7
Lake Quinault, WA 98575
360-288-2571
www.visitlakequinault.com
On South Shore Road in Olympic NF, this 92-room lodge is some 70 years old.

San Juan Islands

San Juan Islands Visitor
Information Service
P.O. Box 65
Lopez Island, WA 98261
360-468-3663 or
800-468-3701
www.guidetosanjuans.com
Information on area lodging.

Camping

Contact the Washington
State Tourism Division for
information on private campgrounds. Contact the Washington State Parks and
Recreation Commission
Information Center for state
park campgrounds.

Mount Rainier NP

The national park offers five
campgrounds, all on a first-
come, first-served basis.

The Forest Service operates
campgrounds in the sur-
rounding Gifford Pinchot
(360-891-5000) and Mt.
Baker-Snoqualmie National
Forests (425-775-9702).
Some campgrounds may be
reserved (877-444-6777.
www.reserveusa.com). Additional information on the
Great Outdoor Recreation
Pages (www.gorp.com).

North Cascades NP

There are five campgrounds
in Ross Lake NRA; two in
Lake Chelan NRA. All are
first come, first served.

The Forest Service operates
campgrounds in the sur-
rounding national forests.
Contact Mt. Baker-Sno-
qualmie (425-775-9702),
Okanogan (509-422-2704),
and Wenatchee National
Forests (509-662-4335) for
more information. Some
campgrounds may be
reserved (877-444-6777.
www.reserveusa.com). Additional information on the
Great Outdoor Recreation
Pages (www.gorp.com)

Olympic NP

The national park operates
15 campgrounds (4 inaccessible to RVs). All are first
come, first served.

The Forest Service operates

campgrounds in the sur-
rounding forests. Contact
Olympic NF (360-956-2300)
for information. Some campgrounds may be reserved
(877-444-6777,
www.reserveusa.com). Additional information on the
Great Outdoor Recreation
Pages (www.gorp.com).

BRITISH COLUMBIA

Provincial and
National Agencies

BC Ferries
1112 Fort St.
Victoria, BC
Canada V8V 4V2
250-386-3431
bcferries.bc.ca
For ferry information from
the mainland to the islands
off the British Columbia
coast.

Department of Fisheries
and Oceans, Pacific Region
604-666-0561
555 W. Hastings St.,
Suite 400
Vancouver, BC
Canada V6B 5G3
www.pac.dfo-mpo.gc.ca
For saltwater fishing
licenses. Fishing licenses are
also available through many
sporting goods stores and
marinas.

Fishing Regulations Hotline
(Commercial and Sport)
604-666-2828 (also con-
tains shellfish information)

Lady Rose Marine Services
P.O. Box 188
Port Alberni, BC
Canada V9Y 7M7
250-723-8313 or
800-663-7192
Provides transportation to
Pacific Rim National Park
and its vicinity.

Ministry of Environment,
Lands and Parks
P.O. Box 9338
Stn Prov Govt
Victoria, BC
Canada V8W 9M1
250-387-4550 (provincial
park information)
www.env.gov.bc.ca/bcparks
For hunting licenses con-
tact the Ministry's Wildlife
Branch (250-387-9717,

PO Box 9374, Stn Prov
Govt, Victoria, BC Canada
V8W 9M4).

Parks Canada Information –
British Columbia
Box 129
23433 Mavis Avenue
Fort Langley, BC Canada
V1M 2R5
604-666-1280
www.parkscanada.pch.gc.ca
For information on national
parks in British Columbia
(descriptions, fees, etc.)

Super, Natural British
Columbia
604-663-6000 or
800-663-6000
travel.bc.ca
Provides regional information on lodging, camping,
activities, transportation,
and more.

Tourism Association of
Vancouver Island
#K302-45 Bastion Square
Victoria, BC
Canada V8W 1J1
250-382-3551
Lodging, dining, and other
relevant information.

Outfitters
and Activities

Manning Park Stable
and Tours
250-840-8844
(May-Oct.)
Hourly horse rentals and
overnight tours of the park
during summer months.

Outdoor Recreation
Council of British Columbia
334-1367 West Broadway
Vancouver, BC
Canada V6H 4A9
604-737-3058
www.orcbc.bc.ca
Provides information on a
wide range of outdoor
activities, including rail-to-
trail hikes, and on training
and certification courses.

Lodgings

Canada-West
Accommodations
604-990-6730 or
800-561-3223
www.b-b.com
For information on bed
and breakfasts in

British Columbia.

Western Canada B&B
Innkeepers Association
P.O. Box 74534
Vancouver, BC Canada
V6K 4P4
604-255-9199
www.wcbbia.com

Pacific Rim National Park

The Tourism Association of
Vancouver Island can provide
a listing of accommodations
near the park.

Manning Provincial Park
Princeton is the gateway city
for both Manning and Cathedral Provincial Parks. Contact
the Chamber of Commerce
for information on lodging
250-295-3103
www.town.princeton.bc.ca

Manning Park Resort
P.O. Box 1480
Hope, BC Canada V0X 1L0
250-840-8822.
www.manningparkresort.
com
Motel and cabins. Offers
canoe, boat, kayak, and
mtn. bike rentals in sum-
mer; snowshoe, nordic and
alpine ski rentals in winter.

Cathedral Provincial Park
Cathedral Lakes Lodge
Site 4 Comp 8
Slocan Park, BC
Canada V0G 2E0
888-255-4453
www.cathedral-lakes-
lodge.com

In middle of park and inaccessible by private vehicle
(lodge will provide transportation from entrance).
Mid-June–mid-Oct.

Camping

The provincial and national
parks offer a range of
campgrounds; contact the
parks for specifics. Campground reservations for
provincial parks may be made
through the reservation
service Discover Camping
(800-689-9025,
www.discovercamping.ca).

**Hotel & Motel Chains
in Pacific Northwest**
Best Western International
800-528-1234
Choice Hotels
800-4-CHOICE
Clarion Hotels
800-CLARION
Coast Hotels
800-663-1144
Comfort Inns
800-228-5150
Courtyard by Marriott
800-321-2211
Days Inn
800-325-2525
Delta Hotels
800-268-1133
Doubletree Hotels and
Guest Suites
800-222-TREE
Econo Lodge
800-446-6900

Embassy Suites
800-EMBASSY
Fairfield Inn by Marriott
800-228-2800
Fairmont Hotels
800-441-1414
Hampton Inn
800-HAMPTON
Hilton Hotels
800-HILTONS
Holiday Inns
800-HOLIDAY
Howard Johnson
800-654-2000
Hyatt Hotels and Resorts
800-233-1234
Marriott Hotels
Resorts Suites
800-228-9290
Motel 6
800-466-8356
Quality Inns-Hotels-Suites
800-228-5151
Radisson Hotels Intl.
800-333-3333
Ramada Inns
800-2-Ramada
Red Lion
800-547-8010
Sandman Hotels and Inns
800-SANDMAN
Sheraton Hotels & Inns
800-325-3535
Super 8 Motels
800-843-1991
Vagabond Inns
800-522-1555
Westin Hotels and Resorts
800-228-3000

About the Author/Photographer

From his home in Oregon, **Bob Devine** writes about conservation, natural history, and outdoors travel. His most recent book, published by National Geographic, is *Alien Invasion: America's Battle with Non-native Animals and Plants*.

A native of the Pacific Northwest, **Phil Schofield** has worked as a photojour-nalist for 28 years and has shot over three dozen photo assignments for the National Geographic Society. His first, in 1978, was for the book *America's Majestic Canyons*. He and his family reside in Bellingham, WA, on northern Puget Sound.

Illustrations Credits

Photographs in this book are by Phil Schofield except for the following:
cover - David Muench
p. 189 - Alan & Sandy Carey
p. 239 - Paul Chesley

Index

Abbreviations

National Historic
    Landmark=NHL
National Monument=NM
National Park=NP
National Recreation
    Area=NRA
National Wildlife
    Refuge=NWR
State Park=SP

A

Agamemnon Channel, B.C.,
    269
Alava, Cape, Wash., 238
Alien species, 37; fish in
    Crater Lake, 75–76; moun-
    tain goats in Olympic NP,
    Wash., 239
Alpine Lakes Wilderness,
    Wash., 179–181
Alpine meadows: Baker, Mt.,
    Wash., 203; Cathedral
    Provincial Park, B.C., 216;
    Garibaldi Provincial Park,
    B.C., 272–273; Manning
    Provincial Park, B.C., 209;
    Mount Rainier NP, Wash.,
    173; Olympic NP, Wash.,
    232–233; see also Plants
Altitude sickness, 217
Alvord Desert, Oreg., 124
Ann, Lake, Wash., 188
Ape Cave, Oreg., 106
Arago, Cape, Oreg., 31

B

Baker, Mt., Wash., 197,
    200–205
Barkley Sound, B.C., 260
Baynes Peak, B.C., 253
Beachcombing: Deception
    Pass SP, Wash., 244–245;
    Ecola SP, Oreg., 56–57;
    Oregon Dunes NRA,
    Oreg., 39–41; Samuel H.
    Boardman SSC, Oreg., 19
Beacon Rock SP, Wash., 97
Bear Valley, Oreg., 64
Benham Falls, Oreg., 79
Big Beaver Cr., Wash., 190
Big Indian Gorge, Oreg., 122
Bird-watching see Wildlife
    watching
Black Buttes, Wash., 205
Black Tusk, B.C., 273
Blackwell Peak, B.C., 208-209
Blue Lake, Wash., 188
Blue Pool, Wash., 178
Blue Sky, Oreg., 116
Bluebill Lake, Oreg., 36

Boating: Crater Lake NP,
    Oreg., 74; Grand Coulee,
    Wash., 161; Gulf Island,
    B.C., 253; Hanford Reach,
    Wash., 155; Hells Canyon
    NRA, Idaho-Oreg.,
    136–137; Lake Chelan
    NRA, Wash., 194–195;
    Lower Deschutes River,
    Oreg., 152–153; Pacific
    Rim NP, B.C., 259, 262;
    Rogue River, Oreg., 26–27,
    28–30; Samuel H. Board-
    man SSC, Oreg., 18; San
    Juan Island, Wash., 251;
    Sunshine Coast, B.C., 267,
    268–269
Botanical Beach, B.C., 255
Botany Beach, B.C., 255
British Columbia, Canada:
    Cathedral Provincial Park,
    214–217; coastal area of,
    254–277; Garibaldi Provin-
    cial Park, 271–277; Gulf Is.,
    246–247, 253; Juan de Fuca
    Marine Trail, 254–255;
    Manning Provincial Park,
    206–213; Pacific Rim NP,
    258–265; Sunshine Coast,
    266–269
Broken Group Island, B.C.,
    261–262
Buena Vista Ponds, Oreg., 130

C

California: Klamath Basin
    NWR, 64–69
Canoeing: Sunshine Coast,
    B.C., 267; Upper Klamath
    Refuge, 69; see also
    Boating
Cape Arago SP, Oreg., 31
Cape Lookout SP, Oreg., 52
Cape Perpetua Scenic Area,
    Oreg., 43
Cascade River, Wash., 191-192
Cascades Range: North Cas-
    cades, B.C.-Wash.,
    183–195; South Cascades,
    Oreg.-Wash., 60–107
Cathedral Lakes, B.C., 215
Cathedral Provincial Park,
    B.C., 214–217
Caving: Ape Cave, Oreg., 106;
    Lava River Cave, Oreg., 79-
    80; Oregon Caves NM,
    Oreg., 22–24
Central Plateau area, Oreg.-
    Wash., 138–163
Chatterbox Falls, B.C., 269
Cheakamus Lake, B.C., 276
Cheakamus River, B.C., 276
Chelan, Lake, Wash., 194
Chewach River, Wash., 196

China Beach, B.C., 255
Christine Falls, Wash., 172
Churchill, Mt., B.C., 269
Clayoquot Sound, B.C., 265
Clear Lake NWR, Oreg., 64
Cobble Beach, Oreg., 47
Coleman Glacier, Wash., 200
Columbia NWR, Wash.,
    159–160
Columbia R., 154–155;
    Columbia NWR, Wash.,
    159–160; Columbia River
    Gorge, Oreg.-Wash.,
    97–102; Grand Coulee,
    Wash., 161–162
Columbia River Gorge, Oreg.-
    Wash., 97–102
Constitution, Mt., Wash., 252
Cooks Chasm, Oreg., 43
Cove, Cape, Oreg., 43
Cranberry Lake, Wash., 245
Crater Lake NP, Oreg., 70–76
Crescent, Lake, Wash., 234
Crown Point SP, Oreg., 102

D

Darlingtonia State Natural
    Site, Oreg., 42
Debris flows, 174
Deception Pass SP, Wash.,
    244–245
DeGarmo Canyon, Oreg., 117
Deschutes River, Oreg.,
    152–153
Deschutes SRA, Oreg., 152
Desert area, Oreg., 108–137
Desolation Sound Marine
    Park, B.C., 267
Devils Churn, Oreg., 43
Devils Dome, Wash., 197
Devil's Woodpile, B.C., 217
Diamond Head Area, B.C.,
    271-272
Donner und Blitzen River,
    Oreg., 119
Dry Falls, Wash., 162
Dungeness NWR, Wash.,
    240–241

E

Eagle Creek Recreation Area,
    Oreg., 102
Easton Glacier, Wash., 205
Eastsound, Wash., 252
Ecola SP, Oreg., 56–57
Elfin Lakes, B.C., 272
Emmons Glacier, 176
Enchantment Lakes, Wash.,
    181

F

Falcon, Cape, Oreg., 55

National Geographic Guide to America's Outdoors: Pacific Northwest
by Bob Devine
Photographed by Phil Schofield

Published by the National Geographic Society
John M. Fahey, Jr., *President and Chief Executive Officer*
Gilbert M. Grosvenor, *Chairman of the Board*
Nina D. Hoffman, *Senior Vice President*

Prepared by the Book Division
William R. Gray, *Vice President and Director*
Charles Kogod, *Assistant Director*
Barbara A. Payne, *Editorial Director and Managing Editor*
David Griffin, *Design Director*

Guides to America's Outdoors
Elizabeth L. Newhouse, *Director of Travel Books*
Cinda Rose, *Art Director*
Barbara A. Noe, *Associate Editor*
Caroline Hickey, *Senior Researcher*
Carl M. Mehler, *Director of Maps*
Roberta Conlan, *Project Director*

Staff for this Book
Janet Cave, *Editor*
Dorrit Green, *Designer*
Vickie Lewis, *Illustrations Editor*
Caroline J. Dean, Kimberly A. DeLashmit, Rebecca Mills,
  Keith R. Moore, Jane Sunderland, *Researchers*
Lise Sajewski, *Editorial Consultant*
Joe Ochlak, *Map Editor*
Joe Ochlak, Thomas L. Gray, Mapping Specialists, Ltd., *Map Research*
Matt Chwastyk, Gregory Ugiansky, Martin S. Walz,
  Magellan Geographix, Mapping Specialists, Ltd., *Map Production*
R. Gary Colbert, *Production Director*
Gillian Carol Dean, *Assistant Designer*
Meredith Wilcox, *Illustrations Assistant*
Julia Marshall, *Indexer*
DeShelle Downey, *Project Assistant*

Eric C. Ewert, University of Idaho, *Consultant*

Manufacturing and Quality Control
George V. White, *Director*; John T. Dunn, *Associate Director*; Vincent P. Ryan, *Manager*;
Phillip L. Schlosser, *Financial Analyst*

Library of Congress Cataloging-in-Publication Data
Devine, Bob 1951-
    Guide to America's outdoors : Pacific Northwest / Bob Devine; photography by Phil Schofield.
      p. cm
      ISBN 0-7922-7740-6
        1. Northwest, Pacific—Guidebooks. 2. National parks and Reserves—Northwest, Pacific—
Guidebooks. 3. Outdoor recreation—Northwest, Pacific—Guidebooks. I. Title: Pacific Northwest.
II. Schofield, Phil. III. Title
    F852.3 .D47 2000
    917.9504'44—dc21   99-085986
                                                                                    CIP